Dr Cassandra Coburn

Enough.

How your food choices will save the planet

First published in Great Britain in 2021 by Gaia,
an imprint of Octopus Publishing Group Ltd
Carmelite House, 50 Victoria Embankment
London EC4Y 0DZ
www.octopusbooks.co.uk

An Hachette UK Company
www.hachette.co.uk

Distributed in the US by
Hachette Book Group
1290 Avenue of the Americas
4th and 5th Floors
New York, NY 10104

Distributed in Canada by
Canadian Manda Group
664 Annette St.
Toronto, Ontario, Canada M6S 2C8

ISBN 978-1-85675-438-5

A CIP catalogue record for this book is available from the British Library.

Printed and bound in the United Kingdom

1 3 5 7 9 10 8 6 4 2

The information in this book is not intended to replace or conflict with the advice
given to you by your GP or other health professional. All matters regarding your
health should be discussed with your GP or other health professional. The author
and publisher disclaim any liability directly or indirectly from the use of the
material in this book by any person.

This FSC® label means that materials used for the product have
been responsibly sourced.

For my parents, Noel and Frances Coburn, who introduced me to the elephants and also hid me from them in the bathtub.

This book is dedicated to you, with love and gratitude.

Enough is as good as a feast

PROVERB

CONTENTS

CHAPTER 1

THE GLOBAL SYNDEMIC

Let food be thy medicine.

HIPPOCRATES

Subtle, it isn't. Everything at the Heart Attack Grill in downtown Las Vegas is in your face, beginning at the entrance, where a huge sign over the doorway proclaims 'OVER 350 LBS EATS FREE'. If you're not sure if you qualify, there's an electronic cattle scale outside the restaurant you can hop on to check. As you enter the restaurant, waitresses dressed in skin-tight parodies of nurses' uniforms greet you and dress you in mandatory hospital gowns. But it's only once you've been led to your table and are given the menu that you really begin to understand just how blatant the Heart Attack Grill is. Milkshakes are made with butterfat, topped with an actual pat of butter. Everything that is fried is fried in lard – and pretty much everything is fried. 'Fat Bastard' red wine is served in IV bags. The only vegan option on the menu is a '100 per cent leaf, no meat additives'... cigarette. And then there's the crowning glory of the menu: the Heart Attack Grill's world-infamous burgers.

For the wary, there's the 'single bypass' burger, with a mere half-pound beef patty. The 'quadruple bypass' burger, with four patties, is the current holder of the Guinness World Record for the world's most calorific burger, coming in at 9,983 calories, or approximately four times the daily caloric needs of the average adult man. Since Guinness last checked, the Heart Attack Grill has added a further four options, with the 'octuple bypass burger' being the biggest thing on the menu. This monstrous creation is made with eight half-pound beef patties, or about 1.8kg of meat, stacked between all the normal burger accoutrements of buns, cheese, chilli, tomatoes, onions and lettuce. For a mere $7.40 more, you can add 40 extra bacon slices. Placed on a table, it reaches about the same height as a seated man.

The octuple bypass burger clocks in at around 19,900 calories, which is enough to sustain an adult for ten days. But don't think you can just eat your fill and take the rest home with you in a doggy bag as food for the next week: those who don't finish their meals are given a painful spanking by their waitress/nurse (the spanking paddle is also available to take home, for $6.50). However, those who clean their plates are triumphally placed in a wheelchair and are wheeled back outside onto the pavement victorious: alive to eat another day.

The restaurant courts controversy in every way it possibly can. At least three people have had heart attacks on the premises, one of whom was the restaurant's spokesman, John Alleman. He visited the establishment daily and had his own line of Heart Attack Grill sportswear. His cremated remains are on display above the restaurant's bar. The founder, 'Dr' Jon ('a non-AMA recognised physician', the website helpfully clarifies), has been quoted as saying 'death equals business at the Heart Attack Grill'.

'Will it please me if other spokesmen die in the future?' Dr Jon asks, before responding himself: 'Absolutely.'

The Heart Attack Grill is macabre in its honesty: unashamedly crude and extreme in its parody of modern eating habits. The response it evokes in most people is worth sitting with, uncomfortably, for a minute. It is a dark mirror held up to reflect something fundamental and profoundly awkward about how much of the world eats. While (almost) none of us would consider tackling even a quadruple bypass burger on a daily basis, the idea of having a single patty burger a few times a week is not unthinkable. The food that the Heart Attack Grill serves is simply a more extreme example of what we would normally eat. The difference is mainly in quantity: of meat, of oil, of sugar, of fat. But it's cut from the same cloth as our normal diets. And while we can gawp at the outrageous lack of respect for the sanctity of human life that the founder displays, it's really the speed and extreme nature of the diseases that assail his patrons which makes it stand out. Because we know that a lot of the food that we eat is also harming us. It's just that the diseases we induce in ourselves from our relatively less extreme eating habits take longer to arrive than a lunchtime heart attack.

A NEW EPIDEMIC

Even before COVID-19, the world was in the grip of a new disease epidemic, and it's unlike any we've ever experienced before. For a start, we don't know exactly what causes it. There's no single cause, no virus or bacteria, that we can point to. Second, despite it being non-infectious, it is spreading rapidly. Oceans and mountains mean nothing to this epidemic: it is global, and it is on the rise. Third, although we've identified a set of risk factors that are associated with it, we have no way of predicting what kind of disease they will lead to. It's like a ghoulish slot machine: common behavioural risk factors mean that anyone can play, but we have no idea what the outcome will be – or even if there will be an outcome.

What is this plague? It is the rising tide of non-communicable diseases, and it has medical specialists extremely worried. 'Non-communicable diseases' is the catch-all term for a group of ostensibly very different diseases. The main four are cardiovascular diseases (including stroke, heart attacks and hypertension), cancer (in all its myriad forms), chronic respiratory conditions (lung cancer, emphysema) and type 2 diabetes (type 1 is also on the rise, but is considered a different disease type). In 2016, cardiovascular diseases led to 31 per cent of all global deaths, followed by cancers (16 per cent), respiratory diseases (7 per cent) and diabetes (3 per cent). If someone dies before the age of 70, their death is medically defined as premature. In 2016, non-communicable diseases accounted for an estimated 17 million, or 57 per cent, of all premature deaths.[1]

The prevalence of these diseases is the subject of such concern that there's a special campaign for action in the World Health Organization (WHO), which has been endorsed by governments worldwide. The 25x25 campaign aims to reduce the premature mortality of the four worst non-communicable disease groups by 25 per cent by 2025. Despite these efforts, the latest research makes depressing reading. While a handful of Scandinavian countries are on-track to achieve the desired reductions in premature mortality, the rest of the world is lagging far behind. In many countries, the epidemic is worsening. You might think that these diseases are the preserve of wealthy countries. In fact, the opposite is true. A 30-year-old woman in a sub-Saharan African country has a one-in-four chance of dying prematurely from a non-communicable disease. A 30-year-old man in eastern Europe or central Asia has a one-in-three chance.[2] Like all the deadliest epidemics, these diseases do not recognize borders.

So what is driving this epidemic and causing these diseases? Despite their dissimilar nature, affecting different parts of the body and ranging from chronic but manageable type 2 diabetes to the much more deadly bowel cancer, the risk factors for all non-communicable diseases are oddly similar. Leaving aside chronic respiratory diseases, in which the main risk factor is smoking, all the other diseases are believed to be caused by the as yet only partially understood interplay between having a poor diet, drinking too much alcohol and not getting enough physical exercise. These three risk factors interact to create a fourth risk factor: obesity. Being obese has been characterized by medical authorities variously as a disease in its own right, a complicating co-morbidity or as a risk factor or a precursor for developing further non-communicable diseases. The interplay between these disease states is confusing. For example, medical science has identified a non-communicable disease state called metabolic syndrome, which refers to the interplay between diabetes, obesity and high blood pressure, which in turn raises the risk of developing heart disease and strokes. The sheer difficulty of understanding how all these factors interact makes tackling the rise of this epidemic all the more challenging.

However, there is one underlying cause which is clearer cut than the rest and that is, very simply, what we eat. Increasing obesity rates and the growth of non-communicable diseases reliably follow changing diets. The food that we eat worldwide has changed dramatically over the last 50 years. While an unhealthy diet was initially believed to be a Western problem, this trend can now be seen worldwide. Data from an epidemiological study in Tokelau, a cluster of three coral atolls halfway between Hawaii and New Zealand, gives a striking example of this change.[3] In the mid 1960s, before there was much contact with the outside world, the Tokelauan diet mainly consisted of coconut, pork, fish, poultry and starchy fruit and vegetables (breadfruit and pulaka). The average islander ate about 3.5kg of sugar a year. By the 1980s, after a trading post was established on the islands, sugar consumption had increased to 24.5kg a year. Diseases followed suit. At the beginning of the study, 6 per cent of the population was diabetic. Fifty years later, in 2014, 38 per cent of the population had diabetes (and two-thirds were obese).

About two billion people, or approximately a quarter of the world's population, are now classified as overweight or obese. If current trends continue, some estimates suggest that the number of overweight or obese children could rise to 3.28 billion by 2030, with low- to middle-income countries being the worst affected. For example, in China the proportion of overweight and obese adults has increased from 14.6 per cent in 1992 to 32.3 per cent in 2012. By 2030 over half the adult population of China is projected to be overweight or obese.[4]

Rising populations have driven an increase in production of an energy-rich but nutrient-deficient diet which heavily favours processed and ultra-processed staples. This surfeit of energy-rich, nutrient-poor food is changing how we think about malnutrition.

For the first time in recorded history, more people are overweight than underweight. However, irrespective of their weight, millions of people remain undernourished. Fifty-eight million children in sub-Saharan Africa and 91 million in Asia are stunted (which means they have a low height for their age primarily because of nutritional deficiencies), and this number is increasing. Recent estimates suggest that about 11 per cent of people in the world are undernourished, with 795 million people facing hunger on a daily basis and more than two billion people lacking vital micro-nutrients such as iron, zinc and vitamin A.[5] But undernutrition, while shocking, is not a new epidemic. What *is* new – and striking – is the number of people in the world who are simultaneously overweight while also eating insufficient nutrients. For example, in low- to middle-income countries, 3 per cent of children are both obese *and* stunted.[6]

On an individual basis, every diagnosis is a tragedy. On a population basis, this is now looking increasingly like a catastrophe. Estimates put the current cost of obesity (in terms of the cost of healthcare plus lost economic productivity) at about US$2 trillion annually. That's about the same as the entire GDP of all 46 sub-Saharan African countries combined. Even in a business-as-normal scenario, if the world were relatively stable and the non-communicable disease burden was not rising, that would be an almost unaffordable bill. But, as we all know, obesity is not the only worsening problem we are trying to wrap our heads around: the planet we live on has problems of its own.

CLIMATE CHANGE

The seaside city of Cape Town in South Africa is arguably one of the best-located cities in the world. It's cradled in a valley between two oceans and protective, low-lying mountain ranges. Beyond the city are verdant farms and vineyards. Unfortunately, it is precisely because of Cape Town's location and climate that the city has the dubious honour of almost being the first major city in the world to be rendered uninhabitable by climate change.

South Africa as a whole has long been troubled by water shortages, but Cape Town's drought in 2017 was the worst in a century. On 31 May 2017, the city's mayor, Patricia de Lille, delivered a sombre speech at the city's council meeting. She told the assembled councillors that the poor winter rains had dried the rivers and reservoirs feeding the city to such an extent that the city had less than 10 per cent of the useable water supplies needed for its four million citizens. In light of the severity of the situation, the council implemented ominous-sounding 'Level 4 water restrictions': Cape Town residents could use no more than 100 litres of water a day. That sounds like quite a lot until you find out that the average toilet flush uses 13 litres and that an average shower comes in at 65 litres. And Ms de Lille went further. At that point, she said, Capetonians were using an average of 660 million litres of water daily, even though the target was 600 million litres. The current situation was so dire that she was planning to ask the council for further restrictions to be brought in, aiming for a maximum of 500 million litres of water to be used daily. She ended by calling on her citizens to rethink their relationship with water. 'The days of plentiful water supply in Cape Town may very well be over,' she said, adding that 'we need to embrace the fact that water scarcity is the new normal.'

Residents of Cape Town began to use unorthodox means of restricting their water use. In an attempt to get people to think about how necessary flushing the toilet really was, a viral campaign on Twitter featured the catchy and disgusting phrase 'if it's yellow, let it mellow; if it's brown, flush it down'. People began to collect water used during showers in buckets instead of allowing it to run down the drain, and used this so-called grey water to flush their toilets. Households were given strict water quotas, mandatory borehole registration was introduced and garden watering was allowed only on certain days, at certain times, and only ever manually. Pools and sprinkler systems were consigned to the past.

It didn't work.

By early 2018, Level 6 water limitations had been implemented, restricting personal water use to a mere 50 litres a day, half the allowance of the previous restrictions. The conversation had stopped being about if a disastrous water shortage would hit, and became about when. The day everyone dreaded was designated day zero. Day zero would be the day that keeping the city's water supply running became untenable, and the taps would be switched off. It was agreed that when reservoirs held 3.5 per cent of useable water, the whole water system would be shut down except for areas of critical need such as hospitals. At that point, residents would only be able to access water by collecting it manually in jerry cans at collection points throughout the city, and each resident would be given precisely 25 litres of water a day. On 29 January 2018, the city of Cape Town activated a disaster operations centre to ensure that its water disaster plan would be in place in the event of day zero.

Using data from the city's dams and projected residential and agricultural usage, the city initially estimated that day zero was likely to occur on 16 April. Critical laws were mooted: the government considered introducing punitive drought tariffs for those using excessive water but there were concerns about how they might play out in areas with such economic disparity. A satellite map of the city was introduced online where Capetonians could check to see if they – or their neighbours – had been awarded a green dot for achieving water-saving targets. Farmers in the region let crops shrivel and die as they gave up their rights to water. And so the people of the city waited anxiously – and parched – praying for rain.

Biblically speaking, heavy rains signal the arrival of floods as punishment for mankind's sins. For Cape Town, the winter rains of 2018 were showers of redemption. Stunningly low water use and heavy rains combined allowed the reservoirs to begin to fill again. At the time of writing in 2020, Level 1 water restrictions still apply, and the city's water supplies are fuller again, sitting at around half capacity. So important are they to everyone in the community that you can monitor the reservoir capacity levels live online through a government site. And so, for the moment, Capetonians can continue to live relatively normal lives.

What caused this emergency? How was a city brought so perilously close to having to switch off its taps? The issues which almost brought Cape Town to its knees are seen by many experts as a microcosm of what the world as a whole is currently facing: climate change, population growth and unsustainable food systems.

A SERIES OF CRISES

First, climate change. Scientists believe that this particular drought had its origins in an especially strong El Ninõ effect, which affected the region's normal winter rainfall. With rivers drying upstream, and no rain falling to replenish them, reservoirs created by building dams to provide a more reliable supply of water inevitably also dried up. Steps that could have been put in place earlier hadn't been, partly because the unpredictable effects of climate change make modelling future weather patterns much more complex.

Second, population growth. Cape Town's population increased by about 80 per cent between 1995 and 2018 (from 2.4 million to around 4.3 million), but water storage did not follow in step, increasing by only 15 per cent.[7]

Third, unsustainable food systems; in this instance the unsustainable irrigation needs of agricultural food producers. The city of Cape Town and the farmers of its heartland in the Western Cape share water resources (the Western Cape Supply System). On 4 February 2018, the government announced for the first time that the agricultural sector had used their allocated quantities of water, as agreed with the National Department of Water and Sanitation. In previous years, there had been no firm restrictions.

But in 2018, the situation was sufficiently dire for the national department to shut off supply to the two local agricultural irrigation boards, decreasing agricultural use from the usual 30 per cent of the supply to 15 per cent in March and to 10 per cent in April. Farmers allowing their crops to die combined with the return of the rains, meant that Cape Town could drink another day. But that came at a price: production of major crops dropped 20 per cent from 2016/17 to 2017/18 (US$415 million worth of lost crops), and more than 30,000 agricultural jobs were lost.[8]

Cape Town's story is of one drought, affecting one city, over the course of one year. But it is repeated with variations all round the world as we begin to deal with the effects of what scientists are calling the Anthropocene: a man-made geological epoch. Epochs are periods of geological time marked by changing weather and environmental conditions. Around 11,000 years ago the world's last ice age marked the ending of the Pleistocene epoch and the beginning of the warmer Holocene. Now, scientists believe we have entered the Anthropocene.

The Anthropocene was first defined in 2000 by Nobel prize-winning atmospheric chemist Paul Crutzen. The beginning of this epoch is roughly dated as starting in the mid-18th century, as a result of the Industrial Revolution. There is a growing body of research showing that the impact of human activity on its own habitat is now akin to a force of nature, like a super-volcano or the tectonic shifts of continents – but much, much faster. The Anthropocene is marked not simply by climate change, although this is a large component part, but by a wide variety of man-made environmental changes. And there are a lot: a recent report shows that 75 per cent of the world's land has been 'severely altered' to date by human actions, as have 66 per cent of the world's seas.[9]

Society is belatedly awakening to the way that human activity is shifting the parameters of our own environment so dangerously that the survival of future generations is at stake. The concern we now feel is best summed up by a conversation I had with a board member of Conservation International: 'Fuck the rhino,' he said, a sentiment not often voiced in environmentalist circles, 'the question is, can we save ourselves?'

OUR FOOD, OUR PLANET AND US

What links these twin burdens of rising non-communicable diseases and our rapidly – and detrimentally – changing environment?

The answer is simple: our food.

We may think of factories belching out clouds of noxious gases as the main culprit, but food systems form the single biggest driver of environmental change on the planet. Agriculture takes up 50 per cent of global habitable land, while food production as a whole emits 26 per cent of global greenhouse gases and uses 70 per cent of fresh water.[10] Consider for a moment the Heart Attack Grill and the mountains of flesh it serves to its customers: if cattle were their own nation, they would be the world's third-largest emitter of greenhouse gases. Even if we were to magically switch to renewable energy overnight, much of the harm done by mass-scale agriculture would continue.

It's not just that we're using too many of our resources. We're spoiling them while we're at it. Just under a quarter of the world's land is less productive than it was because poor agricultural methods have degraded it.[11] Fifty million hectares of forest were cleared in the decades between 1980 and 2000 for farming and ranching, leaving about 68 per cent of the world's forests intact, compared to a pre-industrial level. More than half of the oceans are used for commercial fishing, and a third of all marine stocks are overfished. Food production drives much of the change that is contributing to the Anthropocene's erosion of the ecosystem as we have known it for millennia.

The world's growing population only exacerbates the problem. Current projections predict that the global population will hit about ten billion people by 2050. To feed them, scientists estimate that we will need to produce more food in the next 35 years than we have done in the entirety of human history. Extrapolating from current demand for food and assuming we keep producing it in the same way and in similar conditions, producing this quantity would require 120 per cent more water and 42 per cent more arable land than we currently use; it would also destroy 14 per cent more of the world's forests and produce 77 per cent more greenhouse gas emissions.

But shifting climate conditions and striking new evidence suggest that it is becoming harder to make even the most basic assumptions about the conditions in which people will live. In a far-sighted experiment, cereal crops and legumes were grown under changed atmospheric carbon dioxide levels. When scientists increased the carbon dioxide up to the elevated levels forecast to be the norm by 2050, they found that the crops lost their nutritional value: they had reduced zinc and iron levels compared to normal crops.[12] If the crops we grow have a lower nutritional value, we would have to grow more of them to feed the same number of people, taking up further land and emitting even more greenhouse gases. Another uncertain factor to consider is the effect of a declining number of pollinating species such as bees. Approximately US$577 billion worth of annual global crops are believed to be at risk from pollinator loss. Yet another variable is the loss of arable land to floods and hurricanes, and other catastrophic weather events brought about by climate change. The list goes on.

All the above mean that it might not take overpopulation to bring about food shortages. Climate change is expected to affect food production via two mechanisms: while gradual changes in ambient temperature and weather patterns will adversely affect the crops which now grow best around the world, increasingly frequent extreme weather conditions such as floods, hurricanes and droughts could wipe out regional food stocks entirely. In 2019, there were examples of the latter worldwide. Destructive floods in the USA's breadbasket states of Illinois, Iowa, Missouri and Nebraska in mid-2019, and a year-long Australian drought are harming food production by the day. Look further back and there are many examples of the way extreme weather conditions can disrupt food production. In 2008, Cyclone Nargis flooded large proportions of Myanmar's rice paddies with salt water, effectively removing around 65 per cent of the country's capacity to grow rice. The frequency of these 'climatic shocks' is estimated to triple by 2040. Such huge loss of food in our extremely interconnected and interdependent world will affect food availability and prices. Changes in food availability or cost have knock-on effects beyond mere hunger. We don't need to model these scenarios: we have already seen what the consequences can be.

In March 2008, the global market price of wheat increased 130 per cent in comparison to March 2007. The price of soy rose by 87 per cent and the price of rice by 74 per cent in the same period. These jumps translated into substantial hikes in the retail price of food. For example, in Britain, the price of tinned food increased by 15 per cent, and the prices of luxury goods such as croissants and ham jumped by almost 50 per cent. The causes of this spike were complex, and not entirely related to climate change. Drought played a contributing factor, but people believe that rising oil prices, international stock speculation on grain and increasing the proportion of crops grown for biofuel instead of food also contributed.

In Britain, a wealthy country, the rise in food prices hit the poorest hardest, so fewer of them could afford healthier food such as fruit and vegetables, relying instead on cheaper, less healthy, processed food. In less wealthy countries, such as Syria, the price rises triggered riots in which people died. Analysts believe that these rising food prices, and a second spike in 2010/2011, were contributing factors to the spate of popular uprisings, anti-government protests and riots that became the Arab Spring, which in turn helped trigger the Syrian civil war. If catastrophic climate events begin to happen more often, countries may well end up going to war over fresh water and flour. Governments are taking these possibilities seriously, and many have begun setting up task forces to ensure their readiness in the new arena of food security.

Right now we are living on borrowed time, and we are borrowing that time from our children. The world's food systems are producing food that is harmful both to us as individuals and to the planet as a viable ecosystem – and an increasing population will only worsen these effects. In a recent collaborative international report produced under the aegis of the World Obesity Federation, the authors coined a new term to describe the synergistic interaction between the epidemics of obesity, malnutrition and climate change: the Global Syndemic.[13]

What can we, as individuals, do to try to alter the course of a syndemic? It's easy to feel utterly helpless and hopeless. Many of the world's brightest policymakers seem stuck as well. We have now got to the stage where experts are writing studies about how policy is failing to enact the changes needed, dubbed policy inertia. In the World Obesity Federation report the authors note: 'a principal source of policy inertia related to addressing obesity and climate change is the power of vested interests by commercial actors'. Or, to put it another way, industry seems to be against changing the status quo. If we're battling against earth systems *and* industry giants, you could be forgiven for thinking that there's nothing we can to do to force a change.

Fortunately, you would be wrong.

If food is the thread that runs through this syndemic, then we as consumers have the ability to influence how it plays out. Altering what we eat means it is possible to ameliorate, maybe even reverse, the harms that we are enacting on ourselves and the planet.

WHAT YOU EAT CAN CHANGE THE WORLD

*T*he Lancet is one of the oldest and best respected scientific journals in the world. I have an obvious bias: I work for the Lancet group, as Editor-in-Chief of the title *The Lancet Healthy Longevity*. But fortunately it is an objective fact that the journal *The Lancet* has been in existence since 1823 and, by any metric, is one of the scientific world's most frequently cited and influential publications.

In February 2019 *The Lancet* published a scientific report catchily entitled 'Food in the Anthropocene: the EAT-*Lancet* Commission on healthy diets from sustainable food systems'.[14] This report – otherwise known as the planetary health diet – was the product of a partnership between *The Lancet* and the EAT Forum. This foundation is a Swedish non-profit organization, founded with the stated aim of catalysing a transformation in food systems. It was established as a collaboration between the philanthropic Stordalen Foundation, the biomedical charity the Wellcome Trust and the Stockholm Resilience Centre (where the concept of planetary boundaries originated).

Commissions are something of a *Lancet* speciality. Its Editor-in-Chief for the past 25 years, Richard Horton, defines a *Lancet* commission as 'a scientific review, inquiry and response to an urgent, and perhaps neglected, or understudied, health predicament'. Journals such as *The Lancet* spend most of their time assessing and publishing research submitted to them by other scientists, whereas commissions are, well, commissioned – hence the name – by *Lancet* editors and published as separate stand-alone issues.

Where commissions differ from normal scientific research is in their breadth. Instead of focusing on a single question, they aim to tackle broader problems and propose workable solutions to these. Almost all commissions involve anything from tens to hundreds of experts from around the world and several disciplines, working in unison. These major research projects often take years to write and, in addition to scientists, bring together many players. These include policymakers, members of non-governmental organizations such as charities, large international humanitarian organizations such as the WHO and the United Nations and, sometimes, entire branches of government. Contributions from the latter are especially fun to coordinate at launch events.

Like all scientific research published by reputable journals, commission reports are peer-reviewed. Peer review involves multiple stages of review and revision. Anonymous scientists selected by editors for their expertise in relevant areas deliver detailed critiques of the report; these comments are then shared with the authors and they're asked to revise the manuscript in response. The revised manuscript can then be peer-reviewed again if the editor thinks it's necessary and so on, until everyone is happy with the final version. This means that any peer-reviewed research has been subjected to critique and rebuttal before it sees the light of day. While no scientific discovery is without controversy, peer review is the best method we have for ensuring that the conclusions people reach are as scientifically valid as possible. Don't get me wrong: there are people, including scientific experts, who have taken issue with peer-reviewed research (and the planetary health diet is no exception). But while academics will always disagree, the process by which the recommendations were reached has not been questioned.

The EAT-*Lancet* Commission was the product of more than two years' work by 37 experts from 16 countries.[15] The breadth of this group's membership was to ensure that the proposals the commission came up with were not only scientifically sound, but also feasible in a real-world setting. Although it's a complex read, written by more than 30 experts whose expertise spans environmental, agricultural and medical fields, the crux of the paper is simple. The authors believe that changing the way we eat should be enough to combat both the environmental destruction that we face *and* the rising tide of non-communicable disease. This new way of eating – the planetary health diet – is intended to be less of a burden to the planet as a whole and simultaneously healthier for each and every one of us (even faced with the scenario of ten billion hungry mouths by 2050).

Taking into account the myriad regional climates and cultures in which people live, this is not a diet in the sense of providing a set of recipes for everyone on earth to start cooking. Instead, the planetary health diet makes recommendations for quantities of different nutrients: for example, instead of suggesting that we eat bread, it suggests that about 32 per cent of our daily calories should come from a wholegrain source. It also gives ranges for each nutrient, so diets can be mixed and matched according to local produce: the foods available in Japan are not going to be the same as those available in Uruguay or Ethiopia. The diet offers recommendations in the same way that nutritional food pyramids do: while the foods themselves differ worldwide according to local availability, the main food groups (protein, carbohydrates, fats, etc.) will remain the same.

The authors modelled what might happen if we all changed our eating patterns in line with these suggestions. The results were, to put it mildly, encouraging. The scientists estimated that eating the planetary health diet could prevent 11 million premature deaths from diet-linked non-communicable diseases, every year – globally about 20 per cent of current premature deaths world-wide. The authors also believe that we could halt the destruction caused by current agricultural practices which push many critical environmental processes and systems to their limits. In a best-case scenario, they predict that greenhouse gas emissions could be reduced by 85 per cent, cropland use halved, nitrogen and phosphorus fertilizer application brought back to safe levels and two-thirds of the species predicted to go extinct could be saved. In short, we could begin to see a transformation in our food systems which would allow them to feed people in a healthy, sustainable way, without coming at the cost of wilderness or other species.

But what are the changes the diet wants us to make? Do we need to purge our fridges and cupboards of the food we currently have and start over? Do we have to give up festive eating for celebrations? Does a life of monastic veganism await, with only a heady glow of self-righteousness and carrot juice permitted as sweeteners?

Fortunately, the answer is no. The planetary health diet recommendations are not draconian. In fact, they're not even alien. Instead, the recommendations mainly resemble a way of eating which is entirely familiar to large swathes of the world: a diet that includes far less processed food than we currently eat and far more wholegrains, fruit and vegetables. The recommendations focus on increasing the amount of *wholegrain* carbohydrate (the emphasis is important) in our diets as well as increasing sources of vegetable protein and fat (such as beans and nuts), while continuing to recommend at least five portions of fruit and vegetables a day. Dairy, fish, chicken, eggs and red meat are all still on the table, although much less red meat than we might be used to.

In short, these are changes to our eating habits that we can all make. But as anyone who has ever tried to follow a new and unfamiliar pattern of eating knows, making arbitrary changes is hard. It's only if we understand why these recommendations are made, and what impact our following them will have, that we will have an incentive to change how we eat. The rest of this book is devoted to exploring and explaining why these recommendations are made, and the difference you can make to yourself – and everyone else in the world – by following them.

CHAPTER 2

OUR INTERCONNECTED EARTH

*No man is an island entire of itself; every man
is a piece of the continent, a part of the main;
if a clod be washed away by the sea, Europe
is the less, as well as if a promontory were, as
well as any manor of thy friend's or of thine
own were; any man's death diminishes me,
because I am involved in mankind.
And therefore never send to know for whom
the bell tolls; it tolls for thee.*

JOHN DONNE, 1624

If we change what we eat, we can change the world.

It's a great rallying cry, right? But I am a scientist, trained to be dubious about everything unless the evidence demonstrates otherwise. I quite understand if your reaction is to raise an eyebrow instead of squaring your shoulders. Over the course of this book, I hope to convince you with evidence and data that shows why changing our eating habits can have immense consequences, both for our own health and for that of our planet. But because we have not yet taken the steps I describe, it's easy to be sceptical about their outcome. One of the reasons I am not sceptical about the power food has to change the world is because it's something humanity has done before. If we had never started farming, your daily commute would probably be by dogsled. Let me explain.

MAN-GROWN CLIMATE CHANGE

Almost all contemporary societies farm, and it's the only way of getting food that most of us have known or are ever likely to know. Because this is all we've ever really known, it's easy to think that developing farming must be an obvious step in the evolution of human societies, and that consequently it brought significant benefits. In fact, this is an example of hindsight misleading us. Evidence shows that changing from a hunter-gatherer lifestyle to a farming one is actually less healthy and more arduous for individual humans.[1]

Archaeological comparisons of ancient farming societies and their hunter-gatherer counterparts show that those who farmed suffered from more diseases associated with poorer diet and living in close proximity to animals. A study that used height as a proxy measure for health showed that people in societies that adopted agriculture in Europe, Africa, the Middle East, Asia and South and North America all became shorter (irrespective of when the transition occurred).[2] And contemporary 21st-century societies which continue to get food by hunting and gathering have, by some measures, a much easier way of life compared to similarly-situated subsistence farmers – including far more leisure time.

So you could say that farming appears to require more work in order to make us less healthy. If this is the case, why did almost all human societies end up adopting agriculture? This is because agriculture locked humanity into a bit of a bind.

Farming has several benefits when compared with hunting and gathering: first it provides a more stable food supply, and far more supplies than hunting and gathering. Farming also puts an end to an energy-costly and unpredictable nomadic lifestyle: with more food available locally, there's no need to travel long distances in search of it. This allows societies to settle in one place. Settling in one place leads to population growth: there are more calories to go round, there's a denser population and so more chance of finding a suitable partner, and no need to carry infants as you travel, reducing the burden of child-rearing.

This is exactly what happened millennia ago as people adopted farming. The global population of humans stood at a stable five million for the first 190,000 years of our existence as hunter-gatherers. But once we began farming our population grew to around 300 million people – a 60-fold increase in about eight thousand years.[3] Such a rapid growth in population meant more mouths to feed. Fortunately, farmed crops can be readily scaled up to provide greater food yields – then of course greater yields can support more people, encouraging further population growth...and so on. Once the population becomes so big that it cannot be supported by foraging and hunting, people have no choice but to continue to farm as a matter of necessity rather than choice. Thus society is locked into agriculture, with all the benefits and hardships that that entails. (For the record, it's worth noting that farming has also allowed humanity to develop incredibly complex societies, and freed us from hunger to pursue art, science and culture. The observation that we are locked into farming should not be taken as an indictment of farming, simply an observation about why it predominates.)

As societies expanded and needed more food, early farmers began to change an ever-increasing area of land to meet the demand. The most efficient way of clearing a large area of land to create fields is by burning whatever vegetation happens to be there, which is what early farmers did (and farmers in many countries still do). So early farmers burnt their way through grasslands and forests to create arable, fertile farmland for crops such as wheat and barley. As different species of plant and animal were domesticated, people flooded plains to grow rice and allowed ever greater numbers of ruminant animals (such as cattle and sheep) to graze on newly-created pastures. Such changes, although miniscule compared to current food production systems, had a hugely significant impact on the planet.

To properly understand this impact, we need to take a brief diversion into geology. Over the past 2.6 million years – a stretch of time known as the Quaternary Period – the earth's climate has naturally shifted from being relatively mild to being extremely cold, and back again. Known as the interglacial (mild) and glacial (cold) periods, these normally have a cycle of about 100,000 years: an interglacial period begins mild and gradually cools until it becomes a glacial period – commonly known as an ice age. During an ice age, the earth becomes extremely cold and is partially covered with thick sheets of ice. The ice then melts quite abruptly (geologically speaking) in response to various geological pressures and returns us to a warmer interglacial period.

The fossil record shows us that the earth has had more than 50 of these glacial and interglacial periods. The last ice age was around 21,000 years ago, when ice sheets up to 3.2km thick in the northern hemisphere covered most of North America, the UK and northern Europe, as well as Patagonia, South Africa and much of Australia in the southern hemisphere. So much water was locked up in these ice sheets that the ocean was about 120m lower than it is currently – in other words, a drop about the height of the Pyramid of Giza (139m) and more than the Statue of Liberty (93m).

The shift between glacial and interglacial states is controlled by the earth's orbit. I'm afraid your school science textbook was not telling you the whole truth: the earth doesn't orbit the sun in a neat circle. Instead, our orbit wobbles continuously as we roll around the sun. The degree and type of wobble that we experience determines how much of the sun's energy reaches us, which in turn directly affects various mechanisms that interact to create the earth's climate, in a process known as orbital forcing.

To take one mechanism as an example, when the area around the Arctic Circle receives less light and warmth during a summer due to a wobblier orbit, there isn't enough energy to melt all the ice which accumulated over the preceding winter. The white ice that remains reflects more sunlight away from it than it would if it had melted to become water, cooling the surrounding area further (this is known as the albedo effect, and is the reason some people have suggested painting all our cities white to combat global warming). Consequently, when winter begins again, not all the ice will have melted and so the ice will become thicker. As a result of new ice accumulating and thickening on top of the ice that remained from the previous winter, ice sheets gradually form. Known as climate feedback mechanisms, these and others all interact to determine whether the earth is in a temperate inter-glacial or a colder glacial period.

There are three variables which determine how the earth's orbit wobbles (the satisfyingly named eccentricity, obliquity and precession, if you were wondering), and scientists have determined that these variables change in a predictable manner, allowing us to forecast very generally where in the cycle the earth should be at any one time. The short warm interglacial periods last on average about 10,000 years before there is a slow descent into a glacial period. Each warmer interglacial period begins with high levels of greenhouse gases (carbon dioxide and methane) which slowly drop over time. Once carbon dioxide levels reach about 240 parts per million, the earth's climate generally starts to descend into a glacial period which could last for another 80,000 years. What surprised the scientists is that according to this cycle, we should be starting to descend into a glacial period right now.

This puts us in something of a quandary. According to climate science we should be ice-bound, but unless you're looking out of a window at one of the poles, the world is still pretty temperate. Our sea levels are not dropping – far from it in fact. So what has happened? The ice sheets themselves hold the answer.

Deep ice sheets in places such as Greenland and Antarctica have remained fairly stable throughout the glacial and interglacial cycles. By drilling about 3km deep into the ice, we can engage in an amazing form of time-travel. By correlating the depth of the ice with the time taken to accumulate it, the ice cores we extract present perfectly preserved snapshots of the atmospheric conditions of past millennia.[4] If we look at ice cores from 21,000 years ago – the time of the last ice age – we can see from trapped air bubbles within them that the atmosphere years ago contained significantly lower levels of carbon dioxide and methane than we currently have in our atmosphere.

Carbon dioxide and methane are greenhouse gases: gases that insulate the planet, causing the global temperature to rise. That we currently have high levels of greenhouse gases in our atmosphere is hardly news. But we didn't start burning fossil fuel recently enough to have affected thousands of years of glacial patterns: this isn't a recent phenomenon. In fact, the levels of methane and carbon dioxide in the atmosphere began to rise far before the Industrial Revolution. Carbon dioxide levels began rising around 8,000 years ago, and methane levels 5,000 years ago: just as we, as a species, began to farm.

Scientists believe that farming around the world caused the release of greenhouse gases in such quantities that they disrupted the earth's natural glaciation cycle. Carbon dioxide would have been released by farmers either felling or burning natural vege-tation to create fields. Scientists have found evidence for this all around the world. In Europe, we have found grains showing the distinctive shape of domestication in lake sediments that date back 8,000 years, along with grassland pollens which indicate that forests had been cleared, and charcoal deposits which indicate the burning of forests.

Similar evidence exists in China and India. The increased levels of methane are believed to have been caused mainly by increasing irrigation for rice farming in Southeast Asia, which created artificial wetlands. Wetlands – both natural and artificial – are the world's largest source of methane; when submerged in water, for example to create rice paddies, soil microbes and plants have to metabo-lize without oxygen (called anaerobic conditions), which produces methane as a waste product. Methane is a potent greenhouse gas: it has 21 times the global warming capacity of carbon dioxide.[5]

By flooding their fields and cutting down forests, the first farmers released greenhouse gases in such quantities that humanity prevented an ice age from beginning. It appears that we've been living in unnaturally stable and temperate climes ever since.

While from one point of view this discovery is terrifying, from another, we can see it as heartening. It shows us that we can change the world by changing what we eat – because we have done so ever since we began to produce food for ourselves.

THE INTERCONNECTED EARTH

The incredible impact that farming has had on the world illustrates something else: how interconnected our planet is. The earth's orbital wobble, the thickness of the planet's ice sheets, how much greenhouse gases farmers released into the atmosphere by cutting down trees: the interaction of all these factors delayed what should have been an ice age. We often think of the world's natural processes as things that happen to us rather than the other way round: we shelter from wind and rain in our houses and don't consider how we might have contributed to their formation in the first place. But in fact, as we can see from the farming example, we too are very much part of this system. To understand how this system works and why this matters for our food choices, let's take a step back and address a question which seems utterly tangential (but I promise you is not): is there life on Mars?

Well before 1971, when David Bowie first mournfully asked this question, scientists were reasonably sure that there weren't any little red men out there. This confidence would have come as a surprise to 19th-century astronomers who were pretty sure they had already cracked that question by scouring the surface of Mars with wobbly telescopes. From afar, they delightedly identified straight lines criss-crossing the planet's surface and took them for Martian-built canals – and of proof of life on the red planet. It was just over 25 years after Bowie weighed in on the question that the first NASA rover *Sojourner* made it to Mars. The images it sent home were of a desolate, rocky desert surface utterly devoid of water, canals or life: while these images would disappoint the early astronomers, they were received with equanimity by the scientists who had sent the rover. Far before Bowie or *Sojourner*, scientists were confident that their rovers would be unlikely to encounter any curious little red men – or indeed, any alien life at all. How could they be so sure while standing on another planet?

This was a question put to the British scientist James Lovelock in the early 1960s. He was consulting with NASA on an even earlier mission to Mars – the Viking missions. The NASA scientists were trying to design instruments to detect whether life was present or if Mars' surface was capable of supporting life. They asked Lovelock to come up with an instrument capable of detecting *any* life, even alien life.[6] This is a bit of a tall order. How can you design an instrument to reliably detect any type of life when you have no idea what form it will take? After all, even different types of life on earth behave in totally different ways. Humans need to inhale oxygen whereas for anaerobic bacteria oxygen is a deadly toxin.

Lovelock eventually reasoned that one of the hallmarks of any form of life is that it spends energy on maintaining itself. You are an extremely complex and beautiful machine which works furiously and efficiently to turn coffee and cake into skin cells. While not everything has the luxury of cake, this is true for all living things. As opposed to the messy jumble of atoms bouncing around outside, living things consist of complex, ordered molecules built again and again, until they form a perfect eyeball or fin or tentacle or leaf. It takes two things to create these organic bits of machinery: raw material (food, oxygen, water) and energy. We don't, however, use everything that we take in. What we don't need once we've finished building and maintaining ourselves is released as waste. Human waste includes carbon dioxide, urine, faeces – but it doesn't have to be so: depending on the form of life you take, you might excrete anything from oxygen to lactic acid.

Irrespective of what you need to take in and what you excrete, any living creature is like a little factory, taking in raw materials,

using them as needed and discarding the waste back into its immediate environment. As anyone with a baby knows, children are
superb at doing this, often right after you have put on a fresh
nappy. Now imagine what a huge difference trillions of living
beings, all excreting various waste products, might create. This
was Lovelock's big insight. He realized that when you have enough
living creatures in one place, the amount of modified material
excreted as waste over time would build up to such a degree that it
would change the non-living world around it.

Specifically, Lovelock had this insight when it came to the
chemical composition of our atmosphere. The thin layer of gases
covering our planet contains a lot of different elements that, chemically speaking, shouldn't be able to exist next to one another
indefinitely. Normally, chemists would expect some of the elements
of the air to react with each other, turning into different forms, or
for other elements never to make it to the atmosphere and instead
be absorbed by the earth's oceans. In other words, for this 'unnatural' mix of gases to exist, some force has to actively maintain it.

Lovelock realized that the force actively maintaining this
strange chemical mix was life: the sum of activity from all living
things. Billions of different organisms, all taking in bits of the
world, using them and spitting them out as something new over
millions of years, have permanently changed the chemical composition of the atmosphere. For example, we shouldn't have as much
oxygen in the atmosphere as we do. Our atmosphere is about 78
per cent nitrogen and 21 per cent oxygen, with trace mixes of other
gases. The atmosphere of Mars, on the other hand, is predominantly carbon dioxide and about 3 per cent nitrogen (similar to
other planets like Venus). The reason for our oxygen-rich atmosphere is that early life, known as cyanobacteria, used sunlight and
carbon dioxide to survive, and excreted oxygen just as plants do
today. Over the aeons they produced enough oxygen to form our
atmosphere.

From this insight, Lovelock realized that life on Mars seemed
very unlikely. Mars' atmosphere looks just as one would expect

it to without anything interfering: a random jumble of chemicals, totally as expected (chemically speaking). There's no indication that there's anything alive on Mars which is excreting some interesting gases that mess with the chemistry of the atmosphere. So far, and four Martian rovers later, we're yet to find any little red men, so for now Lovelock's theory on Mars holds.

But Lovelock's insight had a much more important implication, and that was what it meant for life on earth. We're used to thinking about how the inorganic world can have an impact on us and our lives: as little organic life forms, we huddle under artificial shelters against the much bigger inorganic and arbitrary forces of wind and rain. It seems contradictory to turn this round and think that we can influence such factors. But Lovelock's theory implies precisely that – and this began his now (in)famous Gaia hypothesis. Named for the Ancient Greek goddess of the earth, this hypothesis proposes that living beings and their inorganic environments are integrated, forming a single and self-regulating complex system. This system, consisting of both living and inert parts, maintains the conditions for life on earth.

Like any radical idea, this hypothesis has been taken up and contested by various factions, come under fire, been unpicked, reformulated, and so on, and there remains great contention over what it can and cannot imply. But its central thesis highlights something that is both intuitive but hard to grasp: we can look at all the different parts of the world as combining to form a single interconnected system. The oceans, the land, living beings, the atmosphere: each one of these elements is in itself an unbelievably vast and complex sub-system, but none of them exists in isolation. The oceans change the land; the animals and plants change the land; the land changes the ocean, and so on for every permutation imaginable.

Thinking about our world in this way was one of the early concepts that fed into what is now known as earth system science. Earth system science proposes that to understand the world we must acknowledge it as a single system – a vastly complex one with a million different interconnecting components, yes, but ultimately one system. Like a complex, changing tapestry, all the elements of the earth come together to form a single picture.

And importantly, even though it's easy to forget it, we are all part of this system. Every individual is just as much a part of the earth system as any other animal, or a river, or the bedrock. Every component of your life, including the air you exhale, the waste you excrete – and, of course, the food that you eat – is part of it. We might live in concrete jungles but what we tend to forget is that those jungles are built from components we've taken from the earth, smashed, smelted, moulded and plonked back on the earth. And so everything we do has an impact. Our individual actions might be minute: we have a tiny, almost immeasurable impact. But when you take the actions of nearly eight billion people, the numbers add up much faster.

The problem with the beautiful theory of the earth as a single system is that it has a very scary implication: changing one part of the system, even if seemingly small, has the potential to profoundly change the whole. And this is exactly what we are doing. We are changing the world so much that geologists have created a new word for the time in which we are living: the Anthropocene (see page 10).

For the first time since our planet came into being, its future is not being dictated by aeons-long processes such as the movement of tectonic plates, or catastrophic events such as meteorite strikes. Instead, the surface of the world is being reshaped by much more mundane human actions. For example, people move more soil, rock and sediment annually through activities such as construction than are moved by any natural processes – oceans, rivers, landslides and waterfalls – combined. We remove more nitrogen from the atmosphere for the production of fertilizer and other human activities than any natural process does; scientists term this atmospheric mining. We have cut down about three trillion trees, halving the number that existed before we started farming.

In short, the reshaping of the natural environment which we first began with early farming has now gone further than ever before. We have become a natural force in our own right. We are enacting geological-scale changes over a human timespan. And our actions have consequences for the entire world.

GOLDILOCKS AND THE PLANETARY BOUNDARIES

You will probably be familiar with this fairy tale. A small girl named Goldilocks (who clearly lacked a basic moral education) was walking in the woods one day when she came across a lovely little house. Instead of passing it by, she let herself in, and, finding that no one was at home, she went exploring. In the kitchen she found three bowls of porridge, and rather rudely decided to eat them. The first she found too hot for her liking, the second too cold, but the third she found was just right – so she ate it all up. She then proceeded to try various chairs and beds for size and comfort, breaking a chair in the process, and ending up asleep on the comfiest bed. Unfortunately for her, the residents of the house, who happened to be three bears, returned to find her asleep. Most versions of the story have her waking up to the sight of the returned home owners and running away. The story is usually intended to teach children about the consequences of taking something that is not theirs. (One wonders whether allowing the bears a small blonde meal might not be a sharper, clearer lesson, but I digress.) Here however I tell it to illustrate a different lesson.

Our world can be thought of as the porridge in this story. It is capable of being in many different states. Taking temperature as an example, although there was one bowl of porridge at a temperature Goldilocks found to be just right, the other bowls of porridge were presumably just right according to the preferences of the other two bears, though a little too hot or a little too cold for Goldilocks. The porridge itself was no different, but the temperature varied.

Our world is now just right for humanity. We're told that an increase in temperature of any more than 2°C (3.6°F) could have catastrophic implications for our world. What experts often forget to clarify is that those consequences would be catastrophic *for us*. The planet is a dynamic system and the nature of such systems is that changes in one part of it will affect other parts. To use the tapestry metaphor, changing the threads that make up a tapestry might not destroy the fabric of the tapestry itself, but its design will look very different. There is no natural dynamic feedback mechanism which will kick in to warn us that we have pushed the planet too far: the planet doesn't care. What will happen is that the system will just change and the uncaring world will simply cease to be just right for human civilization as we know it.

Scientists call this just-right state the safe operating space for humanity.[7][8] (The acronym may just be coincidental.) This is the space in which the earth system creates an environment which is favourable to human life. This space is defined by the limits to which we can push the processes that make up the system and keep it going. Scientists have identified nine processes which we can directly affect, and which in turn change the whole of the earth system.

Let's take the best-known of the earth system processes, climate, as an example. There are many different factors that contribute to a given area's climate, including the topological features of the area (mountains, oceans), its location on earth (equatorial or polar), the composition of the atmosphere above it, and so on. So while we *could* change the climate by nuking a mountain range, it's (fortunately) not something humanity does all that often. However, what we have been doing – incrementally but persistently – is changing the composition of the atmosphere by emitting increasing quantities of insulating greenhouse gases into it. Increasing carbon dioxide and methane emissions causes a change in climate because it changes the composition of the atmosphere. In this example, releasing greenhouse gases into the atmosphere is a way of pushing a process out of alignment. At some point, if we continue, we will

31

have exuded so much carbon dioxide and methane into the atmosphere that we will have changed the earth's atmosphere, and thus its climate, irrevocably. Passing this limit would mean we have transgressed what scientists call a planetary boundary.

It is important to make a distinction between an earth system *process* and a *boundary* of that system. Let's return to the idea of the world as a tapestry made up of many different threads. The safe operating space for humanity is the pretty picture that the different threads currently combine to make up. Each planetary process can be thought of as a contributing thread. Each planetary boundary is the degree of leeway we have in changing that thread's colour, or how tightly or loosely it is woven, before we start to affect the overall picture. The tapestry will remain whole regardless, but depending on what we do to the thread, the picture might change dramatically.

We can think of the boundaries as tipping points for each process: if a thread is currently a sort of turquoise we can nudge it a little more towards either the green spectrum (one boundary) or a little more towards the blue (another boundary) without seeing much change in the overall picture. But if we were to make it bright pink, it would probably violently disrupt the overall image. With almost all planetary processes, we're pushing towards the green or blue boundaries of things. But the problem is that even while we might not be changing the process all that much, we're certainly changing it enough for us to not know what the picture is going to look like as a result of that change. This is known as the zone of uncertainty, and it's something we're in much more often than we'd like to be.

There are nine earth system processes in total which we are pushing to their limits. While many of the processes feed into climate change, all of them are vital in their own right: overstepping the mark on any one of them will have an impact on how we maintain our safe operating space. The other eight might not enjoy the same media attention as climate change, but they are equally – and in some cases more – worrying. Of the nine, I will only describe and focus on the five which most directly relate to food and its production. They are extremely dry and difficult to understand when listed as they are below (I will explore and explain each term more fully in subsequent chapters), but that's science for you. The good news is that I will spend the rest of this book investigating these bland scientific terms to understand exactly what they mean and how our daily food choices bring us into contact with them every day.

An important thing to note about these boundaries is that they are not hard and fast: they all have areas of uncertainty around what is 'safe', and about what exceeding a boundary might mean. Exceeding a boundary doesn't automatically cause harm. But the problem is, we cannot be sure what it will lead to – only that it will probably affect the earth system in unforeseen and unforeseeable ways.

Earth system process	How we measure the planetary boundary
Climate	Greenhouse gas concentration in the atmosphere
Biogeochemical flow	The amount of nitrogen and phosphorus circulating in the earth system
Freshwater use	How much water we use
Land-system change	Change in land-use area (e.g. deforestation)
Biodiversity loss	Number of species going extinct

Earth system processes and planetary boundaries associated with food

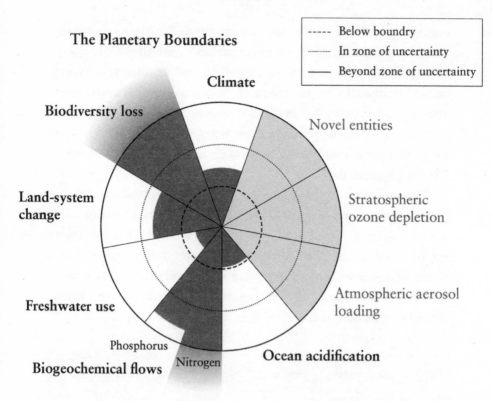

The Planetary Boundaries

Climate
Biodiversity loss
Novel entities
Land-system change
Stratospheric ozone depletion
Freshwater use
Atmospheric aerosol loading
Phosphorus
Nitrogen
Ocean acidification
Biogeochemical flows

----- Below boundry
.... In zone of uncertainty
—— Beyond zone of uncertainty

This figure shows the nine planetary boundaries, and how far we have come to exceeding each one.[9] Novel entities, stratospheric ozone depletion and atmospheric aerosol loading are beyond the remit of this book, and are not affected directly by our food production. Ocean acidification is also not directly related to food production, but because it is directly related to climate change, we will touch briefly on it on page 201. Of all the planetary boundaries directly related to our food production, we are in the safe zone (below the boundary) for freshwater use only. We are in the zone of uncertainty for land-system change and climate change – and we have far exceeded the zone of uncertainty for biodiversity loss and biogeochemical flows.

CLIMATE CHANGE

The first and best-known process is climate change. Scientists and politicians have realized that it is not possible to maintain civilization as we know it without continuing to release at least some greenhouse gases into the atmosphere. So instead of aiming to preserve the climate exactly as it is, the aim is to ensure that it doesn't change too much. This aim has been enshrined in international law thanks to the Paris Agreement. This agreement, reached on 12 December 2015, was made between countries that have signed the United Nations Framework Convention on Climate Change. By early 2020 the agreement had been ratified by 187 countries.

The fundamental aim of the agreement is to ensure that global temperatures this century do not rise above 2°C (3.6°F) more than pre-industrial levels (with the hope, if possible, that we might be able to limit the change to 1.5°C/2.7°F). In effect the target was determined backwards: if we can keep the temperature rise to +2°C (+3.6°F) or less, then we should be able to adapt to the effects of climate change. In order to achieve this target, the world has a 'budget' setting out how many greenhouse gases we can emit into the atmosphere. This is a science-based target because the way in which we can control the change in global temperature is through regulating greenhouse gas emissions. There are two planetary boundaries for climate change. The first is keeping the concentration of greenhouse gas carbon dioxide equivalents to lower than 350 parts per million. We have already exceeded this boundary; the concentration currently stands at over 415 parts per million. The second boundary is known as radiative forcing and is a bit more complex, so I won't go into detail about it here.

The planetary boundaries aim to supply similar science-based targets for all the processes which make up the earth system. If we look specifically at climate change, although carbon dioxide is the most infamous of all greenhouse gases, methane and nitrous oxide emissions also contribute. We can regulate their levels in the atmosphere in several ways. We can release fewer gases into the environment; protect greenhouse gas 'sinks' such as forests and soil which can absorb greenhouse gases and lock them up; or we can create artificial sinks which remove gases from the atmosphere.

BIOGEOCHEMICAL FLOW

The second boundary is biogeochemical flow. This refers to the extraction, application and run-off of two critical elements found in fertilizer: nitrogen and phosphorus. Both of these elements are vital for growing crops: lack of either element limits crop growth and yield.

Nitrogen gas comprises 78 per cent of the atmosphere, but it is in an inert form which plants can't use. For plants to take up nitrogen, the element needs to be 'fixed' into ammonium or nitrate which can be taken up by plants. Fortunately, we can synthesize ammonia artificially using something called the Haber-Bosch process, a discovery so important that it won its inventors Nobel Prizes in both 1918 and 1931. Unfortunately, this process requires a huge amount of energy; ammonia production accounts for 1 per cent of all global carbon dioxide emissions. Phosphorus, on the other hand, is a mineral which can only be extracted by mining. Estimating the earth's current phosphate reserves is contentious but there is no doubt that they are finite and depleting.

Fertilizer is over-applied in many parts of the world to achieve maximum crop harvests. Many countries' governments subsidize fertilizers to ensure that harvest yields are met. Unfortunately, excessive application of fertilizers has terrible environmental consequences: eutrophication. This happens when too many nutrients flow into bodies of water and cause a variety of problems including deoxygenating large areas of ocean, killing animals and causing huge algal blooms to grow which cut off light to the animals and plants beneath them.

So here we have resources which are either finite and depleting, or infinite but polluting and costly to produce, which we over-apply and then lose to the environment, harming it in the process. In this case the planetary boundaries are the global and regional flows of phosphorus and nitrogen from fertilizers into soil and water, measured in teragrams (a billion kilograms). We have not just exceeded the planetary boundaries for these losses – we currently lose more than double the boundary limit for our safe operating space. We urgently need to curb our use and close these loops, but some damage is already done.

FRESHWATER USE

The third boundary is freshwater use. Of the 1,400 million cubic km of water in the world, only 0.003 per cent is freshwater which can be used for drinking, agriculture, bathing and industry. And not even all of this relatively tiny quantity is accessible to us: much is locked in hard-to-reach lakes and rivers underground, or in other inaccessible locations. But we're a thirsty species: humanity's water use grew almost twice as fast as its population in the 20th century, and agriculture accounted for 70 per cent of that use. The United Nations Food and Agriculture Organization (FAO) estimates that by 2050 there will be a 50 per cent increase in irrigated food production.[10]

But there is good news: with new technologies and careful water management, this 50 per cent increase in food production might come with only a 10 per cent increase in water use. In fact, despite the very visible effects of desertification in some parts of the world, freshwater use is the one boundary which we are far away from exceeding. The trickiest problem is that quantities are not evenly distributed throughout the world: some areas are inherently more arid and in other areas human actions disrupt water flows into ecosystems, such as damming or diverting rivers for irrigation.

When people are persistently systematically deprived of such a precious resource this may lead to water wars, and policymakers become concerned that tensions over freshwater use and management will increase regional tensions and unrest.[11] So even though water is a plentiful global resource, freshwater use for agriculture needs to be carefully considered to ensure even distribution throughout regions. The global planetary boundary for freshwater use is 4,000 cubic km per year, and we currently use only about 2,600 cubic km. The biggest issue with freshwater use is its fair distribution.

LAND-SYSTEM CHANGE

Land-system change or land-use change, the fourth boundary, is the area of land which changes from being wild to being used by humans. This generally refers to forested land, but can also apply to grasslands, mangroves and other ecosystems relatively free of human interference. While land can change for reasons other than agriculture, for example to build a new town, agricultural conversion is the driving force around the world. Between 1980 and 2000, 100 million hectares of tropical forest was cleared by humans, of which 42 million hectares was for cattle ranching in Latin America.[12]

To put that into perspective, the total land area of the UK is about 24 million hectares: so in 20 years, an area almost twice the size of the UK was converted from forest to cattle ranch.

Such changes represent a huge loss of habitat for wildlife, but that is not the concern when it comes to this particular earth system process. The issue is that the water, forests and soil of natural habitats are superb organic carbon sinks. Destroying them not only removes natural ways of mopping up excess carbon dioxide, it actively releases yet more greenhouse gases into the atmosphere, for example as vegetation is burned or left to rot. We're reaching a critical point in our land-use. At the moment, just over half the world (51 per cent) qualifies as an intact ecosystem, untouched by human changes.[13] We need to ensure that it stays this way, at the very least, if we're to be able to combat climate change. This means that agriculture cannot take any additional land from wild spaces, and this in itself poses problems as we face having to feed an increasingly large world population.

BIODIVERSITY LOSS

B iodiversity loss, planetary boundary number five, refers to the number of species we are losing every year from the world as they become extinct. Large-scale extinction events in which the earth loses more than 75 per cent of its species have been surprisingly common throughout earth's history: so far, five have been recorded. Scientists believe that we are now in the middle of a sixth. The difference between the threat today and the preceding events is the speed and scope of the extinctions. For example, in the last 100 years, about 200 species of vertebrate animal have gone extinct: this is a rate of about 100–1,000 times faster than previously recorded.[14] The current planetary boundary is set at less than ten extinctions per million species years. A 'million species years' is a way of measuring how many, of all existing species, are expected to go extinct over a million years. The exact background rate of extinction (i.e. how often species would go extinct without any interference from mankind) is around one extinction per million species years. Simply put, this means that if there was a background extinction rate of one per million species years, and there were a million species on earth, we'd expect an average of one species to go extinct every year. Or, if there was only one species, we'd expect it to go extinct within a million years. Our current extinction rate is difficult to calculate accurately – current estimates suggest we are losing somewhere between 100 and 1,000 species per million species years.

Those species that survive are losing habitat and are thinning in numbers: for example, of a sample of 177 mammals between 1900 and 2015, all had lost 30 per cent or more of their ranges and more than 40 per cent had experienced severe population declines. The scientists behind these findings termed them 'biological annihilation'.[15] Extinctions come about as a result of habitat loss, fragmentation or degradation.

Setting aside the more abstract or moral implications of the above, such biodiversity loss has real implications for humanity. Take pollinators such as bees as one example. More than three-quarters of all food produced by humans relies on animal pollination[16] and crops worth between US$235 billion and US$577 billion annually are threatened due to pollinator loss. Other living creatures provide the global earth system – and humanity's systems of production – with resilience in ways that we tend to only understand once we see the effects of losing them.

On our interconnected earth, every action we undertake has consequences for multiple processes. This means that all these boundaries are interconnected. To take just one example, deforestation (land-use change) releases carbon dioxide into the atmosphere through burning or felling vegetation (contributing greenhouse gases, affecting climate change). Deforestation reduces biodiversity – so there are fewer trees – but it also removes habitats for animal species, potentially driving some species to extinction. Also forests play key roles in regulating local rainfall patterns, so deforestation often drives a change in freshwater availability.

In other words, in our interconnected tapestry of the world, pulling on one thread has the potential to affect dozens of others. But while the implications of this can seem scary, they don't have to be. It also means that we have the potential to improve matters by pulling on a single thread. And that thread is food.

THE POWER OF YOUR PLATE

Our food system has a huge impact on the world – and consequently is one of the main contributing factors to where we stand on our planetary boundaries. Exactly how food impacts on all the boundaries is the focus of most of this book, but just to give you a snapshot, consider the following.[17] We use 51 million square km for agriculture – that's half the habitable land on the planet. The amount of land used for raising livestock is 40 million square km – an area the size of North, South and Central America combined. We use 11 million square km, or an area of land the size of the East Asia-Pacific region, to grow crops. Global food production accounts for 26 per cent of the world's total greenhouse gas emissions – but these are not the result of flying in exotic fruit and veg to satisfy middle-class consumers. In fact 31 per cent come from farming livestock and fish, 27 per cent from crop production and 24 per cent from continually changing land-use to sate our ever-expanding appetites for more food. *All* food transport – not just air-freighted perishables – accounts for just 6 per cent of the total emissions produced by food. Agricultural run-off from fertilizers was responsible for 78 per cent of ocean and river eutrophication worldwide.[18] [19]

As a result, food and and how we produce it is hugely important when we consider how to stay within the world's safe operating space for humanity. The planetary health diet takes the planetary boundaries into account when formulating dietary recommendations – so the changes they recommend we make to our diets are not only designed for our health but are also formulated to move us back into the safe zones of these various critical planetary processes.

But while I may have convinced you over the course of this chapter that food production systems at least have the power to harm the world, I wouldn't be surprised if you remain unconvinced that your food choices as an individual have enough power to heal the world. Sure, the planetary health diet says they do, but that's just one piece of evidence. How can we be sure that this is enough?

The planetary health diet is a unique piece of research because it gives a systematic breakdown of the foods that we should be eating in a way that guides us to make changes to our eating patterns. I will discuss exactly what those changes are throughout the book, and in specific detail at the end, so once you've finished reading it you will be able to apply the recommendations to your own eating patterns, no matter where you are in the world. But the planetary health diet is not the only piece of research that supports the notion that changing our diet has the potential to change the world.

Let's take, for example, a truly staggering piece of research published in another world-leading scientific journal, *Science*, in 2018. Modestly entitled 'Reducing food's environmental impacts through producers and consumers' the article describes how the authors took on the task of quantifying the environmental impact of 40 different types of the most frequently eaten food in the world, representing about 90 per cent of all calorie consumption.[20] To ensure an accurate measurement for each foodstuff that took into account the huge variation in farming practices throughout the world, they assembled data on 38,700 commercial farms from 119 countries and then assessed each food's impact on land-use change, freshwater use, greenhouse gas emission, and eutrophying and acidifying emissions. They didn't simply include farming data: they looked at the impact along the entire supply chain, from food production to retail. It is a remarkable piece of work. It is this study that provided the figures above, and I will return to exactly what they did and what they found at several points throughout the book. But one of their most incredible findings, and something which almost gets lost in the reams of data they generated, is the following: 'Today, and probably into the future, dietary change can deliver environmental benefits on a scale not achievable by producers.'

In other words, the power we have through the decisions that we make about what to eat outstrips anything that producers can do. And other scientists agree. There are countless papers that show that changing our diets is perhaps the most effective way in which we can help slow or even reverse environmental harms. And it is very encouraging that the recommendations the planetary health diet makes are echoed again and again throughout the scientific literature.

Another paper entitled 'Multiple health and environmental impacts of foods' was published in 2019 in another top scientific journal, *Proceedings of the National Academy of Sciences*,[21] which assessed 15 types of food for their health and environmental impacts. The study concludes:

> 'We find that foods associated with improved adult health also often have low environmental impacts, indicating that the same dietary transitions that would lower incidences of noncommunicable diseases would also help meet environmental sustainability targets... Global diets have been shifting toward greater consumption of foods associated with increased disease risk or higher environmental impacts and are projected to lead to rapid increases in diet-related diseases and environmental degradation. Reversing this trend in the regions in which it has occurred and instead increasing consumption of...foods that are consistently associated with decreased disease risk and low environmental impacts – would have multiple health and environmental benefits globally.'

In other words, this is not just one group of scientists with an agenda. The planetary health diet represents a specific set of recommendations, and these exact recommendations have been and will continue to be contested. Should we eat slightly less meat and slightly more grain? Fewer nuts but more fruit? These details remain up for debate. But the big picture is the same. What we eat *can* change the world, and we the consumers have the power to make that happen more than any other force.

Over the next five chapters, I will set out the planetary health diet guidelines for each of the major food groups: carbohydrates and sugar; fat; fruit and vegetables; and protein (both animal and vegetable). Within each chapter I will describe the recommendation and why we might need to eat more or less than we do currently for our health. I will also discuss a specific planetary boundary to show you how all the food that we eat relates to the interconnected earth. As I hope you have already realized, this is something of an artificial demarcation, because everything is

– well – interconnected. But picking examples is the easiest way of illustrating these connections.

Finally, in Chapter Eight I will unpack the planetary health diet in full to guide you through how to change your eating habits so that you too can contribute to this planetary change. The recommendations are either radical or totally mundane, depending on your current eating patterns – though they are not alien and they are not unattainable. But they are important. To end with another quote from the authors of the heroic *Science* paper mentioned above: 'Communicating average product impacts to consumers enables dietary change and should be pursued. Though dietary change is realistic for any individual, widespread behavioural change will be hard to achieve in the narrow time frame remaining to limit global warming and prevent further, irreversible biodiversity loss.'

Communicating average product impacts (which means explaining the environmental impacts food has on the world) is exactly what this book aims to do. Not only can what we eat change the world, we need to start making those changes before it's too late.

CHAPTER 3

CARBOHYDRATES AND ADDED SUGARS

> **PLANETARY HEALTH DIET RECOMMENDATION**
>
> Daily recommendation: three to four portions of wholegrain source carbohydrates, such as wholewheat bread, brown rice or oatmeal, substituting one portion of starchy root vegetables (e.g. potatoes) every two to four days. One small portion of food containing added sugars is optional (e.g. two small biscuits).

Consider the vending machine. The next time you walk past one – and that will probaby be soon – pause briefly and look at the food products it offers you. The serried ranks of crisps, chocolates and carbonated drinks are lined up behind the glass like colourful jewels. Each one promises you not only a tasty treat, but also some kind of relief from the humdrum. Have a break, have a Kit Kat. Once you pop, you can't stop. One of Coca-Cola's most iconic slogans was, 'The pause that refreshes'; it is now 'Taste the feeling'. You'll note that none of the food that fits neatly into a vending machine tray is marketed as something to fill you up when you're hungry or slake your thirst, but instead as something to divert or please you. Ultimately, these products are not really sold as food but as entertainment. Their taglines are honest: the product might be edible – but that's not really the point.

All these foods have something in common. They are all either processed or – more often than not – ultra-processed. And their ubiquity is becoming a problem.

PROCESSED FOOD

Food scientists have started to classify food into four groups depending on the degree of processing required to create them (the NOVA scale of food classification).[1]

The first group comprises unprocessed or minimally processed foods. Unprocessed food is defined as edible portions of plants, animals, fungi, algae and water. For example, an apple is an unprocessed food. Minimally processed foods are unprocessed foods minus the inedible parts or food that has undergone a basic cooking process such as roasting or refrigeration. So a whole fresh pineapple is an unprocessed food, and a packet of fresh pineapple slices with the spiky skin removed is a minimally processed one.

The second group includes processed ingredients such as oils, butter, sugar and salt, which are derived from group one foods through processes that include pressing, refining, milling or drying. So for olive oil the group one food is an olive and the oil obtained by pressing it is the group two food.

Group three foods are processed foods, and are the result of combining group two ingredients with group one foods: food such as tinned fish, cheese, bread and most meals which have been processed in some way. These foods tend to have two or three ingredients, are processed using techniques such as non-alcoholic fermentation and general cooking methods, and, crucially, are recognizable as modified versions of group one foods. With enough time and practice you would be able to make a group three food (although, if your bread-making skills are anything like mine, people will not necessarily thank you for it).

However, unless you have a lot of bizarre machinery in your kitchen you wouldn't be able to make anything in group four.

Group four foods are ultra-processed foods, and it is worth quoting the definition in one scientific paper: 'These are industrial formulations manufactured mostly or entirely from sugar, salt, oils and fats, starches and many substances derived from foods but not normally used in kitchens, and additives including those used to imitate the sensory qualities of natural foods or to disguise undesirable qualities of the final product.'[2]

Examples of ultra-processed foods include (but are not limited to): 'sweet, fatty or salty packaged snack products; ice cream, chocolate, candies; mass-produced packaged breads, cookies, pastries, cakes; breakfast cereals; "energy" bars; preserves; margarines; carbonated drinks, "energy" drinks; milk drinks, including "fruit" yoghurts; cocoa drinks; infant formulas, follow-on milks, other baby products; "health" and "slimming" products such as powdered or "fortified" meal and dish substitutes; and many ready-to-heat products including pre-prepared pies and pizza dishes, burgers, hot dogs, poultry and fish "nuggets", and other reconstituted meat products, and powdered and packaged soups, noodles and industrial desserts'.[3]

The term 'ultra-processed' refers to the many processes required to extract and combine the often large number of ingredients into the final product. Almost none of these processes would be recognizable to a home cook (or feasible in a regular kitchen). Such ultra-processing creates foods which are convenient (long-lasting and easy to eat) and, due to the low cost of the ingredients, extremely profitable for the producer.

Foods in group four are a relatively new phenomenon: ultra-processed food has only been around for approximately 60 years. But what ultra-processed food lacks in history, it makes up for in apparently insatiable popularity. Every item offered in a vending machine would be classified as an ultra-processed food. Critically, you also find ultra-processed foods in many aisles of all supermarkets worldwide: while the vending machine might represent the most highly concentrated grouping, these foods have become ubiquitous in our lives.

Using the definition above, a paper published in 2018 estimated that in the UK an average of 57 per cent of a person's
daily calories come from ultra-processed foods.[4] A different study
using older data, looked at similar data across Europe, and put
the number at 51 per cent for the UK, which comfortably beat
Germany and Ireland (both 46 per cent) to claim the top prize.[5]
(For those wondering, the countries with the lowest proportions
were Portugal at 10 per cent and Greece at 14 per cent, although
the data used was pre-2008 and might have changed as a result of
the financial crisis.) About 71 per cent of all foods in the USA are
classified as ultra-processed.[6]

And these foods are not limited to high-income countries. They
are rising in incidence and popularity in low- and middle-income
countries too. For example, in Latin America and the Caribbean,
packaged and processed food rose from being about 10 per cent of
all food sales in 1990 to 60 per cent by 2000.[7]

In short, the whole world is digging into group four foods
with gusto. People are depending increasingly on processed and
ultra-processed foods – whether from a vending machine or off
a supermarket shelf – for their daily calories. This change in our
eating habits has serious implications for both ourselves and the
environment.

FAT AND STARVING

It will probably surprise no one to hear that ultra-processed
foods are not good for us, and data linking such foods to the
rising incidence of obesity and other non-communicable diseases
abound.

So you can fully appreciate how critical these data are, I want
to quickly run through different types of scientific findings. The
media may portray it differently, but not all science is created
equal – some types of findings are a lot more robust than others,
and knowing this is crucial for assessing how big a pinch of salt

you need to take when contemplating any finding. (This is also why there are so many studies which come up with apparently contradictory results.)

In clinical science – that means anything to do with people – the best way of testing a theory is to run a clinical trial. This broadly means that you assemble a group of people, give them some new intervention (a drug, an exercise regime, a technology) and assess what difference it makes. To be consistent, you have to define any difference you're expecting to see *before* giving them the new intervention – are you checking whether it's safe? Or are you expecting to see some change in health, and if so, what kind of change?

Clinical trials come in three phases. Phase 1 trials are for the newest interventions, and are done on small groups of people, often in carefully managed stages, to see whether the intervention is safe or not. Assuming it is, scientists move on to phase 2, in which you assemble slightly more people to see if the intervention results in any beneficial change. The biggest and best clinical trials are phase 3 trials, which compare the new intervention to one that's already been proven to work (the control treatment) to see which works better. Patients are randomly assigned to either the active treatment or the control treatment, and this is known as a randomized controlled trial. Often these trials are blind or double-blind. When a trial is done blind, participants don't know which treatment they're getting. This is to prevent the trial being affected by the placebo effect, which is the odd and poorly-understood phenomenon whereby just getting some treatment, even a sugar pill, improves people's health conditions. In a double-blind trial neither the participant nor the researcher knows which treatment the participant is getting. This prevents any accidental bias on the part of the researcher.

Of these three phases of trial, phase 3 is the most rigorous, and often a requirement for a new treatment to be legally licensed as a valid therapy. But the gold-standard evidence is something called a meta-analysis, which takes this one step further. A meta-analysis takes *all* the trials that looked at a specific question and carefully and rigorously combines the data to see an average result. Data from a meta-analysis is held as the most reliable. Wherever possible in this book I will attempt to flag the kind of evidence I'm referencing so you know how sure we can be about a particular statement.

Back to the data on ultra-processed food and health. A small randomized controlled study by the US National Institutes of Health took a group of healthy adults who were fed for two weeks on two different sets of food which had been identically matched in terms of calories, energy density, macronutrients, sugar, salt and fibre. The only difference was that one group's food was ultra-processed and the other's unprocessed. The volunteers were told to eat as much as they wanted of both. At the end of the two weeks, the volunteers were weighed and their diets swapped, so those who had been eating only the ultra-processed foods ate only unprocessed foods, and vice versa (cleverly allowing each volunteer to act as their own control to make the results more robust).

The results were striking. When eating the ultra-processed foods, participants ate on average 508 more calories a day, consuming more carbohydrate and fat than those eating the unprocessed foods. Weight changes followed: participants gained almost a kilo of weight during the two weeks on the ultra-processed diet, but lost exactly the same amount while eating the unprocessed foods.[8] This study shows that even when every other factor is exactly the same, increasing the processing of food can lead to weight gain, which in turn acts as a risk factor for becoming overweight or obese and developing a non-communicable disease.

The United Nations Food and Agriculture Organization (FAO) produced a much wider-ranging report in 2019 which systematically assessed the data available between 2015 and 2019 on eating ultra-processed foods and non-communicable diseases.[9] Combining all the available data, they also found that eating more ultra-processed foods was significantly associated with obesity and developing cardiovascular and metabolic diseases.

They also found that this relationship was dose-dependent – the more ultra-processed food you eat, the stronger the association. This and other evidence points to a significant link between the rising prevalence of non-communicable diseases and the rise in consumption of ultra-processed food. But it is more complicated than people simply carrying excess pounds.

Although more people than ever before carry extra weight, this does not mean that they are getting the nutrients they need from their food. It is possible to be both overweight *and* malnourished. This phenomenon is called the double burden of malnutrition.

In 2018, about 155 million children around the world under the age of five were classed as 'stunted' (short for their age group, which implies that they had not eaten sufficient nutrients to grow and develop normally), and 52 million children were classed as 'wasted' (light in weight for their height; being emaciated).[10] But in 2014, 41 million children were also classed as overweight or obese.[11]

Although we are used to thinking of malnutrition as a health issue resulting from not having enough to eat, researchers now include the problems associated with eating too much food in malnutrition as well. This double burden of malnutrition arises when people eat insufficient *nutrients* but too many *calories*.[12] Estimates suggest that in 2010, about 38 per cent of low- and middle-income countries faced this double burden of malnutrition, with the highest prevalence in sub-Saharan Africa, south and east Asia and the Pacific.

It would be unfair to characterize ultra-processed food as the only factor driving this change. There are many other complex factors at play, including historical and genetic predispositions, and the global decline in people taking exercise linked in large part to technological advances. But ultra-processed food is widely believed to be one of the main causes underpinning this phenomenon.

Although there seems to be an infinite number of ultra-processed foods, the FAO report flags that 'some ultra-processed products are...especially problematic. These include carbonated soft drinks, sweet and savoury snacks, biscuits (cookies), confectionery, and cakes, pastries and desserts.'[13] What is it about these foods which is so especially problematic? It's that they are predominantly refined carbohydrate products, with added sugars to make them sweeter and added fats to make them feel nicer in the mouth. We'll come on to added fats in the next chapter. For now, we need to examine what causes such concern about sugar and refined carbohydrates.

HEALTHY CARBOHYDRATES?

Contrary to what fans of the Atkins diet might think, eating a carbohydrate-rich diet is neither new nor bad. In fact, it is the diet that people have subsisted on for almost their entire existence. We began the domestication of wheat (our oldest crop) in Southwest Asia 11,000 years ago. Today, there are more than 50,000 edible plant species in the world, and yet just 15 crops provide about 90 per cent of the world's energy intake. Of these 15 crops, just three grains – rice, maize and wheat – are responsible for feeding about four billion people, providing 60 per cent of the world population's energy intake. Rice alone feeds approximately half of all people.[14] We call such grains our staple foods with good reason: we depend on these supplies of carbohydrates.

However, when asked what a carbohydrate is, most of us think for a second and then say, 'bread?'. The confusion arises because we use the word carbohydrate in everyday language to refer to many different food types, when it is actually a technical chemical term. There is a big difference between a food which contains carbohydrates and a carbohydrate itself: carbohydrate is an umbrella term for a whole class of molecules. Chemically speaking, a carbohydrate is an organic molecular compound made from carbon, hydrogen and oxygen (hydrogen and oxygen associate with carbon in the same ratio as they do in water, thus creating hydrated carbon – or carbo-hydrate). Calling foods 'carbs' simply means that the food contains, among other things, a large quantity of these molecules. But there is room within this group for extreme variety and complexity: carbohydrates exist in many forms.

The differences are to do with how long and complex a carbohydrate molecule is. The simplest form a carbohydrate can take is as a monosaccharide, giving us the carbohydrate molecules we've heard of, such as glucose and fructose. Other forms of carbohydrates can quickly start sounding like a list of alien species: fructo-oligosaccharides, galactose, raffinose... The different molecules can be roughly categorized as being either sugars – which are the smallest molecules – or starches – which are polysaccharides, and form longer and more complex molecules.

What makes them different? Despite being technically similar, the amount of energy we obtain from each type of carbohydrate and the way in which we can (or, in some cases, cannot) process different molecules varies.[15] For example, the sugar you put in your coffee is technically a disaccharide made up of two monosaccharides, fructose and glucose. Despite both being small sugar molecules, fructose and glucose are processed in different ways. Our bodies are not built to metabolize all carbohydrates at the same rate – or even to break them down at all.

Our ability to break down a particular carbohydrate depends on the enzymes available for the job. For example, cellulose is a complex carbohydrate found in plant walls. We can't digest it, which is why we don't eat grass. Cows and other ruminants don't have the necessary enzyme either but have cunningly formed a symbiotic relationship with specialist bacteria which do make the right enzyme (cellulase) and live in their multiple stomachs. The bacteria digest the cellulose and the cows absorb the by-products that are produced.

So not all carbohydrates offer us equal energy sources. The type of carbohydrate, the way in which it is molecularly packaged in a food along with other components such as fat and protein, all affect how our bodies respond to eating a particular carbohydrate.

Is it possible to class any given carbohydrate as healthy or unhealthy? The short answer is no, not really: it depends on the proportion of the carbohydrate in the diet as a whole. There is great debate around this topic, but some points have emerged clearly. The most important is that unrefined carbohydrates – those which are wrapped up with the rest of the grain that they grew in – are the healthiest carbohydrates to eat.

In 2019, the World Health Organization (WHO) commissioned a group of experts to look in detail at the evidence behind eating carbohydrates, so that the WHO could update its recommendations. The WHO's group of scientists carried out a systematic review and meta-analysis of all the available evidence they could find relating to the health effects of eating carbohydrates.[16] They looked at the health effects of different aspects of eating carbohydrates in the same way that clinicians look at the effects of a medical intervention such as a new drug: does it harm or benefit? If it benefits, to what extent, and in what way? In this instance they wanted to ascertain whether eating carbohydrates increased or decreased the risk of dying, including the more particular risk of developing non-communicable diseases such as type 2 diabetes, heart disease or colorectal cancer.

Looking at wholegrain carbohydrates specifically, they found unambiguous results: eating high quantities of wholegrains was significantly associated with living longer, and reduced the likelihood of developing multiple non-communicable diseases. In addition, the results were dose-dependent: so the more wholegrains people ate, the stronger their effect.

Looking at the same question from a slightly different perspective, a study in 2017 attempted to estimate the proportion of deaths which were directly caused by different diets. The research group normally uses vast databases to examine which diseases are causing premature deaths worldwide in a country-by-country analysis called the Global Burden of Disease. More than 3,600 researchers from over 145 countries have been compiling and analysing the data since 1990. In their 2017 study they examined whether any specific diets might also contribute to early deaths, or a reduced quality of life. The unit of measurement for this is the somewhat bizarre sounding 'disability adjusted life years', which means losing a year of healthy life, or a year in which disease or accident does not hinder your daily activities. They found that a diet low in wholegrains was one of the leading causes of death and disability in 2017, causing approximately three million premature deaths and costing 82 million disability-adjusted life years.[17] So both of these extensive, rigorous studies concluded that we should consume more wholegrains. The planetary health diet takes this and other data into account when prescribing wholegrains as the bulk of our ideal carbohydrate intake, suggesting that they should form a third of our total daily calorie allowance.

So it's clear that quality of carbohydrate matters. What about quantity?

Another recent study called the PURE study was published in 2017 and followed 135,335 people individually in 18 countries for 7.5 years, assessing what they ate using food frequency questionnaires.[18] The investigators wanted to see if they could identify any link between the individuals' food, and their risk of early death and major cardiovascular events (including heart attacks, stroke and heart failure). This study found that eating an excessive quantity of carbohydrates generally was associated with an increased risk of premature death, although not with any of the cardiovascular events. What can explain this apparent contradiction with other studies' findings?

The answer lies in a combination of quantity and quality. The PURE study found that more than 50 per cent of the people they followed ate a high-carbohydrate diet, which they defined as providing at least 60 per cent of the person's energy requirements. They also found that about 25 per cent of people got 70 per cent of their energy from carbohydrates. For comparison, the planetary health diet suggests that about a third of our daily calories should come from carbohydrates. The PURE study also didn't report exactly what kind of carbohydrates people were eating, but given current global eating patterns, it was much more likely to be ultra-processed foods than wholegrains.

THE GOOD LEFT ON THE FACTORY FLOOR

What is wholegrain and why is it so important that we eat more of this kind of carbohydrate? Wholegrain, as the word implies, means eating the entirety of a grain. A grain is the seed of a plant: it provides the genetic material to make a new seed, and nutrients and energy to help the seed germinate. A grain is made up of three component parts: the bran (yes, like the bran flakes breakfast cereal), the germ and the endosperm. The bran is the outermost part of the grain, which is high in fibre, various vitamins and some minerals (although our ability to absorb the minerals in the bran depends on how the grain is prepared). The germ of the grain is actually the plant embryo, and has vitamins, minerals, fats and protein. Finally, the endosperm is the seed's food supply: it is this part of the grain which contains all the carbohydrates we've been discussing, plus a smaller amount of protein.

Refining a grain means removing and discarding the bran and germ, leaving only the carbohydrate-rich endosperm. When people refer to wholegrains, they either mean eating the entirety of the grain without any refinement, like a grain of brown rice, or they can mean that the entirety of the grain is present in the food, like when the whole grain is milled into wholegrain flour.

Critically, processing carbohydrates leads to throwing away much of the grain's fibre content. Fibre is another general term which has been a little misappropriated. It is a catch-all phrase for all the plant-produced carbohydrates which we cannot digest. For example, cellulose is a type of dietary fibre. The health benefits of fibre are absolutely unequivocal. For example, in the WHO-commissioned study mentioned above, people who ate the most fibre had a 15–50 per cent decrease in risk of death from any cause, or from heart attack, as well as a similar reduction in the risk of other types of heart disease, stroke, type 2 diabetes and colorectal cancer compared to those who ate the least fibre. Thanks to their bran outer layer, wholegrains are an excellent source of fibre, although there is fibre in all plant-derived foodstuffs (fruit, vegetables, nuts and pulses). While estimates vary depending on the population, it's generally accepted that most people eat less than 20g of fibre daily. Many of the health benefits the WHO study found were linked to an ideal consumption level of about 30g of fibre a day.

Fibre isn't simply a proxy measure for an otherwise healthy diet: it brings benefits of its own, and I look at fibre's many benefits in Chapter Five (see page 126). But staying with carbohydrates for the moment, the case seems to be pretty clear. Carbohydrates in their unrefined, natural forms such as in wholegrains or unrefined flours are one of the healthiest things that we can eat, and we should be eating more of them.

SUGAR, SUGAR

The problem is that we're not eating enough unrefined carbohydrate. Instead our changing consumption patterns tell a very different story. We are increasingly eating more processed carbohydrates, often in the form of sugar or refined carbohydrates. For example, in autumn 2020, the international sandwich chain Subway suffered something of an odd setback in Ireland. The chain had been trying to claim that they should be exempt from paying VAT on their bread rolls on the basis that bread is a staple product, with zero VAT. However, under the strict regulations of Ireland's VAT act of 1972, bread ingredients such as sugar and fat cannot exceed 2 per cent of the flour in the dough. The five judges in Ireland's Supreme Court ruled that Subway's rolls, in which sugar content is around 10 per cent of the flour in the dough for both white and wholegrain varieties, cannot legally be classified as bread in Ireland.[19]

Looking at food consumption patterns in America over the past few decades, proportionally the biggest change has been the quantity of carbohydrates consumed as a percentage of total calories. This has increased from 40 per cent to 55 per cent of total calorie consumption.[20] Looking at a breakdown of these figures, it turns out that we're not eating more carbohydrates evenly. People's consumption of starch, the carbohydrates more likely to be found in grains, has increased by only 2 per cent. However, our consumption of fructose – one of the simple monosaccharides in table sugar – has doubled in the last 30 years. Fructose is what makes sugar taste so sweet and is an 'added caloric sweetener' in food (meaning a substance which sweetens food and has calories). It has been implicated as one of the causes of our rising epidemic of non-communicable disease.

Eating foods which have a lot of added sugar (or calorie-containing sweeteners such as high-fructose corn syrup) is associated with weight gain and an increased risk of developing type 2 diabetes, and it also increases the risk of death from cardiovascular diseases.[21] The harmful effects of eating too much sugar are very well known. But the problem is that the hidden sugar content in food is rising insidiously. This is happening for three reasons: first because more ultra-processed foods are available, second because sugar is (ironically) an excellent preservative, and third because when food producers cut their fat content as a 'healthy' signal to consumers they add sugar to make food more appealing. The planetary health diet recommendation for added sugar is 31g per person daily or about 5 per cent of total energy consumption. 'Added sugar' is the planetary health diet's term for 'free sugars'. These include sugars added to food to sweeten it as well as sugars released by blending or juicing, and those in juice concentrates, purees, pastes and syrups.

The planetary health diet's daily recommendation of 31g of sugar is roughly a handful. Unless you watch what you eat like a hawk, it's extremely hard to stick to this when buying what most people consider normal food. In the UK, most adults eat an average of 60g or two handfuls of sugar per day (12 per cent of energy consumption). Children aged between 4 and 10 eat 54g of sugar per day, and children aged between 11 and 18 eat a whopping 73g of sugar per day – probably three or four handfuls of sugar.[22]

Despite governments worldwide making noises about attempting to keep the sugar content of food down, it is rising. An eye-opening paper looked at the sugar content of British cakes and biscuits in 2018, two years after the British government introduced a sugar-reduction programme. This asked manufacturers to reduce sugar by 20 per cent by 2020 in the nine categories of food which provide the most sugar in children's diets. The paper assessed 381 types of cakes and 481 types of biscuits, comparing values per 100g to make them comparable. They found that, on average, British cakes contained 37g of sugar per 100g and biscuits contained, on average, 30g of sugar per 100g, making a slice of cake, or a handful of biscuits, well above the recommended sugar intake. 100g of cake, on average, clocked in at 406 calories (around 20 per cent of the British recommended daily energy intake for women and 16 per cent for men). 100g of biscuits was 484 calories (24 per cent of the British recommended daily energy intake for women and 19 per cent for men). Of course, a single biscuit weighs between 10g and 20g, making eating one biscuit well within sugar limits; the problem is whether anyone eats just the one biscuit.

At least with cakes and biscuits, we know we're eating a sweet treat and can think about it appropriately. What's striking is how much added sugar there is in products we don't think of as containing sugar. To get an idea of how many items we eat that might contain sugar we don't know about, I did a quick assessment of how many of the most frequently bought products in the UK contain added sugar. Using the 2019 consumer price inflation basket of goods and services, I looked at the most frequently bought foods in the UK. I excluded all unprocessed foods, so foods such as chicken breasts were excluded, but rotisserie-cooked chickens were included. I then went to a supermarket website and typed the food category into the search bar (to exclude any bias on my part I used whichever unsponsored example came up first), and looked through the ingredients to see if there was any reference to added sugar. An important caveat: this is not a scientific or reliable survey, it was just to give me a rough estimate (although it would be an interesting exercise to do properly). Based on this very unscientific survey, I was stunned to find that exactly 50 per cent of the most frequently bought NOVA type three and four foods (processed and ultra-processed) in the UK have added sugar. What really surprised me was the types of foods which had added sugar. Sugar is unsurprising in cake, but it is surprising in salami. Or pizza. Or a salty cracker. Or mayonnaise.

The message here is that avoiding sugar is difficult, unless you eat only unprocessed foods. Some of the worst offenders are drinks. The quantity of sugar in our drinks has become ridiculous. The Queen Mary University of London runs the group Action on Sugar which makes detailed assessments of the sugar content of various foods (some of their researchers were behind the cake paper mentioned above). In winter 2019 they released data on the sugar content in many seasonal special drinks offered by the large coffee shop chains. The findings were tooth-clenching: a venti Starbucks signature caramel hot chocolate made using oat milk contained 758 calories and 94g of sugar – as much sugar as three cans of cola (a 330ml can of Coca-Cola contains 35g of sugar). A venti Starbucks gingerbread latte (also made using oat milk) contained 523 calories and 57g of sugar.[24] Obviously these are the extremes (and were made with oat milk, which has more free sugars than dairy milk, making the numbers higher), but it's worth bearing in mind when we begin to think of the quantities of sugar we can ingest unconsciously. Drinking the gingerbread latte is equivalent to eating two 48g Snickers bars in terms of sugar and calories.

Governments worldwide are beginning to crack down on adding sugar to soft drinks. Taxes on drinks with added sugars have been introduced by 14 countries worldwide, and by some US states, with other countries planning to roll these out. Different countries have picked different thresholds, but the aim is similar: to try to use a 'sin tax' to force us to change our behaviour. The rationale is similar to adding a hefty tax to cigarettes or alcohol: indulge in this bad behaviour if you must, say governments, but it will cost you. There is some data showing that such taxation works. Mexico was one of the earliest countries to impose a tax in January 2014 and showed about a 10 per cent drop in consumption of sugary drinks by the end of 2015.[25] Some studies predict that such a drop will lead to a significant decrease in the diabetes and obesity epidemic which is worse in Mexico than most countries.[26] We still don't know if such taxation will lead to a real drop in health problems – it's too early to tell from the data – but it does encourage public awareness that excessive sugar consumption is harmful (at least, ideally it does; some have derided it as a tax on the poor).

People around the world are clearly eating more sugary and refined carbohydrate foods, and more frequently. While these foods provide many calories, their nutritional value is negligible or even absent. Eating too many of them is directly implicated as a cause of the non-communicable disease epidemic which is stalking our world. In short, to continue to eat an increasing quantity would be extremely bad for us. It would also be extremely bad for the planet.

THE GREEN REVOLUTION

As you would expect for crops which we have been growing for over 10,000 years, we have proved extraordinarily adept at coaxing grains from the soil. During the last century farmers improved yields even further, with the advent of the so-called Green Revolution in the 1960s. During this period a number of innovations massively increased crop productivity all round the world. They included cross-breeding cereals to create high-yielding varieties, introducing chemical fertilizers and controlled irrigation, often using greater mechanization to make the advances less labour-intensive. The man who pioneered many of these ideas, Dr Norman Borlaug, has become known as the father of the Green Revolution. He was awarded the Nobel Peace Prize in 1970 for his achievements, and for good reason: some estimates show that he might have saved about a billion people from starvation through his pioneering work. But despite his successes, Dr Borlaug's Nobel acceptance speech showed prescient concern for humanity's future:

'The green revolution has won a temporary success in man's war against hunger and deprivation; it has given man a breathing space. If fully implemented, the revolution can provide sufficient food for sustenance during the next three decades. But the frightening power of human reproduction must also be curbed; otherwise the success of the green revolution will be ephemeral only.'

His words were more accurate than he might have wished. Even as he spoke, the world's population was increasing rapidly – and it is still increasing today. Current projections predict that the global population will hit about ten billion people by 2050, and world food production systems are desperately trying to keep up.

To feed our increasing population, we have been producing ever-larger quantities of food and especially carbohydrates: cereal crop production has increased by 240 per cent since 1961. In 2017, the top four crops we grew globally were sugar cane (1,842 metric tonnes [a metric tonne = 1,000kg]), maize (1,135 tonnes), wheat (772 tonnes) and rice (770 tonnes)[27] and we grew an estimated 2,722 million tonnes of cereals (wheat, rice and corn) in 2019, the most ever recorded. This is a triumph of agriculture, the combined efforts of dedicated research and innovation in plant science and farming, and is not to be discounted. Nor can we afford to produce less without risking mass starvation. But it comes at a growing environmental price.

BIRD POO WARS

In terms of conflicts, arguing over who has the rights to scrape bird poo off a rock would be pretty low down most people's lists. And yet during the 19th century, this is precisely what happened. Spain occupied Peru's Chincha Islands in 1864 in an attempt to monopolize trade in guano (the Incan term for seabird droppings). The Chincha Islands were famous for their guano deposits, which were more than 30m deep in some areas. However, the Spanish troops were forced to withdraw after Peru and Chile defended the islands, later helped by Ecuadorian and Bolivian forces. The deposits of guano, known at the time as 'white gold', were safe.

Why were five armies mobilized for, if you'll excuse the pun, such a shit reason? The answer is that what guano lacks in terms of appetizing smell and appearance it more than makes up for in its chemical constituents: it's one of the richest sources of reactive nitrogen, phosphorus and potassium in the world. These elements – reactive nitrogen in particular – are essential nutrients for plant growth. Without them harvest potential is limited, leading to low yields and risking starvation. This is exactly what was happening in Europe and North America in the early 19th century where the fertility of the soil had declined. The discovery and use of 'white gold' to restore soil fertility led to a guano boom. Islands where seabirds habitually nested were stripped bare of the stuff, levelling the land, until the once plentiful supply was almost depleted in the late 20th century. A guano bust followed the boom, with European farmers mourning their loss.

The reason for tapping such an esoteric source of nutrients is that both reactive nitrogen and phosphorus are scarce in the natural environment, but are absolutely vital for plants. Nitrogen is needed to create amino acids, the building blocks of proteins, which in turn make up our bodies. Nitrogen is also critical for plants to make chlorophyll, the chemical which allows them to synthesize energy from sunlight and water. Among other things, phosphorus is needed to create DNA – our how-to blueprint for reproduction – and to make up an energy-carrying molecule called ATP, which provides energy in all cells. Nitrogen and phosphorus are absolutely vital for all life, along with carbon: without these elements we'd all look very different (if we existed at all).

It's important to distinguish between the different types of nitrogen that biological organisms can and cannot use. To remind you of your school chemistry: atoms are the building blocks of the world and come in different elements (all the different squares on the periodic table). When you join these atoms together in various combinations you create molecules. For example, a carbon atom (O) is one of the elements. Under normal conditions pairs of atoms react together to form a stable molecule (O_2), which we also call oxygen – this is what we breathe. Under different conditions, three oxygen atoms can come together to form ozone (O_3), which has totally different properties.

Nitrogen atoms bond together in the same way as oxygen atoms to form the unreactive molecule nitrogen (N_2). In this form, nitrogen is chemically stable, unreactive and totally useless to living beings: we cannot process it. Unfortunately, this is also its most common form: about 78 per cent of the air in the atmosphere is N_2.

However, there are multiple different forms of nitrogen which organic beings can use; for example, when a single nitrogen atom joins three hydrogen atoms it forms ammonia (NH_3), or a nitrogen atom can join three oxygen atoms to make nitrate (NO_3). Both of these forms, amongst others, can be absorbed and used by living beings. In these forms, it is known as reactive nitrogen. Unfortunately, reactive nitrogen in these forms doesn't occur naturally very often. It can be made in the soil when lightning strikes the ground, or through specialist bacteria which can convert inert nitrogen to one of its reactive forms. These bacteria form a symbiotic relationship in the roots of some legume plants; when the plants die the soil is enriched with reactive nitrogen. This is why traditional farming practices included crop rotation, to take advantage of the reactive nitrogen left behind in different fields.

By contrast, the other vital element for plant growth, phosphorus, is extremely reactive: for example, pure phosphorus will spontaneously combust when exposed to air. Phosphorus is never found in its pure form, perhaps fortunately, because it's so reactive. Instead it always reacts to form compounds within minerals. Phosphorus can be taken up by plants only if it's dissolved in the soil, and so only occurs naturally at low concentrations in decomposed plant matter.

Both reactive nitrogen and dissolved phosphorus are relatively rarely found in soil, and lack of them is the most common reason for poor plant growth. Fortunately we have figured out how to improve soil fertility by applying artificial fertilizer, which contains both elements in high concentrations.

In the early 20th century Fritz Haber discovered a process by which fixed, inert nitrogen could be converted to reactive nitrogen in the form of ammonia; this process was then modified by Carl Bosch to become an industrial process for fertilizer production. Named after its two inventors, the Haber-Bosch process is considered one of the most important discoveries of the 20th century. Because both fixed nitrogen and hydrogen, the two elements required to make ammonia, are so abundant, reactive nitrogen went from being an elusive element to something that was relatively cheap and easy to make. However, while the process might not require much in the way of raw materials, producing it requires an enormous amount of energy. Burning fossil fuel to create fertilizer means that the Haber-Bosch process accounts for 1 per cent of all global carbon dioxide emissions today.

Phosphate is a different story. The only way we can obtain more phosphate is by mining phosphate rock from the ground. Once it's extracted we can separate out the impurities, creating pure phosphorus. The problem here is that phosphate is not found everywhere: the largest deposits in the world are mainly in Morocco, Algeria and Western Sahara, a disputed, war-torn territory claimed by both Morocco and the Polisario Front. Other countries, such as the USA, Brazil and China, have smaller supplies.[28]

There's currently a fierce debate raging over how long our supplies of phosphorus will last. Some estimates suggest we only have about 50 years' worth left; others say we have enough for 1,000 years, but that accessing these reserves will be so costly and energy-consuming that it would not be worthwhile. Added to this the fact that two-thirds of all phosphate comes from only three countries, all of which are a little more politically turbulent than you'd ideally want from your sole supplier of a rare and vital resource, and it's clear that we cannot blithely assume that we will have indefinite supplies of phosphate.

So while we now have the means and mechanisms to obtain both these vital nutrients, their sourcing is expensive, and in the case of phosphorus, time-limited and potentially dangerous. Given this and the importance of the elements in question, you'd think that, to keep costs low, we would carefully apply the minimum quantity of fertilizer required and recycle as much of it as possible.

Wrong!

In fact, exactly the opposite has been happening. Faced with such quantities of nutrients, the world has been overusing fertilizer. Since the 1960s, we've tripled our use of synthetic phosphorus fertilizer, and now use nine times more synthetic reactive nitrogen fertilizers.[29] In 2020 alone we're predicted to use about 118,700,000,000kg of fertilizer globally, which is a number so huge it's almost impossible to understand or visualize. That's the weight of around 9.5 million London double-decker buses – or about twice the weight of the Great Wall of China. It's a lot.

The problem with applying fertilizer is that it doesn't stick around. Only about 20 per cent of the reactive nitrogen and 25–75 per cent of phosphorus is taken up by the plants (the range is so large because it depends on soil conditions, plant types, and so on). So to maintain soil fertility farmers continuously apply extra fertilizer. These excess nutrients are washed off fields into rivers and, eventually, into oceans as agricultural pollution. This pollution is seriously damaging water all round the world.

SUFFOCATING SEAS AND EUTROPHICATION

Lake Erie, straddling the Canadian and US borders, is the fourth largest of the five Great Lakes in North America. Of all the Great Lakes, it has the most cities on its banks and the most people living in its drainage basin. But it has had something of a mixed ecological record during the second half of the 20th century and the beginning of the 21st. For centuries the lake was a fishing hotspot with clear water, but by the late 20th century industrial waste and sewage run-off had polluted the lake to such a degree that it was declared dead in 1970 (shortly after the Cuyahoga River, which feeds into the lake, caught fire, somewhat cementing the ecosystems' status as a joke). The lake's predicament caught national attention in the USA and is credited with kick-starting the Environmental Protection Agency and the Clean Water Act. After sewage and industrial waste treatment laws were passed, Lake Erie recovered to become a living lake once more. But its tribulations were not over. In 2011, the lake was covered with a toxic algal bloom so thick that people described the water as looking like green paint. The algae (photosynthetic organisms which occupy an odd niche, neither plant nor animal) grew to such numbers that it became difficult to sail a boat through the water. Algal blooms such as this are a direct result of agricultural run-off into water – and they're a growing and dangerous problem all round the world.

Under normal conditions, lack of nutrients limits the growth of all types of aquatic plants and algae. However, when water suddenly fills with nutrients as a result of fertilizer run-off, the nutrients allow the algae to grow extremely rapidly. You will have seen algal growths on the surfaces of lakes and rivers – better known as pond scum – but the algal growths created when nutrients are washed into coastal waters form masses so huge that they can be seen from space as enormous hazy fractal patterns, suffocating the coastline.

These algal blooms are problematic for a number of reasons. First, the species of algae that bloomed on Lake Erie in 2011 endangers human (and aquatic) health because the algae produce many toxic chemicals, making the water unsafe to drink or swim in. Second, by multiplying in such vast numbers, the algae cause eutrophication.

In this process algae grow in huge quantities as a result of an increase of nutrients in the water. But there aren't enough nutrients to keep all the algae alive, and they die and decompose into the lake. The decomposition process requires oxygen. This doesn't normally cause a problem, but when decomposition happens on a vast scale, it deoxygenates the water, so oxygen levels fall too low to support marine life. This eutrophication is an appalling occurrence. Without oxygen, no marine life can survive and everything in the water dies. Photographs of thousands of dead fish covering oceans and lakes in a grisly silver blanket testify to the toxicity that follows. If this happens repeatedly, the water cannot recover, and these areas are designated dead zones: oxygen-free or low-oxygen regions of water where almost no aquatic life can survive.

There are more than 500 dead zones in the world's waters,[30] and they're growing in number and in size. The largest is in the Gulf of Oman, part of the Arabian Sea. We've known about it for more than 50 years, but the area was only properly surveyed in 2018 (piracy and geopolitical situations made it hard for scientists to get to the region and this survey was done by aquatic robots). The researchers were horrified to find that the dead zone was much larger than previously estimated and covered almost the entire Gulf of Oman. This area of ocean, which is larger than Scotland, was devoid of oxygen.[31] There are also huge dead zones in the Gulf of Mexico and the Baltic Sea. In the Gulf of Mexico, the dead zone forms so reliably on a seasonal basis that an American government department, the National Oceanic and Atmospheric Administration (NOAA), issues predictions about its size. The largest dead zone occurred in 2017 when it reached about 22,730 square km, approximately the size of the state of New Jersey.[32]

Such is the power and prevalence of these dead zones that they're stripping oxygen from our waters. Recent estimates suggest that the oceans have lost 2 per cent of their oxygen since the middle of the 20th century.[33] This may not sound that much until you consider how vast the oceans are: this loss of oxygen is 145 billion tonnes of the stuff, which is a quantity so vast that it even dwarfs the quantity of fertilizer that we use annually. While the figure might be small proportionally, because the oceans are so huge it has a correspondingly vast footprint.

Deoxygenation of the ocean isn't solely the result of nutrient run-off from fertilizers, but along with warming waters as a result of climate change, it's the biggest attributable factor. Warmer waters can hold less oxygen than colder waters. This is an example of how two different processes act synergistically together in the whole earth model. And while dead oceans are the most visible effect of unprecedented quantities of reactive nitrogen and phosphorus pollution in the world, the problems don't stop there.

Excessive nitrogen and phosphate in the ecosystem causes many other harms. Reactive nitrogen can take the form of nitrous oxide (N_2O), which is a greenhouse gas 300 times more potent than carbon dioxide and depletes the ozone layer. Eighty per cent of all nitrous oxide emissions come from agriculture and it has an atmospheric lifetime of 114 years, meaning that no matter what we do to mitigate our increasing production of it, we're going to have to deal with this problem for generations to come.[34]

Nitrogen in other reactive forms (nitrates, nitrogen oxide – NO – and nitrogen dioxide – NO_2) can form particulate matter in the air which makes us ill (respiratory illness and heart disease); about 60 per cent of the world's population in urban areas is estimated to be exposed to toxic levels of these airborne chemicals. And, in an ironic twist, the excessive application of fertilizer can make soil quality *worse*. Surplus reactive nitrogen in the soil can acidify it and liberate heavy metals in the soil, both of which can stunt or kill plant growth. Because these harms aren't visible, it's easy to dismiss them, but it would be foolish to do so. Taking into account the effects both on ecosystems and human health, scientists have estimated that excessive nutrient pollution might cost the world about US$3,400 billion annually,[35] or, to put it another way, more than the GDP of the UK in 2018.

BIOGEOCHEMICAL FLOWS

The toxic effects described above are the reasons that nitrogen and phosphorus wastage represent one of the planetary processes we need to respect: biogeochemical flows. It is important to note here that the boundary is not the quantity of nitrogen and phosphorus we apply to our crops. It is the amount that is *not used* by our crops: the excess washed into our waterways. Today, we haven't just passed these boundaries, we've obliterated them. Our planetary boundary (see Chapter Two, page 30) for phosphorus flow is 11 teragrams or Tg (one teragram is a billion kilograms) per year – and we currently wash away 22Tg. If you can believe it, our annual nitrogen loss is even worse. The boundary is 62Tg of nitrogen per year, and we currently lose more than double that amount: about 150Tg annually.[36] (It's important to note that these are global figures; there are also regional boundaries but these are more complicated.) No wonder we are already seeing these harms.

There is an obvious problem with curbing fertilizer application: we need to keep producing crops. Fear of failed harvests and subsequent widespread starvation is something Western countries have relegated to the past, but failed harvests remain a real and present danger in many countries. Richer countries can buy grain if their crops fail: others do not have this luxury. It's hard to convince countries with an increasing population that they should use less fertilizer: they have mouths to feed and if we can ensure they are fed there can be little debate around the issue. How can we keep everyone fed while respecting this planetary boundary? The good news is it can be done. And there are ways of changing how we eat that will help.

Countries around the world are slowly becoming aware of the harm caused by excessive fertilizer application and the subsequent consequences of nutrient pollution. In both China and India, countries where fertilizers have previously been subsidized and therefore routinely excessively applied, governments have legislated to reduce usage. In 2015, China brought in legislation, Zero Growth of Chemical Fertilizer and Pesticide Use by 2020, in an attempt to curb spiralling application rates, and in 2017 India's prime minister called for farmers to halve their fertilizer use by 2020. In 2019, Sri Lanka and the United Nations Environment Programme spearheaded what has come to be known as the Colombo Declaration, in which signatory countries pledged to aim to halve nitrogen waste by 2030.

The key word here is 'waste'. Eutrophication (see page 66) and all biogeochemical pollution are the result of inefficient use of nitrogen and phosphorus. The quantities of fertilizer we apply are only excessive in the sense that many of the nutrients are not taken up by the plants they're intended for. The majority are left in the soil and washed away as waste. These are the pollutants which cause the harms. So we are missing an expensive trick here: scientists estimate that halving the quantity of wasted nitrogen (the amount lost to the world's waterways and air) could save about US$100 billion annually.

Preventing this waste is critical if we're going to be able to feed the world in a sustainable fashion. To ensure we have enough food for everyone, we need to make sure that every part of the world producing food is doing so at maximum capacity. But there are inequalities in fertilizer application around the world. If we return for a moment to thinking about the earth as a single system, we're currently pulling much too hard on the biogeochemical lever in some parts of the world, but not hard enough in other parts. For farmers in sub-Saharan Africa, for example, fertilizer is often unaffordable. These farmers are producing less food than the land is capable of yielding: a great inefficiency from the point of view of a planet which needs every resource to feed its population. By reducing waste where nitrogen and phosphorus are excessively applied, we effectively free up these nutrients from one part of the system and allow them to be used elsewhere. If they are used moderately – as needed to ensure maximum crop yield but no more – then we will no longer exceed a planetary boundary.

We know that fertilizer waste can be reduced without reducing crop yield because it has been done. Some countries have been sounding the alarm for decades. For example, Denmark, where 60 per cent of the land is used for agriculture, has been working on this since 1983. By 2012, as a result of dedicated agricultural policies and action plans, they had reduced nitrogen input by a third with no drop in yield. Similarly the Netherlands have reduced nitrogen fertilizer application while doubling yields.[37] In the UK, the quantity of fertilizer used is strictly controlled according to the Nutrient Management Guide (known by everyone in the industry as RB209) which stipulates the recommended fertilizer applications required to achieve both high yields and grain quality, depending on soil type and nitrogen content.[38]

In short, making gains (and grains!) without using excessive fertilizer seems not only possible, but feasible, assuming we treat fertilizer as a precious resource to be applied sparingly.

As well as reducing what we put on the fields, it's also important to use other opportunities to reclaim nutrient waste. With apologies for bringing us back to scatological considerations, other important sources of nutrients are animal waste and human sewage. We are not efficient converters of nutrients: we all excrete significant quantities of both reactive nitrogen and phosphorus which also ends up in waterways. By aiming to recover these through dedicated facilities in sewage plants or by collecting and purifying animal manure, we can recycle nutrients instead of having to use energy to mine or create more, as well as reducing the amount flowing into our oceans.

It's all very well suggesting that farmers apply an optimum amount of fertilizer to their barley crops. What does this mean for us? How can our food choices influence this planetary boundary? Our choices matter because eating sustainably and healthily leads to sustainable and healthy food production.

Take sugar consumption. Most of us eat far more than the planetary health diet's recommendations of 31g of added sugar daily. In response, we grow more sugar cane than any other crop on earth: more than wheat and rice combined. And yet sugar cane gives us only excess sweetness which at best is nutritionally neutral and at worst contributes to the growing burden of double malnutrition, obesity and diabetes. When you look at refined carbohydrates, a similar story is true. While grains can give us amazing nutrients, by refining them we throw much of the goodness away, making them a worse foodstuff to eat so we then need more food to make up the nutritional shortfall.

By eating excessive refined sugars and carbohydrates, we eat inefficiently. If we ate less sugar and refined carbohydrate, and so reduced demand for it, we would free up space for other crops to be grown instead. Fertilizers would still be needed for those crops, but they'd have more nutritional benefit, making them a more efficient choice for the world as a whole and people's health in particular.

There is one final issue to consider when we think about wholegrains and carbohydrates. We are not the only animals eating them. Instead, huge quantities of farmland are devoted solely to growing grain for livestock. From a nutrient cycling point of view, this is extremely inefficient. Of the 80 per cent of nitrogen and phosphorus in grains and grass that is used to feed livestock, only about 20 per cent ends up in human diets. If we ate only plant-based products, we would require significantly less nitrogen and phosphorus.

In fact, some have suggested that the Green Revolution which introduced chemical fertilizers has really enabled a livestock revolution. Cheap grain has mainly led to the intensification of livestock farming, rather than bringing direct nutritional benefit to those in need.

In short, one of the easiest ways to ensure that we can sustainably produce wholesome carbohydrates would be to eat less meat. Reduced consumption of meat would diminish demand for animal feed and potentially free up grains for us to eat. I will examine this, and the other thorny implications of eating meat, in Chapter Six.

CHAPTER 4

FATS AND OILS

PLANETARY HEALTH DIET RECOMMENDATION

Daily recommendation: four portions of unsaturated vegetable oil, equivalent to about four tablespoons, and small quantities of animal-derived lard or tallow and palm oil, as part of meat intake or processed foods.

Athens, Greece's capital city, can come as something of a shock to tourists whose images of the country are of ancient temples and crystalline waters. Athens is an entirely modern, loud, bustling city, described by some as vibrant and others as chaotic, depending presumably on whether you have to be somewhere in a hurry. It can be difficult, when you're stuck in traffic behind a dump truck, hemmed in on all sides by low apartment blocks and lines of parked cars, to believe that this city is one of the oldest in the world: Athens has been continuously inhabited for over 7,000 years. But the city is full of surprises. Turning a corner in a residential neighbourhood brings you abruptly to a sunken plot of land with a small plaque which casually informs you that the ruins of the building you see before you are more than 2,000 years old. And if this fails to impress, there's always the Acropolis. This huge rocky outcrop towers over the modern city and still houses the remains of the ancient Athenian citadel. You can climb up to its peak and walk through the sacred site, seeing the famous Parthenon and other temples dotted around the rock's flat top. And in among these ancient buildings, you will see something which is not ancient nor a temple, but no less sacred or revered: an olive tree.

Ancient Greek legend has it that when Athens was a young city two rival gods, Poseidon, god of the sea, and Athena, goddess of wisdom, vied to be its patron (and so control Athens and the surrounding land). When the rivalry began to verge on war, Athena lived up to her name by suggesting an alternative: both gods could give the citizens of the city a gift, and whichever proved more useful would win. The contest would be held atop the Acropolis and the Athenian king, Cecrops, would judge it. Poseidon went first. He struck a rock with his trident and water gushed forth. Initially excited, the citizens found that it was salt water – not useful for drinking or farming. Athena went next. She used her spear to plant an olive tree on the Acropolis, explaining that its fruit and oil could feed and heal the city's citizens, that they could burn the oil in their lamps for light and that they could use its wood for shelter and fuel. In perhaps the earliest recorded example of a no-brainer, Cecrops chose Athena as the winner and Athens acquired its name and patron. (Poseidon was a sore loser: when he failed to win the city, he cursed Athens so that it would never have a ready supply of water, a problem which plagues the city to this day.)

While the olive tree you'll find on the Acropolis today is not quite as old as the buildings that surround it, it is considered just as important. Olives, and especially their oil, had near-sacred status in Ancient Greek legend and history. Hippocrates, the world's earliest physician, referred to olive oil as 'the great healer', and Homer, author of the epic poems *The Iliad* and *The Odyssey*, called olive oil liquid gold. Ancient Greek athletes lathered themselves in it before competitions, and the victors were crowned with olive branches. While we no longer watch oiled-up young men wrestling in the altogether (at least, not on public television), olive oil has retained something of its mythical status in public health circles.

FOOD AS MEDICINE

Although the connection between what you eat and how you feel has long been known, it took a while for science to catch on to the idea that we could rigorously assess foods' health benefits like any other medical intervention. Until then, science was limited to observations made by travelling physicians, who described the people they encountered in different parts of the world experiencing either exceptionally good or exceptionally bad health as geographic pathology. For example, the Dutch professor Cornelis de Langen moved to Indonesia in 1900 to teach internal medicine. There, he was surprised to find that Indonesians had extremely low levels of cholesterol and chest pain caused by coronary heart disease compared to the Dutch he had left behind in Holland. Professor de Langen attributed this to the Indonesian diet, which at the time was almost entirely vegetarian.[1] More than 50 years later scientists began formally exploring how different countries' diets influenced their citizens' health.

In the late 1940s, there was an American epidemic of apparently healthy middle-aged men abruptly dropping dead from heart attacks. The American physiologist Professor Ancel Keys was one of the first to try to figure out the difference between those who had a heart attack and those who remained healthy. In the early 1950s, Keys was on sabbatical at the University of Oxford, and was invited by the Neapolitan Professor Bergami to come to Italy to see an interesting phenomenon. Keys travelled to Naples, where the two discussed the curious fact that extremely poor Neapolitan men had many fewer heart attacks than wealthy American men.

This and other observations catalysed one of the first large international prospective studies, called the Seven Countries Study.[2] A prospective study recruits and follows participants aiming for a specific outcome, rather than simply surveying them retrospectively. The study looked at the link between health and food. Keys and his collaborators began by looking at men in the

USA, Finland, Japan, the Netherlands, the country then known as Yugoslavia, Italy and Greece. These countries varied dramatically at the time in terms of their cultural traditions and eating habits. The scientists were curious to see whether anecdotal data about different countries having varying levels of coronary heart disease and cardiovascular disease (and associated deaths) was true. If they found that it was, they wanted to see whether different eating habits and other risk factors played a role.

You've guessed the punchline: the researchers found that heart disease varied dramatically between countries, with diet being one of the biggest contributing factors. The highest rates of heart disease were in the USA and northern Europe, with the lowest in southern Europe, Mediterranean countries and Japan. Keys attributed the differences in rates of heart disease in different countries to people eating varying quantities of animal fats; in Greece and Japan, which had the lowest rates of heart disease, people ate very little animal-derived fat. Using this data, Keys went on to popularize the idea of eating diets very low in animal fats as a way of protecting against heart disease. This idea took firm hold in Western countries throughout the second half of the 20th century, and was behind the decisions people made to avoid eating eggs and fatty meats, as well as encouraging manufacturers to create the now ubiquitous low-fat or no-fat food products.[3] The impact of these changes is still being felt today and I will explore them later.

One of the other effects of the Seven Countries Study was that it recognized that there might be something important about the diet of people in the Mediterranean region of Southern Europe. Data from the study and a huge amount of later research led to the formation of a new set of dietary recommendations, known as the Mediterranean diet. This diet aims to replicate the way people in the Mediterranean regions ate in the 1950s and 1960s and is characterized by eating a lot of vegetables, legumes (such as beans and other high-protein-containing vegetables), fruit, nuts, unrefined cereals, a moderate amount of fish, low-to-moderate amounts of dairy produce predominantly in the form of cheese or yoghurt, very little poultry or red meat, regular but low wine consumption, and, crucially, lots of olive oil.[4] Strikingly, the study discovered that one of the cohorts of men from the Greek island of Crete got about 40 per cent of their daily calories from olive oil alone![5]

Over the next half century, observational studies (where researchers observed how people ate, without any active intervention) confirmed that the Mediterranean diet did seem to provide extensive health benefits to those who ate as it recommended. Then in the early 2000s a group of Spanish researchers decided to put the Mediterranean diet to the test. Rather than simply see who ate what and how it affected their health, they aimed to assess the Mediterranean diet as they would assess a new drug by running the gold standard of scientific tests, a randomized clinical trial. The PREDIMED trial (the name is short for PREvención on DIeta MEDiterránea, or 'Prevention with the Mediterranean diet') actively encouraged participants to eat different diets and then followed them for years to see how these affected their risk of developing cardiovascular disease (defined as heart attack, stroke or death from cardiovascular-related illness).[6]

They recruited 7,447 people who were at risk of developing cardiovascular disease (defined as having diabetes or a number of risk factors, including being overweight or a smoker) and randomly assigned them to one of three groups. The first two groups were recommended to eat a Mediterranean diet, defined as one high in olive oil, nuts, fruit, vegetables, white meat, fish, beans and (optionally) wine. Eating foods such as bakery goods, red and processed meats, fizzy drinks and margarine was discouraged. The third group was recommended to eat a low-fat diet, defined as eating low-fat products, carbohydrates such as bread, potatoes, rice and pasta, fruit, vegetables, lean meats and seafood; they were discouraged from eating vegetable oils (including olive oil), nuts, anything fried, bakery goods, spread fats, red, processed and fatty meats or fatty fish such as tuna.

In addition everyone who signed up was given a free gift, along with individual and quarterly group educational sessions, which is unusual in clinical medicine. The nature of the gift varied depending on the group. Of the two groups assigned to the Mediterranean diet, one group was given a free litre of extra-virgin olive oil a week, and the other about an extra 200g of mixed nuts (hazelnuts, walnuts and almonds). The group assigned to the low-fat diet got non-food gifts. The trial was single-blind: this means that the physicians overseeing the trial did not know which group their patients were in, and so were unaware of any dietary changes they were making. (Most medical trials are double-blind, which means that the patients also don't know what group they're in. However, there's no way to slip an extra weekly litre of olive oil into someone's diet unnoticed.)

As with all good randomized controlled trials, an independent data monitoring committee oversaw the results. This committee was not blind to the different groups: its purpose was to assess data as it started to come in, rather than waiting until the end of the trial to uncover which group followed which diet. Most trials are carefully designed to run for the minimum time needed to tell whether there are any statistically significant differences between the groups receiving different interventions. This is mainly for safety: for example, if you're testing an unknown compound as a potential new drug, you don't want to wait until the end of the trial before realizing that the group who received it all suffered complications. To minimize harm you would need to stop them taking the drug early on, as soon as a significant difference was detected. Equally, if the new drug was a miracle cure, you'd want to know as soon as possible; it would be unethical not to give it to everyone on the trial.

Almost unbelievably, this is what happened in the PREDIMED trial. The independent data monitoring committee stopped the trial early after doing an interim analysis: they found that people who were eating the Mediterranean diet were at significantly lower risk of major cardiovascular disease events than their counterparts eating a low-fat diet. Eating the Mediterranean diet reduced the risk of heart attack, stroke or death by about

30 per cent compared to the risk of those not eating it.[7] The trial was stopped because it was deemed unethical – and potentially harmful – to keep participants on the low-fat diet. Although there wasn't a difference between the two different groups eating the Mediterranean diet in terms of cardiovascular outcome, what was striking was that those in the group given olive oil lost more weight than those in the group given nuts, and this weight loss came off their waist measurements, which suggests that they were losing the fat surrounding their internal organs (visceral fat) – a critical risk factor for cardiovascular disease.

In short, modern science is in the process of painstakingly validating something that an Ancient Greek doctor two millennia ago understood: eating fat is not bad for you. The science indicates that the reverse is true. But there is a caveat. Not all fats are created equal – and eating some types of fats is still extremely harmful.

GOOD FATS? BAD FATS?

When we talk about fat, we're actually talking about a vast variety of different molecules, in much the same way that carbohydrate is a huge umbrella term. When we use the term fat we're really referring to chemical compounds called lipids, which are generally defined by the fact that they don't dissolve in water (hence the old adage about mixing like oil and water). There are many different sub-categories of lipids and I will not bore you with them in detail. Most dietary fats are made up of a variety of these lipids in different proportions, which is what gives different fats different properties. For example, the most obvious difference between types of fat is between fats and oils: fats are solid at room temperature, whereas oils are liquid. That fat's state is temperature-dependent is no surprise to any of us who have left a cooling meat-roasting pan for a little longer than we should: what begins as delicious *jus* when warm ends as a solid white lump that takes a lot of elbow grease to dislodge. (As a side note, this is part of the problem with the growing number of fatbergs which various authorities have to work to dislodge from our pipes. People wash warm, liquid fats which are normally solid at room temperature down the sink; the fats then solidify into giant masses as they cool in the sewage system.)

In terms of how fats affect our health, the biggest difference between dietary fats is their molecular structure. Fatty acid molecules are one of the biggest components of dietary fats. When drawn in a chemical diagram, fatty acids look a bit like a sperm: they have a fat acidic 'head' and then a length of carbon and hydrogen molecules as a 'tail'. The main difference between different types of fatty acid is how long this carbon-hydrogen tail is, how the tail is joined together and what the hydrogen to carbon atom ratio is. Carbon atoms can link to each other using either a single or double bond. They share either one pair of electrons in a single bond or two pairs in a double bond. A fatty acid is said to be saturated when none of the carbons in its tail are joined together with double bonds. The electrons that could double bond with another carbon are instead used to bond hydrogen atoms. The fat is saturated because there is no way to add more hydrogen atoms to it. However, if the tail has even one carbon double bond, it is said to be unsaturated. Theoretically you could split apart that carbon double bond and add extra hydrogens (the carbons would remain bonded by a single bond). Monounsaturated fats are those with just a single carbon double bond, whereas polyunsaturated fats have multiple carbon double bonds.

Different types of fats and oils are a mixture of saturated and unsaturated fats. Many vegetable oils contain monounsaturated or polyunsaturated fats. For example, olive, rapeseed (canola), peanut (groundnut) and sesame oils all contain mostly monounsaturated fats, as do many nut oils, whereas sunflower oil, soybean oil and the omega-3 fats found in fatty fish such as salmon and tuna are mainly polyunsaturated. By contrast, almost all animal-derived fats mostly comprise saturated fats. These include the dairy fats in milk and cream, as well as fatty meats, such as beef and the fat of chicken skin. Generally speaking, unsaturated fats are liquid at room temperature, like most oils, whereas saturated fats are solid at room temperature.

You may recognize some of these terms: some of the above information has entered the general consciousness with the understanding that saturated fat is somehow 'bad', whereas unsaturated fat is 'good'. This is related to the way the fats interact with our cholesterol levels – another term that may ring alarm bells.

Cholesterol is another type of lipid that our bodies make from the fats we eat. Despite its current bad reputation, it is actually an essential molecule that our bodies need for cell membrane function. It's also a required ingredient in creating a lot of other vital compounds, such as vitamin D. We get cholesterol in two ways: we can eat it (this gives us about 20 per cent of our intake) or we can produce it in the liver. Once in our bodies, it is carried around the body in the blood on transporter molecules called lipoproteins.

There are two different types of lipoprotein: high density (HDLs) and low density (LDLs). HDLs are sometimes called 'good cholesterol' because they absorb the cholesterol and transport it back to the liver, where it can be flushed from the body, whereas LDLs are sometimes called 'bad cholesterol' because they can build up in your body's system and clog your arteries. Too much arterial clogging is known as plaque; in the same way as the plaque on your teeth, it sticks to the walls of arteries, which makes them less elastic in responding to changes in blood flow – hence hardening of the arteries. More seriously, plaque can break off in chunks and travel around the body, and can block crucial blood flow to your brain (causing stroke) or heart (causing a heart attack). This is why people take cardiovascular health so seriously: strokes and heart attacks are leading causes of death and disability around the world.

Everyone has HDLs and LDLs in different quantities, with the majority being LDLs. The proportion of HDLs to LDLs is important; higher levels of HDLs means you're more likely to be efficiently clearing your system of cholesterol, reducing your risk of cardiovascular disease. And – drumroll – you can effectively manage this ratio by eating more unsaturated fats than saturated fats. This is why unsaturated fats are seen as 'good' versus the 'bad' saturated fats.

The planetary health diet reflects this. It recommends that 450 calories a day come from fats (that's 18 per cent of the diet as a whole), but of those 450 calories almost all (354 calories or 79 per cent) should come from unsaturated vegetable oils (olive, soybean, rape, sunflower, peanut). That's about four tablespoons of oil. The remaining calories can come from the (optional) inclusion of lard or tallow (rendered animal fat), and palm oil (which is technically an unsaturated vegetable oil but is in a category of its own, which I'll explain later – see page 88). Dairy fats are included separately.

Fat is a vital part of our diets. Current UK guidance is that up to 35 per cent of our energy intake should be derived from fat. Aiming to limit the total fats we eat to diminish the risks of cardiovascular disease is not recommended.[8] But, as with any balanced diet, the quantity, form and what we eat alongside fats is key. Both saturated and unsaturated fats are healthy when consumed in moderation: it's only when we overconsume fats, and especially when we eat significantly more saturated fats than unsaturated fats, that we threaten our cardiovascular health (especially when these are combined with high levels of refined carbohydrates). For example, one study estimated that in 2010 about a quarter of a million deaths as a result of coronary heart disease worldwide were caused by people eating saturated fat instead of unsaturated fats.[9] Unfortunately, these deaths are a direct reflection of the way people's eating habits have changed around the world.

CHEAP FATS

The popularity of processed and ultra-processed foods relies on manufacturers catering to people's taste for sweet or salty and fatty foods, and so there is a huge demand for cheap sources of fat. For many decades manufacturers found a solution in something like a chemical magic trick: the creation of a fat called trans fat which is chemically speaking an unsaturated fat, but has all the useful properties of a saturated fat. In the USA and Canada trans fat is listed on food nutrition labels, but in most of the rest of the world, it's not acknowledged. Trans fats can occur naturally, but they're rare. Almost all the ones we eat are likely to have been made artificially in a process known as hydrogenation.

To return to vegetable oils: these are relatively cheap fats which are liquid at room temperature. A few centuries ago – exact dates are contested – scientists discovered that if you added hydrogen gas to unsaturated fats such as vegetable oils with a catalyst, the fats develop interesting new properties due to a change in their molecular structure. After this hydrogenation, fatty acids remain unsaturated (so they keep their carbon double bond) but, in a molecular quirk, the process causes one of the hydrogen atoms to change sides, turning it into a 'trans' formation.

Normally, the carbon double bond in unsaturated fats makes the fatty acid tail develop a little kink or bend – in contrast to saturated fats, which have straight tails. However, when unsaturated fat is turned into a trans formation, this single structural change straightens the chain out again. Structurally, this makes a trans fatty acid molecule look and – fascinatingly – *behave* much more like a saturated fat. So hydrogenation suddenly gives the newly-created trans fatty acid properties similar to saturated fats, all of which are commercially advantageous. First, trans fats are solid (semi-soft) at room temperature, making them easy to transport and store. Second, they go rancid less easily than other fats, which gives them (and products that contain them) a much longer shelf life. Third, they can be repeatedly heated and cooled without breaking down in the way other fats do. And, finally – although this is an unintended consequence of the molecular change – they are much cheaper than other animal-derived solid fats. With this discovery, partially hydrogenated vegetable oil had arrived.

Although the process of hydrogenation was discovered a while ago, it was some time before companies understood the properties of these new fats. The first commercial application was in America, with the 1911 launch of Crisco,[10] a type of vegetable shortening which Proctor & Gamble created by hydrogenating cottonseed oil (the name Crisco came from an abbreviation of crystallized cottonseed oil). Trans fat very quickly became a common ingredient in margarine, prepacked baked goods and snacks and fast food restaurant deep-fat fryers: in short, a mainstay of processed and ultra-processed foods. In the 1970s and 80s trans fat became the primary added fat in many processed and prepacked foods; by the 1990s the Food and Drug Administration in America estimated that about 95 per cent of all biscuits, and all crackers and other salty snack foods in the USA contained trans fats. This is how the new trans fats became a major dietary source of fat and calories for huge numbers of people worldwide; a review estimated that in 2006 trans fats accounted for about 3 per cent of all calories consumed in the USA.[11]

The reason for their ubiquity was twofold: apart from being cheap, animal-derived saturated fats in dairy products and meat were widely perceived as unhealthy as a result of findings from the Seven Countries Study and others. Unsaturated vegetable fats, which trans fat could technically be classified as, were perceived as healthy. So adding these fats to products made them a win-win: cheap *and* supposedly healthy.

Unfortunately, even in food science there is no such thing as a free lunch. Trans fats were soon found to be far worse for human health than much-decried saturated fats. No formal clinical trials were ever carried out, interestingly, on the basis that trials would be unethical, which says something about a supposedly innocuous substance found in foods industry-wide. But the overall pattern of trans fats' effects on health was striking and concerning. Researchers found that getting even 2 per cent of your daily calories from trans fats raised the risk of coronary heart disease by 23 per cent![12] Even more concerningly, one study suggested that they were associated with a tripling of sudden death from cardiac causes.[13] It appears that trans fats mimicked saturated fats a little too well: they also increased the ratio of LDLs to HDLs in the blood, mirroring some of the worst effects of overconsuming saturated fats.

Denmark led the way in responding to these findings in 2003 by becoming the first country in the world to introduce a cap on trans fat in food products. The Danish government forced manufacturers to cap additional trans fats to 2 per cent or less of the total added fats. Despite being challenged by the European Union on the basis that it would interfere with the free movement of goods within the EU's borders, Denmark stuck to its guns, citing extensive public health concern, an argument with which the EU eventually agreed.[14] Over the following 15 years or so, reductions, caps or even outright bans on the additions of trans fats to processed foods have been imposed worldwide. In 2018, the US banned trans fats completely;[15] manufacturers were given a deadline of 1 January 2020 to remove products containing trans fats from circulation.

However, not all countries have followed this example. In 2018, the World Health Organization (WHO) estimated that about half a million people still die annually from heart disease caused by the addition of trans fats to food.[16] The WHO has launched a plan to eliminate trans fats from the world's supply chain. There is no legislation on trans fats in foods in the UK, where manufacturers have signed up to a voluntary reduction scheme. While this appears to be working – national dietary surveys indicate that the quantities of trans fats in British diets has been steadily declining since 2007 – it does not solve the problem altogether. Trans fats continue to be added to processed foods around the world, and processed and ultra-processed foods are predominantly eaten in significant quantities by those who cannot afford fresh produce. So lack of regulation of the addition of trans fats to certain food products might be disproportionately affecting those of lower socioeconomic status, adding to the health burdens of more marginalized groups. Currently about 160,000 people die of heart and circulatory disease in the UK annually, with up to 3,000 estimated to be dying as a result of chronic conditions caused by eating food with trans fats.[17]

In 2016 about half a million people worldwide died of coronary heart disease caused by eating too many trans fats. High-income nations have a notably higher number of coronary heart disease deaths attributable to trans fats than lower income countries. This is presumably because people in these countries were able to buy more fast food (this is underlined by the fact that those who died from eating excessive trans fats were younger). The highest mortality attributable to eating excessive trans fats was in North America, with an estimated 488 deaths per one million adults.[18] But low-income countries are also affected: for example, in Pakistan fake cooking oils sold as ghee (a type of clarified butter traditionally used for cooking), have been found to contain about 7 per cent trans fats. Widespread use of these oils is believed to be contributing to the country's escalating rate of heart disease.[19]

Despite this there is an overall trend towards removing trans fats from diets worldwide, spearheaded by the WHO guidance. For example, India aims to be trans fat-free by 2022, and Brazil aims to keep the trans fat content of food to less than 2 per cent of all added fats by 2023. But as I have mentioned before, the consumption of processed and ultra-processed food is rising worldwide, and one of the biggest factors in this food's success is its low cost. To allow manufacturers and fast-food chains to continue to make money, there is – and there will continue to be – increasing demand for a new source of cheap fats. But it seems that the new source of cheap fats comes at an environmental – as well as a health – cost to the world. I refer to palm oil – although the story is not as simple as you might think.

OUR RELATIONSHIP WITH PALM OIL:
IT'S COMPLICATED

One of the odder Christmas traditions to emerge in the UK over the past few years is that every major retailer produces a lavish TV advert extolling their ability to provide Christmas spirit at a reasonable cost. In 2018 the retailer Iceland went about things a little differently. Their advert was an animated short film originally made by the environmental organization Greenpeace featuring an adorable baby orang-utan which unexpectedly takes up residence in a little girl's bedroom. To the girl's dismay (narrated in a poetic voiceover) the orang-utan wreaked havoc, throwing away her chocolate and howling at her toiletries. Naturally, the girl sent the orang-utan sternly away, but just before the baby ape knuckled out of the room, the girl stopped it and asked why it was in her bedroom in the first place. The response, laid over stark black-and-white animated scenes of destruction and despair, was that there was a human in the orang-utan's forest, who had taken away its mother and was burning down the forest to produce palm oil to put in products such as chocolate and shampoo. So the baby orang-utan is homeless ('I thought I'd stay with you'). The advert ends with a pledge by the supermarket to stop using palm oil in their own-brand products until all palm oil causes zero rainforest destruction – and was dedicated to 'the 25 orang-utans we lose every day'.

In an unexpected twist, the advert was banned before it could be aired because it was deemed to be too political: political advertising is not allowed on British television. This arguably helped to disseminate its message more widely than airing it might have done (the advertising executives might have known this). It was watched more than 30 million times online and a petition calling for its reinstatement on television collected over a million signatures. In short, it touched hearts and minds and helped to establish palm oil as a demon crop responsible for the decimation of the forest homes of orang-utans and thousands of other animals. While banning palm oil from our shelves might benefit orang-utans, it is likely that this would cause worse harms elsewhere. And this is mainly due to the extraordinary nature of palm oil.

African oil palms are beautiful plants, which, despite looking very much like trees, are technically classified as woody herbs. They originally grew in Africa and were taken to Southeast Asia in the late 19th and early 20th centuries. They were originally exported as ornamental plants, designed to prettify colonial estates, but the extraordinary properties of their fruit meant that they were soon given plantations of their own. Palm oil is now one of the world's most lucrative cash crops – the industry is worth US$33 billion, and palm oil (and its derivatives) is one of the world's top 100 most traded commodities.[20]

One of the reasons palm oil is valuable is that it is astonishingly versatile. The fruit can be used to produce two different types of oil: the fleshy fruit can be squeezed to make crude palm oil, and the fruit's kernel can be crushed to produce palm kernel oil. Both these oils can be used whole, or further separated into different oil types, each with their own properties. Palm oil derivatives can be used in food as an added fat, as a frying oil, in cosmetics to give smooth textures, as a foaming agent in shampoo, liquid soap or detergent, as an addition to animal feed, as a lubricant and even burned as biofuel.[21] Almost half of all packaged products use palm oil in some form or another.[22] The palm itself is almost factory-like in its efficiency. At the peak of its fertility, a tree can produce a crop of palm oil every ten days – and each crop can produce 20–30kg of oil.

Most importantly, palm oil functions as an almost identical replacement for rendered animal fats such as lard or beef tallow, giving manufacturers an easy way of making some products both vegetarian and cheaper at the same time. Despite being a vegetable oil, palm oil is semi-solid at room temperature, making it much easier to transport than other vegetable oils and so logistically more attractive. It is odourless and tasteless but has a wonderful 'mouth feel' (the term for how a food feels in the mouth, as distinct from its taste; think about the difference between butter and margarine). Apart from enhancing food texture, it is also a natural preservative, effortlessly extending product shelf life. Because of these properties, palm oil now accounts for 40 per cent of all vegetable oil consumption worldwide and is the most consumed oil worldwide.[23]

Part of the reason for this very high consumption is that when the trans fats were found to be detrimental, producers looked for a new fat to replace them. Palm oil was the most frequently chosen replacement, which is one reason it has found its way into so many of the products we consume. Added to this, it is also cheap to produce, and because it is a vegetable oil it is seen as a healthier alternative. However, one of the reasons palm oil is more similar to rendered animal fats is that it contains far more saturated fats than most comparable vegetable oils. Compared with, for example, soybean oil, palm oil has only 9 per cent polyunsaturated fats versus soybean's 60 per cent; conversely palm oil contains 53 per cent saturated fat versus soybean's 16 per cent.[24]

Processed palm oil raises the ratio of LDLs to HDLs in the same manner as saturated fats. Consequently, eating it might also increase the risk of heart disease compared with eating vegetable oils with a higher proportion of unsaturated fats. These studies are small, so we still don't have a definite answer. It's most likely that palm oil sits somewhere between other vegetable oils and animal fats in terms of health benefits. In the same way as saturated fats, palm oil's composition wouldn't be a problem if we consumed it in moderate quantities. But because palm oil is such a wonderful fat for preserving and extending the life of processed food, it has become a near-ubiquitous part of our diet. As people continue to eat an ever-greater proportion of processed and ultra-processed food in their diet, they will also overconsume these fats at the expense of unsaturated fats, which will in turn contribute to the rising incidence of heart disease.

The 2016 study mentioned earlier (see page 88) also looked at the effects of eating too much saturated fat or carbohydrate at the expense of unsaturated fats, and found that about 711,000 deaths from coronary health disease were caused by this imbalance.[25] However, the problem is excessive consumption of palm oil and very few other unsaturated fats, not eating palm oil itself.

So to improve our health, there are two options: either eat fewer processed products, consuming less palm oil as a by-product, or agitate for producers to change their fat supply to something healthier, replacing palm oil where possible with a truly unsaturated vegetable oil such as rapeseed or olive oil. Iceland, by stating that none of its own-brand products would contain palm oil, albeit for environmental rather than health reasons, was implicitly promising that they would change the composition of their products. But there are several problems with this. First, other unsaturated vegetable oils do not have the same physical properties of palm oil so like for like replacements aren't always possible. Much of palm oil's success is due to its amazing similarity to saturated animal-derived fats; ending the use of palm oil would probably lead to an increase in the use of saturated animal-derived fats, with all the associated health and environmental harms I've discussed. Second, switching away from palm oil would increase the price of food with the burden of this likely to fall on those who can afford it least (people in lower socioeconomic groups are likely to be the most dependent on processed food). And finally, most importantly (and counter-intuitively): switching away from palm oil would most likely worsen the environmental impact of producing processed food.

Palm oil has become the poster child for causing harm to the environment. This is both true and unfair at the same time. One study which looked at satellite imagery to find palm oil plantation sites estimated that in Southeast Asia (Indonesia and Malaysia), 45 per cent of the palm plantations assessed were in areas that had been natural forests in 1989; another study suggested that the number was 50 per cent.[26] Between 1980 and 2000, an estimated six million hectares (one hectare is 10,000 square metres) of land were cleared for palm oil production in Southeast Asia.[27] Ever-expanding palm oil production does not threaten only orang-utans. As a result of expanding palm oil production, there are fewer than 3,000 Sumatran elephants left and only 1,500 Bornean pygmy elephants, the smallest (and, to drop the science for a second, the absolute cutest) of all elephant species. But these animals are only endangered. Palm oil production has left other species even worse off, such as the critically endangered Sunda tigers: there are only 400 left in the wild. And there are fewer than 80 Sumatran rhinos today, our closest (currently) living relative to the woolly rhinos.[28]

While these are terrible statistics, they tell only half of the story. It really is no exaggeration to say that palm oil is an almost miraculous crop. Apart from its incredible production rates, it is also an extraordinarily efficient crop. It yields 3.3 tonnes of oil per hectare, almost five times as much as rapeseed, the next most efficient vegetable oil.[29] Palm provides 35 per cent of the world's vegetable oil using only 10 per cent of the land. To produce equivalent quantities of oil from other sources we would have to clear about 40 per cent more land worldwide, causing even more damage to ecosystems. In short, given what we currently choose to eat, palm oil is one of the most effective ways of providing added fats despite causing harms: it is the best of the bad options. If you want to blame something for causing environmental harms, don't blame the cultivation of palm oil plantations: blame our seemingly insatiable desire for unhealthy, processed foods. If we reduce the amount of ultra-processed foods we consume, we could keep palm oil plantation extents as they currently are, and not cause further damage to the environment by expanding into virgin ecosystems. (As a side note, sustainable palm oil does exist, even if it's not the norm. Different manufacturers use sustainable palm oil or transparent, deforestation-free supply chains. To assess the sustainability of the products you buy look up the Roundtable on Sustainable Palm Oil and the incredible WWF palm oil scorecard tool.)[30]

While palm oil might be the least of multiple evils, we cannot deny the harm its excessive cultivation has already caused to otherwise virgin forests. Not only does this represent extreme deforestation, with all the associated harms that land-use change brings, dwindling numbers of species (both animal and vegetable) are a problem too. The number of different species in the world is known as biodiversity, and along with nutrient flow it is the other planetary boundary (see Chapter Two, page 30) whose limit we have already pushed past into the realm of unknown harms. It's important to realize that dwindling biodiversity doesn't simply matter because having fewer cute elephants on the planet makes us feel momentarily sad. Biodiversity, along with climate change, is one of the planetary boundaries which is most intertwined with all others. We are likely to discover the harms that befall us when species disappear only once they have gone. And once species have gone extinct, despite the promises of *Jurassic Park*, they cannot be resurrected. It's time to examine the impacts of our eating habits on the rest of life on earth.

THE SIXTH EXTINCTION EVENT

Dinosaurs, as many four-year-olds will tell you whether you ask or not, were gigantic animals that roamed the earth for an astonishingly long time – almost 180 million years. Unfortunately for them, the dinosaurs' reign ended abruptly around 66 million years ago. It was then that a huge asteroid – believed to be 10–15km wide – crashed into the Yucatán Peninsula in Mexico. The speed at which it was travelling made the asteroid vaporize on impact, creating a crater 150km across and sending out shockwaves of heat and debris. The impact led to gargantuan tidal waves which flooded parts of both American continents, and so much debris was thrown into the atmosphere that almost all sunlight was obscured. However it was not the direct impact of the asteroid which wiped out the dinosaurs; instead it was the consequences of the subsequent ecological disaster. Lack of sunlight stunted or killed plants, which in turn meant that herbivorous dinosaurs couldn't find sufficient food to survive. Diminishing numbers of herbivores led to the death of the carnivores. In total, about 75 per cent of all the animals on earth (including all land animals heavier than 25kg, which was almost all dinosaurs) died at approximately the same time.

The death of the dinosaurs is referred to as the late Cretaceous extinction event. While it is the most famous of all extinctions, and definitely the most dramatic, it was the fifth extinction event to wipe out a significant proportion of life on earth.[31] In terms of size, it wasn't the biggest: the late Permian extinction event, about 250 million years ago, is cheerfully known in palaeontological circles as 'The Great Dying'. Palaeontologists believe that this extinction event was caused by extreme Siberian volcanic activity, and wiped out 90 per cent of all marine animals, along with about 70 per cent of land animals and even many insects for perhaps the first time (insects have generally been less affected by extinction events than other animals).[32]

As none of us was around to witness these events, scientists have pieced together what happened using clues in changing rock strata and the fossil record. None of the mass extinction events – not even the late Cretaceous asteroid impact – occurred on a timescale which we would have been able to observe. They all happened over millions of years: a blink of an eye in terms of geological time, but beyond our conception. So the way we have identified and defined these extinction events is to compare the number of species going extinct over a given time period (generally several million years) with something known as the background extinction rate.

The world is a dynamic and constantly shifting system, so at any given time a certain number of species lose out to other, better-adapted species and go extinct. For most of history, the background extinction rate has remained more or less constant as environments change and animals adapt to these changes (or fail to adapt). However, at times of mass extinction, this number rises significantly: so much so that when they are plotted on a graph the number looks like a series of spikes emerging from an otherwise low-level straight line. All these mass extinctions have occurred in response to one or more apocalypse-like events: gamma ray bursts from space; ice ages; more asteroid strikes; more volcanic eruptions. But now into this mix of catastrophic events that befall earth, leading directly to the deaths of unprecedented numbers of animals, we have to add one more: us.

Using the same methodology as they used to identify the previous five mass extinction events, scientists have identified that we are in the middle of a sixth. The number of species of animals going extinct is significantly higher than the background extinction rate. For example, looking at vertebrates (animals with backbones), scientists calculated that if animals were going extinct at a normal rate, we would have expected nine vertebrate species, at most, to go extinct between 1900 and 2014. (This uses an extremely high estimate of the background extinction rate.) Instead, 477 species of vertebrate went extinct. To put it differently, if nothing unusual was happening, under normal circumstances it should have taken about 10,000 years for that many animals to go extinct – and instead it took 114 years.[33]

This is an old problem. It appears that people have been systematically responsible for causing greater-than-expected extinctions wherever we have been in the world. For example, Australia and New Guinea were once home to a group of huge mammals: giant kangaroos, huge marsupials that resembled rhinos and leopards, a one-tonne lizard, and a large 200-kg flightless bird that looked like an ostrich. These megafauna, as they are known, all went extinct at roughly the same time around 40,000 years ago – about the time that humans first reached Australia and New Guinea. Similarly, around 15,000 years ago, the great plains in Western USA resembled today's Serengeti: they were filled with herds of elephants, camels and horses (as well as giant ground sloths) preyed on by lions and cheetahs. The fossil record shows that all these animals went extinct in the same 5,000-year period, which coincided with the arrival of humans in the region. Several fossils show the animals with spearheads between their ribs. While we cannot *prove* that the arrival of humans led to these species' extinctions, it seems extremely probable that we were a major contributing cause.[34] Large mammals could have posed a threat or been useful food for humans but other species also suffered from contact with people. People colonized the tropical Oceania islands (Micronesia, Fiji and all of Polynesia except New

Zealand) about 2,000 years ago and since then about 1,800 bird species have gone extinct.[35]

So if people have always caused extinctions, why do we need to be concerned now? Why is biodiversity, the measure of the variety of animal and plant species in the world, one of the planetary boundaries? The answer is that not only are we accelerating the loss of species, we're also losing vast numbers of individual animals in the species that remain. This affects how we live. To return to the image of the global earth system as a single tapestry (see page 31), viewing our continued existence on earth as separate from the rest of life on earth gives us a very narrow perspective. If we continue to lose animals in the way that we are, we run the risk of going the way of the dinosaurs, whose extinction was caused not by a single catastrophic event, but by the impact that event had on the ecosystem. It is time to consider the unpaid, hidden and non-glamorous role that the earth's natural systems play in our continued survival.

BIODIVERSITY IN THE WILD

*R*uPaul's Drag Race is an American TV show in which a group of contestants compete to be crowned the best drag queen. The contestants visually transform themselves while remaining consummate entertainers. Once in drag, they sing, dance, act, banter and create visually stunning costumes, all while tottering in heels. Each episode features various outlandish challenges, which the contestants take extremely seriously for fear of being cast out by the judges. Judgements centre around critical issues such as whether a contestant's make-up style is stale, or whether a corset and tights makes a sufficiently interesting outfit.

In season 12, episode four ('The Ball Ball'), the contestants were given a challenge with a different spin. In order to 'raise awareness of the world's declining bee population', they had to create and wear bee-inspired costumes in an impromptu dance-off. The eventual winner of the challenge was given only half the normal prize money, with the other half being given to the Honey Bee Conservancy. The host, RuPaul, prefaced the challenge by saying, 'Bees are a crucial part of our ecosystem, pollinating fruits, vegetables and the grains we eat. So basically, without bees, we are fucked.'

RuPaul might not be a conservation scientist, but he is not wrong. The numbers of bees, along with all other pollinator species – which include birds and small mammals such as bats – are declining dramatically around the world. Pollinators are animals which move between plants, transferring pollen from plant to plant and so fertilizing them. We know more about the decline of honeybees than other insects because we keep them commercially, and so we're more immediately and acutely aware of their population loss. Honeybee numbers are declining dramatically. Two-thirds of American beekeepers lose about 40 per cent of their colonies annually, European and South African beekeepers lose 30 per cent and Chinese beekeepers lose up to 13 per cent. Their bees are suffering from colony collapse disorder, a poorly understood phenomenon in which most of a colony's worker bees vanish, leaving their queen behind, despite there being plentiful food supplies.[36] Colony collapse disorder is believed to result from interaction between multiple factors, including colony infections, stress as a result of moving hives to pollinate various crops, toxins from pesticides and the poor nutritional value of monoculture crops offering an insufficient variety of food.

However, there are about 16,000 species of bee worldwide, and almost all their numbers are declining. For example, a long-term study of central European bumblebees over 136 years found that of 60 recorded species, an astonishing four out of five species have become less abundant, 30 per cent are now classed as threatened and four have vanished entirely and become extinct.[37]

It's not just bees. *All* insect species in the world seem to be in rapid decline. Anecdotally, some readers might have noticed this already: not too long ago, long summer car journeys resulted in a windscreen splattered with the bodies of dead insects. Now that rarely happens. Research looking at historical data over time bears this out: insect numbers are falling so rapidly that we might see the extinction of 40 per cent of the world's insect species over the next few decades.[38]

To demonstrate how widespread this problem is, two studies in countries on different continents which assessed changes in insect biomass over time both found startling drops.

When assessing insect numbers it's impossible to count individual insects flitting about in the wild. One of the ways that scientists estimate insect numbers is by using a Malaise trap. This is a gauze tent with some open sides and a hole at the highest point connected to a collecting bottle. Insects fly into the tent and try to escape by flying upwards, and so are trapped in the bottle. Bottles can then be weighed to assess insect numbers according to their weight, and this is compared to weights of previous collections; the resulting weight is known as the insect biomass.

A study carried out over 27 years in 63 separate areas of protected wilderness in Germany found that insect biomass had fallen by as much as 82 per cent in some areas.[39] On the other side of the world, another study compared insect biomass data between 1976 and 2012 in two locations in the Puerto Rican rainforest, and found a loss of between 78 and 98 per cent (depending on how the insects were collected).[40] In the best-case scenario, we've lost about three-quarters of the volume of insects in both countries in less than 40 years. It's not quite equivalent, but can you imagine what would happen if three-quarters of the pets in the world died? Picture four pets you know – dog, cat, rabbit, hamster – and now imagine that three of them died of some sudden and unexplained malady. That would be front-page news.

But insects are neither cute nor fluffy, and are often seen at best as irritating and at worst as disease-bearing (which is admittedly true in some cases). So why should we care that insect numbers are declining around the world? Because insects are the biggest group of pollinators we have. We need them to pollinate more than 75 per cent of commercial food crops worldwide. Their role is not trivial; without pollinators we risk losing up to US$577 billion worth of crops worldwide every year.[41]

These pollinators are the best examples of wild animals providing something called ecosystem services. Ecosystem services are defined as both the direct and indirect contributions of ecosystems to human well-being. There are two main types of ecosystem service: those that provide renewable resources for people (such as food, wood, water) and those that regulate the environment for our benefit (for example, the way forests regulate climate).[42]

Losing pollinators has a direct, tangible and detrimental effect on people. To quote John Donne and extend his words out from his human-centred lens: if no man is an island entire of itself, neither is any other animal. All animals, ourselves included, exist in complex ecosystems that rely on many interconnecting interactions to create a system resilient to challenges. For example, 80 per cent of wild plants are pollinated by insects, and 60 per cent of birds rely on insects as a food source. So losing insects doesn't just mean that our vegetables go unpollinated: their loss affects the whole ecosystem. Let's not forget that the cause of the dinosaurs' extinction after 180 million years was not the impact of the asteroid itself, but rather the knock-on effects it had on the ecosystem.

There are two component parts to this: loss of numbers of animals and loss of species. When there are very few plants or animals of a specific species left, that species is said to be endangered. If a species goes extinct, there might be no change to the *number* of plants or animals in the world but there will be fewer *species*; in other words, there is decreased biodiversity. Both falling numbers of animals within a species and falling numbers of species can affect an ecosystem's resilience. This in turn affects the ecosystem's ability to provide the services which we need. For example, falling numbers of insects reduces the rate of pollination, as there are fewer insects to go between plants, while decreasing numbers of insect species will affect *which* plants are pollinated. Most pollinators have evolved specific physical adaptations for particular plants and so only pollinate a certain number. But the two are also interconnected: if there are fewer animals of a certain species this will affect other species' ability to survive. As an example, if the number of pollinators falls below a critical threshold, certain plant species will not be able to reproduce, and so the plant species will go extinct. A recent report suggests that there has been an average 60 per cent decline in animal population sizes (about 2 per cent a year) worldwide.[43]

The planetary boundary that encompasses these measures is known as biosphere integrity. It is made up of two elements, which broadly speaking are what I have just described: genetic diversity (or the number of different species) and functional diversity which measures the abundance of animal populations and compares that with pre-industrial times.

The problem is that both are extremely difficult to measure accurately. So scientists have put interim measures in place until we can make more accurate assessments. These are the extinction rate (to assess biodiversity), and the Biodiversity Intactness Index (to measure functional diversity). For a variety of reasons, the Biodiversity Intactness Index only looks at Southern Africa and remains a little hazy, so I will not address it here. The planetary boundary for extinction rate (see page 39) as a measure of biodiversity has been set at less than ten extinctions per million species years.[44] (This is already ten times more than the 'natural' background extinction rate of one extinction per million species years.)

In 2019, the Intergovernmental Science-Policy Platform on Biodiversity and Ecosystem Services (IPBES; an independent non-government agency closely associated with the UN) published one of the most comprehensive assessments of the world's ecosystems ever carried out. Their report on Biodiversity and Ecosystem Services was based on a systematic review of approximately 15,000 scientific and governmental resources. It was written by 145 experts from 50 countries and took three years to write. Their findings were ominously clear. If we do not change how we live, about a million species of animals and plants are at imminent risk of extinction within the next few decades.[45] By way of comparison, there are estimated to be about eight million species of animals and plants on earth, of which 5.5 million are insects. On land, about 20 per cent of species have become less abundant (so have fewer individuals) since 1990, and in the water about 40 per cent of all amphibians and a third of all marine mammals are threatened. Overall, the experts estimate that the current rate of extinction is about 100 times higher than the background extinction rate (although some other reports have put it as high as 1,000 times the background extinction rate, depending on the data modelling used).[46] The authors of the IPBES report attribute these extremely high – and increasing – rates of extinction to five factors. In order of magnitude these are: changes in land and sea use; direct organismal exploitation; climate change; pollution; and invasive alien species. In other words they are almost entirely caused by humans.

While people's actions have been increasing extinctions for hundreds of years, our recent increasing incursions into the natural world have vastly accelerated the rate at which extinctions occur. These have important and concerning implications for both our natural world and for us. When the report was issued the IPBES chair, Sir Robert Watson, commented that 'the overwhelming evidence of the IPBES Global Assessment, from a wide range of different fields of knowledge, presents an ominous picture. The health of ecosystems on which we and all other species depend is deteriorating more rapidly than ever. We are eroding the very foundations of our economies, livelihoods, food security, health and quality of life worldwide.' One of the report's co-chairs, Professor Josef Settele, added that 'ecosystems, species, wild populations, local varieties and breeds of domesticated plants and animals are shrinking, deteriorating or vanishing. The essential, interconnected web of life on Earth is getting smaller and increasingly frayed. This loss is a direct result of human activity and constitutes a direct threat to human well-being in all regions of the world.'

Why does loss of biodiversity concern these eminent scientists so? Biodiversity has been shown to improve or provide a vast number of different ecosystem services. To name just a few, greater biodiversity promotes better plant growth (including commercial crop yield, trees in woodland and fodder on grassland); more stable and resilient fisheries; greater resistance of commercial crops to invasion by exotic species or attack by fungal or viral pathogens; better retention of soil minerals and organic matter; and increased carbon capture and storage. So retaining high levels of biodiversity doesn't just benefit those species which remain on the earth, it also benefits us, just as decreasing biodiversity brings harms.[47] And having a diverse range of species is not just beneficial in terms of wild species and the ecosystem services they provide: it provides resilience for our commercial food supplies too.

BIODIVERSITY IN FARMING

Consider the banana. Have you ever wondered why, unlike the many different varieties of apple we can choose from, almost all bananas seem identical? Apple varieties vary from the green, tart Granny Smith, to the bright red, extremely sweet Gala to the soft yellow Golden Delicious. By contrast, bananas are all the same uniform yellow colour, and the only variation in taste and texture comes from how ripe or not they are. There's a good reason for this uniformity: almost every banana in the world is a clone of a single banana. Instead of being planted as seeds, bananas are grown asexually from offshoots. This clone army is a variety known as the Cavendish. Despite there being more than 1,000 varieties of wild banana, the Cavendish has risen to pre-eminence: 95 per cent of all bananas in the world are Cavendish. Cavendish clones give producers many advantages: having no seeds makes them nicer to eat; unlike other varieties, the Cavendish can survive the weeks it takes to transport them around the world; and their uniformity in size and shape makes for efficient shipping. However, it also has a huge weakness: if one banana is susceptible to a certain disease, then they all are.[48]

This is not idle supposition. In the mid-20th century there was an outbreak of a fungal pathogen which causes something called Panama disease in bananas. At the time, the most widely cultivated banana type was the Gros Michel variety, which was susceptible to the infection. The disease was first discovered in Panama (hence the name) and spread quickly between the genetically identical plants, wiping out whole plantations throughout Latin America, where most bananas are grown. The Cavendish variety was resistant to the disease, and so was adopted worldwide in response.

But in 2019, a different variant of Panama disease known as TR4 reached Latin America. It's not new – the origins of this disease can be traced back to Indonesia in the 1960s – but farmers had desperately tried to stop it in its tracks through worldwide containment methods. Once the fungus takes root in the soil, the spores persist for decades. The only way to contain it is to destroy all the plants on an infected plantation and stop production; fungicides cannot save plants already infected. The emergence of TR4 in Latin America has driven the fear that bananas as we know them may become extinct, as well as imposing huge costs on banana farmers and those who rely on bananas as a staple food worldwide.[49] We might have to accept that if we want to continue to eat bananas, we need to embrace a variety of different shapes, colours, tastes and textures – and even seeds.

While bananas are an extreme example because they're clones, we are cultivating fewer species of animals and plants than ever before. For example, more than 6,000 plant species have been cultivated for food, but fewer than 200 make major contributions to food production – and nine plant species make up 66 per cent of total crop production (sugar cane, maize, rice, wheat, potatoes, soybeans, oil-palm fruit, sugar beet and cassava). Of 8,803 livestock breeds, 594 are extinct and around 2,200 are at risk of extinction.[50] This is the farming equivalent of putting all your eggs in one basket. Animal and plant populations are not equally resistant to disease. The more breeds of animals and plants there are, the more genetic diversity there is within a species. Greater genetic diversity in a population means there is a stronger possibility of developing a mutation with disease resistance which can provide some defence and resilience in the population as a whole – it can offer breeders alternatives if disease rips through the currently farmed variety.

Research has also shown that growing vast quantities of the same variety of crop in the same fields every year (known as monoculture farming) decreases the resilience of both the landscape and the crop. For example, reducing crop biodiversity seems to make crops more vulnerable to being eaten by agricultural pests[51] as well as depleting soil nutrients, reducing yields. This means that farmers need to add increasing quantities of fertilizer to retain fertility, which leads to the problems highlighted in Chapter Three (see page 66). By contrast, growing new and unrelated species of plants on cropland offers unexpected benefits. As an example, the agroforestry practice of planting trees on cropland has been shown to improve soil erosion and land fertility.[52] By adopting these strategies, farmers can make their farms more like a natural ecosystem: creating a more complex ecosystem increases both resilience and productivity.

But it's challenging for farmers to make such changes. For a start, commercial farmers supplying producers might be required to plant only one variety of crop to ensure consistency in large-scale commercial production. Similarly, planting trees in fields might affect how crops are harvested, depending on the size of the field and the machinery farmers have at their disposal. Also, planting trees or other species of plants might seem counter-intuitive for most farmers and they may take up valuable field space. So while there are many benefits to introducing biodiversity, it might be an economic decision which a farmer cannot take.[53] Fortunately, the importance of agricultural biodiversity has been recognized. The United Nation's Food and Agriculture Organization (FAO) aims to make it easier for farmers to adopt measures which support both agricultural and wild biodiversity. Data shows that agroforestry for oil palms, where cocoa and oil palms are grown together (known as intercropping), gives much higher yields than mono-culture farming. Intercropping also replenishes ground water, requires less labour overall and has a small carbon footprint. So innovative farming methods can create win-win situations, both economically and environmentally – and reduce the area of land used for farming.[54] This is vital if we are to keep ecosystems intact and continue to retain their services.

HABITAT LOSS IS EVERYONE'S LOSS

Habitat loss is the single biggest cause of decreasing biodiver-sity – and so reduced ecosystem services. I have explained the climatic and environmental impact of land-use change – the conversion of forests into agricultural land – on pages 38 and 40. These changes also lead to habitat loss. For example, the single biggest cause of insect species loss is believed to be habitat loss as the result of converting more land to intensive agriculture and urbanization. Not only does habitat loss decrease the space in which animals can live, habitat fragmentation can lead to such small numbers of animals living in isolated pockets of space that there is not enough genetic diversity to maintain the species. This is the equivalent of being trapped in a house with only your close relatives as possible sexual partners (yes, I shuddered just writing that as well). Reducing the area of habitat available for animals and plants gives each species a smaller space in which they can live, and research shows that this is one of the biggest risks for going extinct.[55] So it's vital that we preserve habitats. And some-times human activity doesn't simply decrease the resilience of an ecosystem habitat through decreasing biodiversity. We've wiped out some ecosystems completely. This has very real consequences – not just for those animals and plants in an ecosystem, but for us as well.

Mangrove forests are aquatic forests growing in the waters of lagoons, swamps and coasts around the world. They're slightly creepy-looking, with gnarly root systems, prompting thoughts of snapping alligators and black, sucking mud. There are about 152,000 square km (58,700 square miles) of mangrove forests in 123 countries, but the biggest chunk – about a third – is in Southeast Asia.[56] Put together, all the mangrove forests in the world would cover an area only the size of Greece, but they represent an extraordinary ecosystem, acting as a sheltered nursery for many coastal and marine animal species. Mangroves also store almost ten times the carbon of other forests. This means that although mangrove forests represent only about 0.7 per cent of tropical forests, destroying them leads to 2–8 per cent of all carbon dioxide emissions. They also protect people and land against natural disasters.

In 2004 a tsunami devastated countries with Indian Ocean coastlines, killing hundreds of thousands of people and flattening cities. Nothing could have saved the communities near the epicentre of the tragedy. However, evidence suggests that homes in settlements further away were saved by mangrove forests. Researchers looked at villages along the stretch of beach in the Cuddalore District of Tamil Nadu in India and found that villages directly exposed to the coast were completely destroyed by the waves, while villages shielded by mangroves were almost unharmed.[57] Analysis of the harm done by a super cyclone elsewhere in India reached similar conclusions – villages with a wider area of mangroves between them and the coast experienced significantly fewer deaths than those with narrower strips or no mangroves.[58] The World Bank estimates that mangroves are protecting millions of people and property worth about US$57 billion from flooding annually. If they were to lose these mangroves, as many as 18 million more people would be flooded every year.[59] Worldwide, up to 300 million people are thought to be at increased risk of floods and hurricanes as a result of the loss of coastal habitats and other types of protection.[60]

Unfortunately, mangroves are under threat from our agricultural needs. Between 1980 and 2005 19 per cent of the world's mangroves were destroyed to create farmland, build or plant other forests. A recent paper suggests that more than 1,000 square km

(386 square miles) of mangroves were lost to agriculture between 2000 and 2012, with the land used for aquaculture, palm oil plantations and rice paddies.[61]

This destruction has implications for many people, animals and plants. Most immediately, it hugely increases the risk of flooding and destruction for those people who are currently protected against more frequent extreme weather events. But the ecosystem services provided by mangroves go further. They function as nurseries for many commercial fish stocks. An American study found that mangroves in the Gulf of California increase fishery yields: the greater the area and abundance of mangroves, the more fish were available for commercial capture. Many commercially-fished species rely on mangroves to provide food and shelter, including some species of crabs, prawns, mullet, herring, anchovy, snapper and groupers.[62] Overall, the value of global mangrove ecosystem services is estimated at about US$1,648 billion every year. This is approximately equivalent to Russia's GDP.[63] This is an example of how the destruction of one habitat has far-reaching consequences: the nature of ecosystem services and our interconnected earth means that the repercussions are felt everywhere in the world.

BEAUTY

I was three when the elephants ate the house next door. We were in a safari park in South Africa, my country of birth. The lodge was a simple affair: half a dozen rondavels near a watering hole. Rondavels are small, circular huts, basic in design and execution, with mud walls and thatched roofs. They were enclosed by a fence with a largely symbolic protective function; the gate was kept open during the day on the grounds that anything big enough to cause serious upset was likely to be asleep during the heat of the day, and closing a gate would act as no deterrent to smaller dangerous beasts such as snakes. A gamekeeper nominally kept watch to ensure that anything big would be shooed away before joining the tourists, but any animals awake at noon tended to ignore the camp and walk past to the nearby watering hole. Tourists woke before dawn to go on game drives and then retired during the day, to sleep or laze by the main camp at the water's edge, reading books and watching wildlife come and go. So it was quite a shock when the elephants came.

No one noticed at first; not many people were about or awake. Two elephants wandered placidly but determinedly into the camp, making a beeline for something. It was only when they began determinedly gnawing at the roof of the rondavel next to ours that someone raised the alarm.

I remember there being a commotion outside. My mother appeared white-faced, picked me up hurriedly and tried to put me somewhere safe. It says a lot for her frame of mind at the time that the place of safety she decided on was the bathtub: I'm still not sure what protection it might have afforded me (although as she says now, I should try thinking clearly when there are two elephants outside my door). But it turned out that we were quite safe: the elephants were not there for us. The gamekeepers, who knew most of the animals by sight, kept the tourists back (fortunately our next-door neighbours weren't in), assuring them that the elephants were not harmful. And indeed they weren't. Once they had munched a hole in the roof, they extended their trunks gracefully into the hut and pulled out their prize: a succulent bag of oranges, the smell of which had proved irresistible. Once they had eaten the oranges, and had had a further nibble on the roof to check that no one had hidden any fruit in there, they departed as they had come: quietly and harmlessly.

It would be disingenuous to say that this experience left a lasting impression on me: I barely remember it, although it's still fun teasing my mother. But it was a formative experience: growing up in South Africa with wilderness-loving parents, meant that from a very early age I had up close and personal experiences with species other than my own, often on an unnervingly equal footing.

On a different occasion, I remember sitting around an evening campfire, and as dusk slid into night becoming aware that the firelight was reflected in dozens of other eyes which encircled the campfire just beyond where we sat. When I urgently pointed this out to an adult, I was not reassured to be told that it was 'just hyenas – they're too scared of the fire to come any closer, don't worry'. The adult was right; it was fine.

There was also the time when we discovered that a group of mongooses had set up an impromptu nursery beneath the base of one of the camp houses. No circus has ever had as agile acrobats, nor wittier clowns than the tiny scraps of fur which bounced variously from their parents to the trees, to our front steps and back again. On yet another visit, I remember waking to find the camp lovingly entwined with golden netting, stretching great distances between each tree, each with a huge tortoiseshell-coloured spider sitting fatly in the middle. Taking down the golden orb spiders' webs and shooing their creators back into the trees every morning became a daily chore. I have slept – or rather not slept – in a tent in the middle of the bush, hearing the odd belches that lions make which seem to come from all directions and none, and are designed to disconcert their prey and spook them into running headlong into the pride's waiting jaws.

In short, I am privileged because I have experienced an ecological service which is not available to many people: I have experienced the beauty and joy of biodiversity quite separately from any other function it might serve. While I was especially lucky to have experienced the wilderness of the African savannahs, there is beauty in the natural world wherever we live. My flat in north London has no garden, but overlooks a neighbour's tree which is covered with wisteria, and so has formed a sort of apartment block for resident wildlife. As I write, I can watch squirrels chase each other from branch to branch; some tiny chittering birds whose species I don't know fight each other for a prime spot on the bird feeder; a beautiful jay who only recently made this place his home ruffling his feathers impatiently; and a local cat watching them all lazily, tail flickering. I am sure that this lush miniature ecosystem keeps my home well-stocked with improbably large spiders and accounts for some of the scratchings in the walls which I assure myself are definitely mice and not rats. Less welcome denizens aside, watching these small sagas play out in front of me brings me joy.

The other places that bring me joy, even in London, include parks, rivers or canals: I love being outdoors generally. Judging by the numbers of people with whom I jostle for a spot on the grass on sunny days I am not alone in this, even on the days when I run under cold grey skies. Go into any art gallery and the walls are hung with centuries' worth of landscape painting; walk into any office and people's computer backgrounds are almost always some natural scene. Travel agencies and airline adverts entice us with photographs of sunny beaches or snowy mountain ranges. Even when we cannot physically be in natural landscapes, it seems we have a near-universal yearning to be near a representation of one.

I'm not sure we need science to illustrate this point, but it exists. A meta-analysis has found that those of us who feel more connected to the natural world experience greater life satisfaction, a greater sense of vitality (defined as the 'positive feeling of being alive, alert, and energetic') and of happiness than those who are less connected to nature.[64] There's even a scientific term for this: the biophilia hypothesis has been around for decades. This is the theory that humans have a natural predilection to focus on, and feel connection with, other forms of life. You only need to see a pet owner with their dog or cat to see that our ability to love is certainly not limited to our own species – and any suggestion that the love is not reciprocated by their animal companions would be hotly disputed by those owners.

In short, there is greater value to biodiversity than simple ecosystem services. They are vital for our continued survival, yes, but they are more than that. Animals and their natural habitats – the wilderness – are a source of beauty and joy for us all. With each extinction we come closer to a world in which elephants could never quietly and absent-mindedly eat a roof in search of oranges. It would be a less beautiful world; a less interesting world. It is not one any of us would choose to live in.

FATS FOR (ALL) LIFE

To return to where I started at the beginning of this chapter, the planetary health diet recommends eating more unsaturated vegetable oil than animal-derived saturated fats. Trans fats mimic the latter. One of the hallmarks of ultra-processed foods is added trans (hydrogenated) fats, palm oil or high quantities of animal fats. Thus one of the healthiest changes that we can make for ourselves and the planet is to eat less ultra-processed food, and to eat more plant-based food. Both these decisions would lead to a reduction in land-use change and habitat loss. Fats such as palm oil have been somewhat unfairly demonized: it is the demand for processed products which has driven their almost non-stop growth; hopefully if demand falls, their growth will stop and we can make do with what we have (or, whisper it quietly, even less). By making the choice to eat more rapeseed, sunflower, peanut or olive oil and less butter, lard, tallow and processed foods, we can not only improve our own health, but by making small changes can reduce pressure on natural habitats worldwide, and preserve – or even increase – the beauty and resilience of our natural ecosystems.

CHAPTER 5

FRUIT AND VEGETABLES

PLANETARY HEALTH DIET RECOMMENDATION

Daily recommendation: between three and four portions of vegetables, with these including at least one dark-green vegetable and one red or orange vegetable, and a maximum of one portion of legumes. Two or three portions of fruit.

I n 2018, the New York dermatologist Dr Shari Lipner saw a female patient with a strange array of symptoms. Her patient was 40 years old, and had previously suffered from chronic pancreatitis – damage to the pancreas from inflammation – and acid reflux. However, neither condition explained why she stood in the dermatologist's office that day. The patient had developed a rash which had rapidly spread over most of her body. In addition, she was tired and dizzy, had diarrhoea, had begun to bruise easily and was having difficulty walking. Upon examining her, Dr Lipner found that the rash, which looked like a mass of brownish-red freckles covering the skin, was perifollicular haemorrhage: bleeding in the tissues around the hair follicles. The patient's skin was covered in corkscrew-shaped hairs, visible to the naked eye, and her gums were bleeding. Laboratory tests confirmed what was obvious to the doctor: her patient was suffering from scurvy – an ancient disease, first reported in Egypt more than three and a half thousand years ago which plagued mankind until its almost complete eradication in the 20th century. Fortunately for her patient, in 2018 New York the cure was to be found in every supermarket. She was suffering from a deficiency of vitamin C caused by lack of fresh fruit and vegetables.[1]

We tend to think of scurvy as a disease of the past. Reports of scurvy and scurvy-like illnesses are dotted throughout history, but the disease came to prominence as a public health concern when seafaring nations began to send their navies on long ocean journeys. Portuguese, French and English ships began to report 'amalati de la boccha' (curse of the mouth – sailors died with swollen hands and legs and bleeding gums). The disease seemed to ease after ships took on fresh supplies.[2] For these sailors, this mystery disease was far more deadly than anything else faced on the voyages; one British expedition sent to raid Spanish holdings in the Pacific lost 1,300 of 2,000 men to illness. The descriptions make gruesome reading: the commanding officer of the expedition, George Anson, said, 'almost the whole crew' was afflicted by symptoms including a 'luxuriancy of funguous flesh...putrid gums and...the most dreadful terrors'.[3] Despite the seriousness of the malady, it was not until 1747 that someone systematically tried to discover a cure.

James Lind was a Scottish medical apprentice who joined the navy in the late 1730s. On board the HMS *Salisbury* in 1747 he carried out one of the first controlled trials recorded in medicine to try to find a cure for the scurvy that beset the sailors. There was a plethora of suggested cures to choose from, but none had been formally tested. Lind tried them all: he took 12 men suffering from scurvy and tried a different treatment on each pair. The suggested cures ranged from the odd (a nutmeg-sized paste of garlic, mustard seed, horseradish and multiple tree resins, to be taken three times a day), to the ineffective but probably appreciated (a quart of cider a day), to the unpleasant (half a pint of seawater a day), to the probably dangerous (25 drops of elixir of vitriol – a mixture of alcohol and sulphuric acid – three times a day). The least exotic cure was also the most effective: the pair of men given two oranges and a lemon daily recovered their health so rapidly that by the end of the week they had begun nursing the other men back to health. Lind wrote up his findings in his *Treatise of the Scurvy*, a review of the literature of the disease and his original observations, which was published in 1753.[4]

Despite Lind's treatise, it was 42 years before the Admiralty acted on his recommendations, and all British sailors were provided with rations of lemon juice on their voyages. This continued until the late 1860s, when the swap was made to (cheaper) lime juice: because vitamin C had not yet been identified as the curative agent, Lind believed that it was the acidity of citrus fruit which acted as a cure. (This incidentally, is why British sailors, and by extension Brits in general, are still sometimes referred to as 'limeys'.)

It wasn't until 1933 that the structure of vitamin C was published and the link between its deficiency and scurvy was finally established later that century. Calculations now estimate that we need 40–45mg of vitamin C daily,[5] which is fairly easy to get as long as you eat fresh fruit and vegetables: citrus fruits and their juices are the best-known vitamin C providers, but red, yellow and green peppers, strawberries, broccoli and Brussels sprouts are also good sources. Oddly, humans, monkeys and guinea pigs cannot synthesize their own vitamin C, whereas almost all other animals can. In fact, healthy goats make approximately 13,000mg of vitamin C per day – and increase their production to 100,000mg daily when faced with illness, trauma or stress.[6] However, humans have only three of the four enzymes needed to synthesize vitamin C: the fourth enzyme seems to be defective, a paradoxical fact which remains unexplained.

We still don't know everything that we need vitamin C for. It's vital in the synthesis of collagen, the most abundant protein in our bodies, of which there are at least 27 different types in our skin, tendons, cartilage, bone and connective tissue. Vitamin C is also needed to synthesize neurotransmitters and hormones which act as vital messenger molecules in our brains and bodies. There are other possible roles, including helping to synthesize cell membranes, protecting cells from damage and contributing to general growth and repair – but the science is still unclear as to exactly how. What we do know without question is that failure to eat a sufficient quantity of vitamin C has dangerous consequences: without treatment, scurvy is fatal.

And vitamin C is just one of many micronutrients in fruit and vegetables without which we suffer terrible diseases. Micronutrients differ from macronutrients such as protein and fat in that we only need very small amounts to maintain our health: a milligram (mg) is one thousandth of a gram, and a microgram (µg) one thousandth of a milligram. Nonetheless, in the same way that every screw in an aeroplane is a tiny component of the whole but vital to keep the plane airborne, without these tiny amounts of vitamins and minerals, our health suffers. Because we require a huge variety of these micronutrients to be in optimum health we need to assemble them from many different sources, which is one of the reasons eating a wide variety of fruit and vegetables is so highly recommended for good health.

MICRONUTRIENTS: TINY AMOUNTS, HUGE EFFECTS

Micronutrients are something that many of us take for granted because most of us can eat a range of fresh fruit and vegetables, and so never miss out on anything vital. But access is not the same worldwide. One of the biggest public health problems in many developing countries is vitamin A deficiency in children. The World Health Organization (WHO) estimates that about a third of all children worldwide aged between six months and five years are vitamin A deficient, with the highest rates in sub-Saharan Africa (half the population) and South Asia (about 40 per cent). Vitamin A deficiency causes xerophthalmia, a progressive eye disease which begins by drying out eyes and tear ducts and can develop into worse conditions such as night blindness (an inability to see in low light conditions), corneal scarring and even permanent loss of sight. Not getting enough vitamin A also increases the risk of children dying from otherwise potentially manageable conditions such as measles or diarrhoea.[7]

We can eat vitamin A in its whole form in foods such as liver and eggs, or we can eat its precursor molecule, beta-carotene, which the body changes into vitamin A, in yellow, red or leafy green vegetables. (Beta-carotene is one of the colourful groups of molecules known as carotenoids. Carotenoids are the molecules which make carrots orange and tomatoes red – as well as being responsible for giving animals including flamingos and salmon their characteristic pink colour and canaries their yellow hue.)

In an ideal world, children worldwide would be able to eat foods rich in vitamin A, but these foods are either not available or prohibitively expensive in the areas where children need them most. Because Vitamin A is so vital the WHO has set up a supplementation programme for children who are affected by either malnutrition or lack of varied fruits and vegetables in their diet: two doses of vitamin A supplement (total cost: about eight US cents) can prevent vitamin A deficiency. But such a programme relies on continued funding and is vulnerable to local disruption: ensuring a supply of colourful fruit and vegetables would be a more sustainable and robust solution.

A far less common but much grislier health problem is vitamin K deficiency. There are two types of vitamin K: vitamin K1 (phylloquinone) and vitamin K2 (menaquinone). Vitamin K1 is vital for photosynthesis in plants, and so is abundant in leafy green food such as kale (you didn't think we'd get through a book on healthy eating without at least one mention of kale did you?), salad leaves and spinach. More than 90 per cent of vitamin K comes from these dietary sources of vitamin K1. Vitamin K2, by contrast, is mainly found in high-fat dairy foods, liver, eggs and fermented foods – our bodies can also synthesize it from vitamin K1. We don't need very much vitamin K – about one microgram per kilo of bodyweight – so someone who weighs 65kg would need to eat 65μg daily. Eating half a cup of cooked spinach supplies almost nine times more than that, so it's not a difficult vitamin to obtain. However, it is vital for a process we almost never have to think about: blood clotting.

When we cut ourselves, after a short time we stop bleeding and a clot forms on top of the cut. Blood being something we generally want to retain, this is an important mechanism for keeping us from bleeding excessively. Clotting is a reaction between specific blood cells, called platelets, and the liquid part of our blood, called plasma, which bind together to form the solid protective clot over the wound. Vitamin K is required for many of the enzyme steps needed for this clotting. When vampire bats attack their prey, their saliva contains an anticoagulant which keeps the prey's blood liquid and flowing so they can drink their fill. The anticoagulant inhibits the first enzyme in the pathway, factor X (the Roman numeral 10, not a mysterious X-marks-the-spot). Factor X is vitamin K-dependent. Without vitamin K, all our wounds would be as grisly as if they had been inflicted by a vampire bat. The importance of vitamin K for coagulation is reflected in its name: the discovery of the vitamin was first reported in a German journal where it was given the moniker *Koagulationsvitamin*, hence the 'K'.

Vitamin K deficiency is most common in newborn babies because they have low vitamin K stores at birth as it cannot pass through the placenta, and breastmilk contains low amounts, so it takes a while for babies to build up their reserves. In some countries, newborn babies are given an injection of vitamin K as a matter of course to prevent the deficiency. It's rarer in adults but it is possible to have vitamin K deficiency as a result of eating too few green vegetables. And as you would expect, the symptoms are excessive bruising or bleeding. Like scurvy, it's easily remedied by a change in diet, although it's far better to make sure your diet is not deficient in the first place.

While we are often aware of some of the functions of these vital vitamins, we're discovering important new roles played by different vitamins all the time. For example, there are many types of vitamin B: eight to be precise. All are considered essential micro-nutrients and each has its own specific biological contribution to make. Vitamin B9, better known as folate (or its synthetic cousin, folic acid), is found in leafy green vegetables such as spinach and cabbage, legumes (plants which grow seeds in pods; it is worth noting that pulses are part of the legume family but the term 'pulse' refers only to the dry, edible seeds within the pod) and oranges. It is an especially important nutrient for women who are trying to conceive or who are in the first trimester of pregnancy because of the effects it has on neural tube development. The neural tube is the embryonic precursor to the brain and the spinal cord; it begins to develop early in pregnancy and normally closes within the first month or so. However, for reasons we still don't fully understand, when a mother doesn't have enough folate, the tube doesn't develop or close properly, causing neural tube defects such as spina bifida. A baby with spina bifida has a spinal canal which is open along the vertebrae in the back. Instead of being protected by the bones of the vertebrae, the spinal cord and its protective membranes protrude out in a vulnerable sac along the baby's back. The spine can be surgically closed but because of the lack of protection during its development, the spinal cord may be damaged, leading to paralysis, loss of sensation and potentially some learning difficulties. Studies show that the risk of developing neural tube defects (and some other development defects, including congenital heart disease and cleft palate) can be reduced by 80 per cent by ensuring that mothers have good levels of folate before and during birth.[8]

Folate plays such an important role in development that many countries have introduced mandatory fortification of some foods, often grains and cereal products, with folic acid. The US and Canada introduced mandatory fortification in the late 1990s, but the importance of folate for other ages is only now starting to emerge. A clinical trial evaluating the effects of having additional folic acid if you are between 50 and 70 years old found that it significantly improves cognitive functions that tend to decline with age (such as memory and information processing).[9] Recent research suggests that folate deficiency might lead to mental health problems such as depression or even cognitive impairment.[10]

Fruit and vegetables are also vital sources of the minerals we need to stay healthy. The best-known example is iron in spinach (although it's in a non-readily absorbed form, and so needs to be eaten in Popeye-style quantities). We need iron for our red blood cells to carry oxygen, which is one of the reasons anaemia (low red blood cell count or iron deficiency) first manifests as exhaustion: if sufficient oxygen doesn't reach cells they can't work properly. As well as being in spinach and red meat, there is also iron in legumes, nuts, dried fruit, wholegrains and dark-green leafy vegetables such as kale.

But iron is far from being the only mineral that fruit and vegetables give us. They're also a great source of calcium – after dairy products, green leafy vegetables (excluding spinach) and legumes are the best dietary sources of calcium available. Calcium is vital for the development of strong bones and teeth: without adequate calcium during development, children can develop rickets (which makes bones weak or soft) and adults can develop a similar condition known as osteomalacia. Rickets can also develop as a result of a lack of vitamin D, but vitamin D is one we can synthesize ourselves, as long as we get sufficient exposure to sunlight. This can be a problem in countries such as the UK and others in the cloudier, colder northern hemisphere. Potassium is another example of a vital mineral: our body needs it to keep fluid pressure balanced within our cells, and it's also important for keeping our heartbeat regular. Bananas, broccoli, parsnips and Brussels sprouts are full of the stuff.

In short, we can get many of the essential micronutrients we need to keep ourselves in peak condition just by eating a relatively varied diet that contains decent quantities of fruit and vegetables. All the diseases described above are the result of deficiency – of not having enough of the small but important components we need to function normally – as opposed to more complex non-communicable diseases such as heart disease which has complex, multifactorial causes which are still largely not understood. That being said, eating fruit and vegetables seems to help with those diseases too.

NON-COMMUNICABLE DISEASES VS YOUR FIVE A DAY

Multiple studies and meta-analyses systematically come up with the finding that eating more fruit and vegetables is associated with a lower risk of death from any cause. It is strongly associated with a reduced risk of dying from cardiovascular disease, such as heart attacks and stroke.[11][12] Eating more fruit and vegetables also seems to help prevent diabetes, although the jury is still out on cancer. There's some evidence that eating a variety of fruit and vegetables is weakly protective against cancer[13] but no evidence that it's a harmful habit to adopt. In 2019 the American Diabetes Association published a consensus report on nutrition therapy for people with diabetes or prediabetes which assessed a variety of diets as medical interventions.[14] The association didn't make one therapeutic diet recommendation (which would have been impossible considering the huge spectrum of different cultures and diseases the report covered), but it did make macronutrient recommendations. The report found that eating a diet high in fibre from fruit, vegetables, pulses and wholegrains was a means of lowering both blood sugar levels and mortality in people with diabetes.

And it's not just those who have diabetes or other underlying diseases who gain a longer, healthier life as a result of eating fruit and vegetables. The Global Burden of Disease study which I discussed in Chapter Three (see page 54) aimed to systematically assess the impact of different dietary choices on premature deaths and years of healthy life lost. It found that eating insufficient fruit was responsible for about two million premature deaths and 65 million disability-adjusted life years. Eating insufficient vegetables led to approximately 1.5 million deaths and 34 million disability-adjusted life years.[15]

In other words, eating (at least) five portions of fruit and vegetables a day seems to extend our lives, as well as making those extra years more likely to be unaffected by disease. Apart from providing vital micronutrients to ensure that we all continue to function in tip-top shape, what's the magic element in fruit and vegetables? The answer is that fruit and vegetables are great, healthy sources of fibre, carbohydrates, fat and protein. This is why it's possible to eat a vegetarian diet and remain healthy, as long as it's appropriately balanced: fruit and vegetables bring all the necessary macro *and* micronutrients to the table, and generally speaking have a much smaller environmental footprint than animal-based produce.

This is why so much of the planetary health diet is plant-based, and why the fruit and vegetables that it recommends span the macronutrient recommendations. In addition to wholegrain sources, carbohydrates can be obtained from starchy vegetables such as potatoes, cassava and parsnips. We can get vegetable-based protein from legumes (the plants that contain nitrogen-fixing bacteria in their root nodules and so can make protein). Examples of legumes include beans, lentils, peas, soybeans (and soy-derived products such as tofu) and peanuts (which are secret legumes, not 'true' nuts). 'True' nuts like pistachios and cashews are also good sources of protein.

We can get fats in the form of vegetable oils from a multitude of different sources, including palm, olive, coconut, soybeans and rapeseed. And from a colourful array of fruit and vegetables, we can get a variety of micronutrients. The planetary health diet even breaks vegetables down by colour, insisting that a third of what we eat should be dark green, a third red and orange, and a third 'other'. This is because differentiating by colour is a great way of ensuring that we get all the essential micronutrients that fruit and vegetables provide (for example, the beta-carotene in orange and red vegetables signals the provision of vitamin A). And finally, fruit and vegetables bring to the table something that other sources of fat, protein and carbohydrates might not and that is fibre. Lots of it. And this is increasingly believed to be of huge importance for maintaining our health – but not quite in the way you think.

I AM LARGE, I CONTAIN MULTITUDES (WITH APOLOGIES TO WHITMAN)

Who are you? If you're like most people you'll be a little flummoxed by the question. The 'I' that most people think of is a sense of driving consciousness just behind the eyes, a bit like a small person acting from an elevated vantage point who has been left in charge of a large and complex piece of machinery. It is often only when we're injured or temporarily incapacitated that we remember that we 'are' our bodies too. But the strange thing about our bodies is that even though we are our bodies, our bodies are not necessarily all us. In fact, of all the cells within our bodies, only about half are estimated to be human.

Let me reassure you that by *mass* you're mainly human. But by sheer number of cells, you're a bit of a mixture. This is because we act as host to a bewildering array of other life forms. In the same way that cows' stomachs house specialist bacteria which allow them to digest cellulose, we also contain a multitude of bacteria (and other types of life, including viruses and fungi, although for simplicity I will just refer to bacteria). Without wishing to freak you out too much, these bacteria are *everywhere*: not only in our stomachs, but also in our entire gastrointestinal system, reproductive organs, on our skin – even in our eyes. The sum of these microscopic extra life forms that we carry around with us is known as our microbiota, and their genetic material the microbiome. The full extent to which our health depends on our microbiome is only just becoming understood, but already we know that it is sufficiently important for some to suggest that we should consider our microbiome as an entirely separate human organ, and research it accordingly.[16]

Our gut microbiome in particular is extremely important when we consider the impact of food on our health. The latest research is making us rethink some concepts we used to consider as basic. Without considering the microbiome, questions of human health and nutrition are complicated but at least only involve two elements: our nutritional needs and the foods that can provide them. The gut microbiome adds an extra complicating element into this equation: we now need to consider which of the foods we eat are used and processed by the gut bacteria we house. In other words, do we gain nutritional benefit from the foods directly or do we benefit because a crafty bacteria takes the food, eats and digests it and then excretes some separate component which is the useful element that our bodies absorb? And if this wasn't complex enough, when we consider the fact that we all have different types of bacteria in our stomachs (literally different species) and varying quantities of those types, the potential outcomes are almost endless.

We still don't quite understand how our bodies' health, our food and our microbiome interact. Early findings suggest that some of the health benefits we get from certain foods are nothing to do with digesting the foods themselves, but rather result from by-products of bacterial digestion. So not only does the food we eat matter for our health, the kind of species we carry within our microbiome – and how many of them we have – might also have a significant impact as this mix determines the benefits we receive. And the health benefits – or harms – associated with certain mixtures of microbiota are both huge and wide-ranging.

Microbiome dysbiosis is the term which describes having a harmful or somehow imbalanced group of species within your microbiome (this is an extremely loose term as every person's microbiome is different). However, having certain species over-represented can be associated with harms. Microbiome dysbiosis has been linked mainly with diseases which relate directly to energy and nutritional intake: for example, stunting and other forms of malnutrition.[17] But microbiota health is also associated with conditions not directly related to nutrition, such as neurological disorders, including Alzheimer's disease, autism spectrum disorder, multiple sclerosis, Parkinson's disease and stroke. It is striking that the richness of the gut microbiome – the number of different species present in the gut and so the quantity of genetic material – seems to correlate with health. This implies that having a wide array of gut bacteria somehow conveys some health benefit, although precisely what we have yet to determine. This observation has profound implications for how we think about non-communicable diseases and what we eat.

Studies have looked at the link between gut microbiota and being overweight and obese. Several have now found that people who have a less varied microbiome (assessed by gene count) are at greater risk of becoming overweight or obese, of having higher insulin resistance which predisposes them to developing diabetes, and of being more susceptible to inflammation which in turn leads to cardiovascular disease and cancer.[18] There is also evidence to suggest that our microbiome might govern why some people find it easy to lose weight, or never put it on, while others find the opposite. In short, having more species of bacteria in your gut – otherwise known as microbial richness – might be a magic bullet capable of tackling the whole gamut of non-communicable diseases that people face.

So how can everyone achieve this magic bullet? What can increase gut microbial richness? One absolutely disgusting solution being touted by scientists who will need an excellent marketing campaign is called faecal microbiota transplantation, which is exactly what you think it is. A recent review defined it in clinical language as 'the transfer of minimally manipulated, pre-screened donor stool into the gastrointestinal tract of a patient, with the aim of ameliorating the dysbiotic state by increasing overall diversity and restoring the functionality of the microbiota'.[19] Faecal transplantation is already being used as a treatment for certain types of bowel infection, but has been touted as a potential cure in conditions as wide-ranging as bipolar disorder, liver cirrhosis, Parkinson's disease and psoriatic arthritis.

But there is, thank goodness, another way of increasing your microbial richness, and a far more palatable one: eat more fibre-containing fruit and vegetables. A study examining the impact of dietary interventions on gut microbial gene richness found that 'increased consumption of fruits and vegetable and thus higher fibre consumption before the intervention seemed to be associated with high bacterial richness... This finding, although exploratory in nature and requiring replication, supports a recently reported link between long-term dietary habits and the structure of gut microbiota and suggests that a permanent change of microbiota may be achieved by appropriate diet.' The link referred to is a study that showed that you could detect a change in microbiome composition as soon as 24 hours after starting a changed diet, and that this change was sustainable and stable throughout the study.[20] So eating more fibre-containing fruit and vegetables, along with wholegrains, might be an easy way of enriching our microbiome and lead to a variety of improvements in health.

Conversely, one of the ways of depleting our microbial richness and worsening our health might be to eat a diet high in processed foods. The microbiome of hunter-gatherers and more rural populations of people around the world seem generally to be richer than those of people living in modern societies. This has been suggested to be linked to the latter's decreased fibre consumption and increased eating of processed foods.[21] Eating more processed foods doesn't sustain the variety of gut bacteria that we need for optimum health, presumably because processed food makes the bacteria more homogenous and nutritionally similar. Our gut bacteria, it would seem, are pickier than we are.

Fibre in particular seems to be key to driving healthy change by increasing microbiota richness. We do not make the enzymes needed to digest fibre, but our microbiota often can. Some bacterial microbiota can ferment fibre to produce short-chain fatty acids. These fatty acids have been shown to be useful and important energy and signalling molecules for us. They potentially improve our metabolism and immunity and lower our risk of developing cancer.[22] This might also explain why eating a lot of processed foods (which lack fibre) harms the richness of our gut bacteria.

So it seems that eating a varied, high-fibre diet with a lot of fruit and vegetables might improve our health and resilience to a variety of non-communicable diseases through the somewhat odd mechanism of keeping a huge mixture of gut bacteria happily fermenting within. Which is great to know, but something not many of us do judging by how few fruit and vegetables we actually eat.

THREE-ISH A DAY?

The more-or-less universal recommendation that we should all eat five servings of fruit and vegetables a day suggests that a serving weighs on average about 80g. Theoretically, if we all followed that guidance, we'd be chowing down on a minimum of 400g of fruit and vegetables a day. The planetary health diet recommends that we eat even more: an average of 200g of fruit daily (with a range between 100 and 300g), 300g daily of non-leguminous vegetables (between 200 and 600g) and 100g of legumes (ranging from 0 to 225g). To take their average recommendations, that adds up to eating 600g of fruit, vegetables and legumes a day (legumes are included separately as they're categorized as vegetarian sources of protein). Converted into portions, that would be a couple of apples, a glass of orange juice, a red pepper, about three tablespoons of cooked spinach, some asparagus and about six tablespoons of chickpeas.

It should come as no surprise that we're not hitting either our recommended targets or the larger targets suggested by the planetary health diet. For fruit, the global average intake is just under 100g a day, although there is significant regional variation: for example, in sub-Saharan Africa it's closer to 50g daily, whereas the Caribbean comes much closer to eating 200g. (These data come from the Global Burden of Disease dataset, which suggests 250g as the ideal required quantity of fruit daily, and estimates mortality and disability-adjusted life years accordingly.) The quantity of non-leguminous vegetables we eat is a little better: the world average is just below 200g. Some regions, such as central Asia, smash the recommendations, eating about 400g a day, whereas southern Africa and South America trail behind at about 100g. No region of the world eats 100g of legumes a day – the global average consumption is about 45g – but many come close, with sub-Saharan Africa and parts of South America leading the way. Globally, we eat an average of 350g of fruit and vegetables a day, which is about four servings daily (although these vary by region which is discussed below). But this also means that, on average, we eat about 250g, or three servings daily, below what the planetary health diet recommends.[23]

Part of the reason for this is that people eat more of other foods. For example, most of us eat more meat than the planetary health diet suggests, and one of the difficulties of making this diet easier to adopt is the challenge of reducing meat-containing meals. To make up the protein we lose through eating less meat, we would all need to start eating more vegetable sources of protein, which would increase the quantity of legumes we eat and so push the numbers up. But even taking this into account, there are other reasons our intake is still below current, lower recommendations. And one is because eating fruit and vegetables is expensive.

A study surveyed almost 150,000 people in 18 countries to determine how many servings of fruit and vegetables people ate.[24] It found that the average was about 3.8 portions, which tallies with what we already know about the quantity of fruit and vegetables we eat. However, this study looked more deeply into who eats what around the world. What it found was striking and significant, but unsurprising. The consumption of fruit and vegetables was heavily influenced by wealth. In low-income countries, people ate about two servings of fruit and vegetables daily, in lower–middle-income countries it was three servings, in upper–middle-income countries four servings and in high-income countries almost five and a half servings. In low-income countries, the cost of eating five servings of fruit and vegetables a day (two of fruit and three of vegetables) came to just over half the average household income, compared with just under 2 per cent in high-income countries. This means that nearly 60 per cent of people in low-income countries could not afford the recommended servings, compared with 0.25 per cent of people in high-income countries. As low consumption of fruit and vegetables increases the risk of almost all non-communicable diseases, this has worrying implications for those countries fighting the pandemic.

The disparity between high- and low-income countries is not the only cause for concern: a gap between rich and poor exists within countries too. The American Centers for Disease Control and Prevention carried out a study in 2017 which found that only 12 per cent of Americans ate the recommended daily amount of fruit, and even fewer – 9.3 per cent – ate the recommended daily amount of vegetables. The biggest disparities they discovered were by income: while still not extremely high, 11.4 per cent of adults in the highest household income brackets ate the recommended quantities, whereas only 7 per cent of those with the lowest household incomes did this.[25] So lower fruit and vegetable consumption is linked to socioeconomic status – which unsurprisingly also correlates with increased processed food consumption and a greater risk of developing non-communicable diseases.

The factors which make fresh fruit and vegetables widely inaccessible to poorer households in high-income countries include both affordability and availability. One of the biggest problems in making fresh fruit and vegetables available to the poorest members of society in high-income countries is geographic. Areas described as food deserts are described as 'those areas of cities where cheap, nutritious food is virtually unobtainable. Car-less residents, unable to reach out-of-town supermarkets, depend on the corner shop where prices are high, products are processed and fresh fruit and vegetables are poor or non-existent.' A study by the Social Market Foundation found that 10 per cent of deprived areas in the UK – areas in which 1.2 million people lived – were classified as food deserts (defined in the report as containing two or fewer supermarkets or convenience stores). Admittedly the study was commissioned by Kellogg's, not a disinterested party. The report also found that almost half of people who earn under £10,000 believe nutritious food to be unaffordable in the UK.[26]

Given the health benefits of eating five or more portions of fruit and vegetables a day, these are serious issues which need to be solved if everyone is to move towards the planetary health diet recommendations. The difficulties cannot be resolved by science alone: government policy has to change – potentially to subsidize fruit and vegetable costs – in order to ensure that they are accessible to all. But ensuring equal access to more fruit and vegetables also relies on there being plenty of fruit and vegetables available – and that will rely on resolving a different, and rather challenging, distribution problem.

WATER INEQUALITY

Since the 1980s Iraqis have known very little other than conflict. First the Iran-Iraq War in the mid-1980s; then the Gulf War of the early 1990s; the US-led coalition invasion in the early 2000s and, most recently, in 2014, the rise and spread of the Islamic State (IS) terrorist group. For those living in rural Iraq, the emergence of IS arguably had the worst impact of all: the group had strong rural roots and deliberately targeted key regions for food production, prioritizing the seizure of water infrastructure as means of controlling the land. At the peak of its power, IS controlled up to 40 per cent of Iraq's wheat-producing areas, as well as many dams and thousands of kilometres of irrigation canals. Towards the end of the 2010s, IS began to lose ground to the defending Iraqi forces. Those forces eventually declared victory over IS in December 2017.

As military conflict eased, the Iraqi farmers who had been forced from their land began to return – but found that, even defeated, IS had left its vicious mark. Those who returned found their former homes destroyed. Anything of value that could be taken had been stolen, and anything that could not be taken had been destroyed. Nowhere was this more obvious than where there had once been farmland. Fields were burned and orchards and olive groves deliberately sacked, with evidence of axes and chainsaws having been used to level the trees. And wells had been sabotaged: filled with rubble or oil, or their vital pumps, cables, generators and transformers destroyed or stolen. One ex-farmer interviewed by Amnesty International described what he saw when he returned briefly to what had been his family farm as 'pure destruction':

'I had a well – 220 metres deep – as well as a generator and an irrigation pipe system. They threw rubble in my well and filled it to the top. My trees were chopped down – I could see the marks from chopping with a chainsaw. The irrigation system – from the pump to the pipes – was stolen. They did this to send a message: that you have nothing to return to, so if you survive don't even think of coming back…I don't have anything now… just land which I cannot use.'

Even more than food, access to clean supplies of drinking water can make the difference between life and death. Consequently there are, and always have been, conflicts over water access. In fact, people have fought over water rights for so long that there is an entire website, Water Conflict Chronology, devoted to the history of water conflict[27] which starts before 0 BC. A sample entry states: 'Assyrian king dries up enemy's wells' from 669–626 BC and and the timeline continues to the present day: '50,000 people flee their homes in central Mali as conflict escalates over land and water' in 2019.

Water is weaponized in three ways: by restricting or stopping the supply, by destroying its quality or by releasing too much of it as a destructive flood. In a report by Amnesty International, IS was found to have used all three to control territory in Iraq.[28] As their grip on the land loosened and they were forced to retreat, IS poisoned and choked water supplies. The message was clear: you might retake the land, but we have taken the water. And without water, the land is useless.

The world is not equal in terms of water access, as the bloody history of water conflict attests. Many areas of the world are arid or semi-arid and so are said to be 'water-stressed'. In these areas the demand for water is greater than the quantity of water available (or the water quality is so poor that it cannot be used to satisfy demand). According to the UN, about two billion people live in countries that experience high water stress, and about four billion people – more than half the world's population – experience severe water scarcity during at least one month of the year.[29] So while globally there is no shortage of water, an increasing number of regions are becoming chronically water stressed, or suffer from water scarcity for many different reasons.

Of the 1,400 million cubic km of water in the world, only 0.003 per cent is fresh, so we can use only this quantity for drinking, agriculture, hygiene and industry.[30] While this might sound like a tiny percentage, it should be ample for all our needs: freshwater use is the planetary boundary (see Chapter Two, page 30) that we are least at risk of overstepping.

The planetary boundary measure is broken into two parts: the first is the maximum quantity of freshwater available for consumption (in cubic km per year). The second is a measure per river basin of the quantity of freshwater withdrawn as a percentage of mean monthly river flow (in other words, how much freshwater is taken out of the river for human needs each month compared to the average amount of water that flows in). The second measure, while important, is not a planetary boundary itself but measures how we use water from different rivers. The global boundary for consumption of freshwater use is estimated to be about 4,000 cubic km per year, and we currently only consume about

2,600 cubic km per year. So it seems that water is the planetary boundary we need to worry about least. But that offers no consolation to the farmers in Iraq.

There is sufficient water globally to continue to grow the food we need, but at a regional level, many areas are short of water which has an impact on how people live and work, as well as their economic and food security.

First, many regions are chronically short of water as a result of accidents of geography and they have not invested in the necessary tools to manage water supplies. This investment could be in infrastructure, legislation or mediation and could help to ensure sustainable, equitable water access. So one part of a region might have more than it needs at the expense of another area of the region. This unequal access fuels further conflict within and between regions of the world. Second, climate change is beginning to alter global weather patterns, exacerbating drought, desertification and flooding. And, finally, as the world's population increases, so does our demand for water. In fact our demand increases disproportionately: water use grew at almost double the rate of the population in the last century alone.[31] And this increasing water use is mostly needed for agriculture.

About 70 per cent of global freshwater is used for agriculture. As food production rises to meet the challenge of our increasing population, so agricultural water consumption will rise too. Over the last 30 years, food production has increased by 100 per cent: the United Nation's Food and Agriculture Organization (FAO) estimates that it will need to rise by a further 60 per cent by 2050 to feed 10 billion people. While these statistics might sound gloomy, there is good news: the FAO also estimates that while we will need to increase irrigated food production by more than 50 per cent by 2050, that increase may only result in a 10 per cent increase in water use for agriculture, assuming that there will be advances in technology and changes in irrigation habits.[32] The trick is getting the balance right.

TROUBLE IN PARADISE?

We think of California as a part of the world over-endowed with good things. Not for nothing has it kept its moniker as the Golden State 150 years after the gold rush. As well as being the home of world-leading industries ranging from Hollywood to Silicon Valley, California is also one of the biggest agricultural producers on the planet. The value of California's agricultural output is more than the next two American states combined. In 2017–2018, it produced more than US$50 billion worth of goods – about 13 per cent of all American cash crops.[33] In 2018 the state made about US$5.8 billion from the sale of grapes alone.

Most of this produce is grown in the Central Valley, which begins in central California and goes up to the Cascade Range of mountains in the northern part of the state. The valley is a 725-km-long area of lowland hemmed in by two mountain ranges: the Pacific Coast Range in the west and the Sierra Nevada in the east. It's divided into two smaller valleys: Sacramento Valley in the north and San Joaquin Valley in the south. Driving through it is to drive into a kind of American dream. Sunshine from an iridescently blue sky falls on the basin, illuminating the farmland, fruit trees, vineyards and pastures which line the road on both sides as far as the distant mountain ranges. The soil, where you can see it beneath the greenery, is dark and rich: wonderfully fertile. Every few miles you pass a farm shop selling containers of produce so huge and luscious that they look almost like film props: giant fuzzy peaches, succulent figs, every variety of nut, cascading bunches of grapes, endless rows of crisp green lettuces. It's hard not to feel that this represents a sort of earthly Eden: a place of bountiful abundance.

But don't be fooled. This is not a natural Eden. Central Valley's climate ranges between hot Mediterranean in the north and desert in the south. It has an annual rainfall of about 51cm in the north and 13cm in the south (a desert has less than 25cm of rain per year). The lushness of this valley is the result of engineering, not natural rainfall. The water used in farming comes from two sources: surface water pumped from reservoirs elsewhere in the state, or ground water pumped from aquifers deep beneath the surface of the earth. (Aquifers are bodies of permeable rock which can either contain or convey ground water.) In a wet year, about 40 per cent of the water is pumped ground water; in dry years that rises to about 60 per cent. Both these sources are under threat.

Until 2014, ground water access was entirely unregulated. Anyone could pump as much water as they cared to from the underground aquifers – and so they did. So much water was pumped out that the ground in Central Valley began to sink: between 2012 and 2016, a period of especially intense drought, parts of Central Valley dropped by about 60cm.[34] This was the result of sucking the clay (which carries much of the ground water) almost dry: the once-thick layers of clay became compressed, causing infrastructure damage throughout the state. The damage included cracked bridges, roads and irrigation canals. Between 2012 and 2016, the drought was so bad that the subsequent demand for ground water in the southern San Joaquin Valley lowered the water table beyond the reach of most wells: only the deepest wells, stretching a quarter of a kilometre below the surface, still held water. In wet years, enough rain falls to partially refill the aquifers, but this does not completely rejuvenate them, especially after periods of intense drought. Satellite images of water loss confirm the story that the wells told. Together with other data, NASA's specialist Gravity Recovery and Climate Experiment (GRACE) surveillance suggested that between 2003 and 2010, Central Valley lost 20 cubic km of water.[35]

California is not alone in experiencing falling levels of ground water. What we see in the Golden State is replicated around the world. Global withdrawal of ground water is estimated to have grown from 100–150 cubic km in 1950 to 950–1,000 cubic km in 2000.[36] In large areas of South and East Asia, in western Asia, North Africa, and North and Central America, the rate of ground water withdrawal is higher than the rate of natural refill, and so aquifer water levels are falling.

The situation in California (and elsewhere) is complicated by climate change. Previously, one of the ways in which aquifer tables were refilled was through surface water. Thanks to industrial building projects in the 1930s, Central Valley's fertile lands were also irrigated using water which came from the northern parts of the state. Reservoirs, canals and pipelines were built to carry snow meltwater from the northern mountains down to the central and southern valleys. The slowly melting snow kept reservoirs full until water was needed in the summer and allowed aquifers to refill. But global warming and changing climates threaten this system. Annual snowfall is becoming lighter and melting sooner. And as the climate warms, more of the precipitation is likely to fall as rain rather than snow. These factors combined mean that reservoirs will fill faster and so their water will have to be released earlier, before the farmers need it in the spring. This in turn will add to pressure on ground water sources during the hot, dry summers.

And those summers are getting hotter and drier. Southwestern North America (the western USA, including California and northern Mexico) has been especially warm and dry since the beginning of this century, with persistent drought. Researchers used modelling and 1,200-year-old tree rings to measure how dry summer soils have been over past millennia, and discovered that the period between 2000 and 2018 was the second driest period since 800 AD. This period has been called a megadrought: a drought of extreme severity lasting several decades. Through reconstructions, the researchers were able to disentangle the elements of changes which were the result of human activity and they found that 47 per cent of the severity can be attributed to human-caused climate warming. Without man-made warming, the last two decades would have been just another period of lower than normal rain and snowfall.[37][38] All these factors combine to create intense pressure on water sources.

In California, the response to the alarming data on the declining levels of aquifers was that the Sustainable Groundwater Management Act was signed into law in 2014 – the first time that California has legislated on ground water access. The law requires Californian agencies to stabilize ground water levels in the state. This is exactly what needs to happen, according to a 2015 white paper by the FAO, which said: 'innovative and more effective governance mechanisms, together with investments in water technologies and infrastructure will be needed to mitigate the impacts of growing water shortages to ensure water is allocated in such a way as to secure its efficient use, protection of the natural resource base, and to ensure access to water for household use and agricultural production'.[39]

There are a variety of ways in which California can act to refill depleted aquifers. First it can simply ensure that less water is used for the same tasks: efficient use of water can be incentivized or legislated for, for example by demanding that households use water-efficient appliances such as low-flush toilets and water-conserving shower heads. Second, farmers can vary or change the crops they grow (for example, switching from alfalfa to grapes uses less water), or some fields can be left fallow in times of drought. And another suggestion is simply to reduce levels of agricultural production in California. Some have called for precisely this. Agriculture uses 80 per cent of the water consumed in the state. To stabilize aquifers in the San Joaquin Valley, farmers would have to reduce current irrigated cropland by about 10 per cent, with concomitantly large losses in food production (and revenue), a move that most farmers vehemently oppose and which pits two different groups of water users against each other.

In a world that needs more food, not less, reducing water use by curbing food production is not ideal. But fortunately there are ways of reducing water use without reducing the amount of food that we produce through a combination of changing what we eat and (cautiously) embracing new technologies.

FUTURE FOODS

When we talk about genetic modification, people tend to think of scientists growing ears on the back of rats, or making a variety of animals glow in the dark. Almost all this work was done with a serious scientific purpose, but a lot of this gets lost in the headlines – and it's hard not to be creeped out by the idea of creating such unnatural creatures. But genetic modification is a technology which is as old as domestication itself; we just used to call it selective breeding.

Selective breeding means selecting two animals or plants which have certain characteristics to create offspring which are likely to also have the desired traits. Let's imagine you want to breed a cat with pure black fur. If you keep leaving white cats together in whatever setting felines regard as romantic, you're unlikely to eventually achieve black kittens. But if you take a white cat and a white cat with dark spots and leave them together, then due to the magic of genetic mixing during reproduction, you might get a litter of kittens which has a kitten which is partially black. Take that cat, breed it with another partially-black cat, and the resulting litter will probably, all things being genetically equal, have kittens in a variety of colours, with the possibilities ranging from almost all white to almost all black. Take the latter cat, breed it with a similar almost all-black cat, and you're likely to end up with a black cat.

This is a simplistic overview of selective breeding: actual results vary depending on the genetics of fur colour. To understand this, let's take a very brief detour into genetics. Genes are bits of DNA which act as instructions for how to make the building blocks of the body: proteins. We have two copies of almost all the genes in our bodies. Because men have both an X and a Y chromosome, they only have one copy of each of the genes that are found exclusively on those two chromosomes. By contrast, women have two X chromosomes: the combination of Y and X chromosomes have different genes which are responsible for making men and women look and reproduce differently. Apart from this specific example, most genes are found in pairs. But even though these genes are instructions for making the same protein, genes can differ in the instructions that they give, so creating slightly different versions of the same thing. Different versions of genes are called alleles: it's helpful to think of them as different flavours, for example, of jelly. Raspberry jelly and lime jelly are both jellies: they have pretty much the same properties, but despite this, they have different colours and tastes.

Not all alleles are created equal. Some are dominant and some are recessive. If an allele is dominant, it will always win out over a recessive allele. The best examples of this relate to eye colour. The alleles for brown eyes are dominant, compared to the alleles for blue eyes. That means that even if you have one allele for blue eyes as well as one allele for brown eyes, your eyes will come out straight brown, rather than a mixture: brown trumps blue. (This is also why two brown-eyed parents can produce a blue-eyed child: each might carry a blue-eyed allele which is hiding in the background.)

The sum of all the genes we contain is called our genotype. The way our genotype translates into physical properties such as how we look and behave – our characteristics – is called our phenotype. So you can have a mixed blue eyes-brown eyes genotype, but because brown eye alleles are dominant, you will have a brown eye phenotype (otherwise known as having brown eyes).

For centuries, selective breeding has worked on a phenotype-first basis. Breeders have selected animals and plants based on certain desired characteristics, and bred them together to try to produce offspring that have more of those characteristics. Without an understanding of the genetics that underpin the phenotypes, quite often such selective breeding efforts are doomed to failure, because of irritating quirks such as dominant and recessive alleles. Genetic modification in the modern era is simply taking a genes-first approach: alter the genes to effect the changes you want in the phenotype. This is by no means a silver bullet: we are a long way away from knowing what each gene encodes, and even further from understanding the complex inter-actions between them and the environment. But where modern genetic modification has an advantage over traditional selective breeding is that you can use genes to introduce new favourable characteristics which the animal or plant might not have origi-nally developed.

An example of this is in engineering insect resistance. Caterpillars of the European corn borer moth are aptly named: they bore holes into all parts of the sweetcorn or maize plant, including its leaves and the corn ear. This causes such huge crop losses that the corn borer has been nicknamed the billion dollar bug, because of the estimated billion dollars they cost farmers annually in lost crops and insecticide use. The soil bacterium (one bacteria) *Bacillus thuringiensis* (otherwise known as Bt) makes hundreds of different crystal proteins which are toxic to many different types of insects, including corn borer caterpillars. Solutions containing large quantities of these crystal proteins have been used as an insecticide since the 1930s. In 1996, advances in genetics made it possible to use these crystal proteins a little differently. A single gene from the Bt bacterium that encoded a crystal protein was inserted into the sweetcorn genome. As the plant grew it also made crystal proteins. If a caterpillar ate the sweetcorn plant it also ate the crystal protein, which killed it.[40]

This had a variety of benefits. First, sweetcorn growers do not now have to use traditional insecticide: there was an estimated decline of about 35 per cent in insecticide use between 1996 and 2008 on Bt maize globally.[41] Insecticide is toxic, and reducing its use reduces the health risk to farmers. Second, importantly, using modified sweetcorn has increased insect and other biodi-versity in those fields when compared with fields of crops treated with traditional insecticide, because it's so specific and efficiently targeted at corn borer caterpillars. Third, sweetcorn quality has increased. Insect damage provides an entry point for plant fungal infections, which can produce highly toxic chemicals within the sweetcorn ear. Reducing the damage caused by the insects and by also reducing the production of fungal toxins, American farmers are estimated to save about US$23 million annually compared with previous costs.[42] Finally, and most importantly, sweetcorn yields have increased: the methods work and reduce crop waste.

Reducing crop loss, and subsequent food waste, is one way in which genetic modification can help to improve water efficiency in areas where it's a scarce resource. Another way plant biotechnology can help is by making plants more drought-resistant, or more resilient when there is little water. This is a much more complex problem than simply engineering one plant to produce a protein which defends it against a single predator. Drought resistance involves a complex interaction between all parts of the plant and a variety of changeable and unknowable factors. But scientists are trying various approaches in order to engineer more resistant crops. The first is to continue to selectively breed drought-resistant crop varieties, as they have been doing for centuries, which continues to produce exciting results. The second is to genetically modify crops so that they have more drought-resistant traits. One such potential pathway is crassulacean acid metabolism (CAM) which is a form of photosynthesis in which the pores in a plant's leaves only open during the cooler night to collect carbon dioxide. Through not opening the pores on its leaves during the warmer day, the plant loses far less water. Genetic analysis reveals that very different plant species – from pineapples to orchids – have 60 genes which separately evolved this water-saving pathway.[43]

Despite the benefits they may bring, there are great concerns about genetically-modified crops. One of the concerns is that they may potentially damage or contaminate the ecosystem, and it would be foolish to deny that the road to hell is often paved with good intentions. The unforeseen consequences of adopting new technologies feature heavily in our past (for example, climate change). Another problem is the potential it offers companies which make genetically-modified crops to tie farmers into high costs. Genetically-modified seeds are patented as intellectual property and so farmers are prevented from saving the seed from one crop to plant the following year. Consequently the farmers have to buy seeds every year. In the case of Bowman v. Monsanto which was adjudicated in the US Supreme Court in 2013, the judge found that by saving genetically-modified soybeans to sow in his fields the following year, the 75-year-old farmer Vernon H. Bowman had infringed Monsanto's copyright.

Both these concerns are important but I would argue that in a world which risks getting hungrier we owe it to those who have less access to supplies of food to negotiate an answer to these difficult questions. The European Union operates the strictest policies in the world related to the safety of genetically-modified crops. Bt corn is the only licensed GM crop in Europe, whereas in the USA and other parts of the world, other modified crops are routinely grown. The EU's policy is to assess genetically-modified foods on a case-by-case basis, but it accepts the principle that they are needed. All such foods are tested rigorously for safety and must continue to be. But it seems unfair to reject innovations that could help feed millions once such modifications have passed those tests. And if these technologies can provide drought-resistant crops, legislation will be passed which will mean they become widely available without continual financial penalties for farmers. In the same way as legislating for fair access to water, access to fecund crops should be a basic human right – and international law must support this.

I've explained the role that unconventional crops can play in protecting us from drought-induced hunger, but there is another rapidly-emerging technology which is looking at growing conventional crops in rather unconventional ways.

GROWING UNDERGROUND

London's Clapham High Street is nothing special to look at. It has the same array of shops to be found on most British high streets: bustling chemists, supermarkets, clothing shops, all the busier because Clapham Junction railway station ('Britain's busiest!') is nearby. But there is something rather special about Clapham High Street, although it's entirely invisible to the casual observer. Deep beneath these south London streets, something is growing. And that something is...salad.

Growing Underground is not only a terrible pun: it is also the name of the world's first subterranean urban farm. Housed in an extensive network of tunnels which were dug as bomb shelters during the Second World War, the farm is an almost entirely closed system. Unlike normal farms which are open and rely on uncontrollable natural elements such as sunshine and rain to achieve optimum growing conditions, Growing Underground can regulate every part of the system it uses without relying on any other input. It receives water from the mains supply, not falling as rain. Light for photosynthesis is provided by LEDs, which also generate enough heat to ensure that the plants are kept at a balmy 22–25°C (70–77°F) all year round. Because the farm is underground it needs no pesticides. The farm is emblematic of the wave of new farming techniques which have been developed in response to concerns about limited natural resources, known overall as vertical farming. Everything at Growing Underground is designed as far as possible to reduce waste. All the energy comes from renewable sources. Plants are grown on discarded carpet. And Growing Underground has the advantage of an amazing location. Everything grown there can be instantly and freshly transported locally – to a bustling metropolis of more than ten million people.

Being able to produce fresh food and vegetables within cities has many positives. First, it reduces transport time and costs, which allows food to remain fresher for longer as well as making them more competitive when compared with long-life ultra-processed foodstuffs.

Second, it cuts down on energy-consuming transport, reducing both cost and local pollution. Growing food in cities greatly reduces the distance between where it is grown and where it is eaten. This is especially important for fresh produce as the last mile in the journey of fresh food is the most costly, both financially and in terms of pollution. This is because most food is transported in bulk from farm or factory to distribution centre. When this is a long distance, the cost and pollution is minimal per item. But transporting food to every supermarket, hotel, convenience store or restaurant from the distribution centre means hundreds of short individual journeys, which push up the cost per item – and this is higher for perishable items which must be transported in refrigerated vans.

Third, growing food in cities reduces food waste. The crops grown in controlled environments are far more consistent and reliable than those produced by open farming. They are untainted by pesticides or pests, so that far less food is discarded. And as demand shifts, vertical farms can change production relatively seamlessly, again reducing food waste as consumer preferences oscillate between rocket and watercress.

All these factors together mean that vertical farming might also contribute to reducing the cost of fresh fruit and vegetables, making them more affordable for all. There is huge excitement about these technologies, even though they are only in their infancy. Ocado, a British online-only supermarket, invested £17 million in vertical farming in 2019.[44]

There is one final factor which makes vertical farming stand out as an important development: water use. The closed system means that far less water is lost, so overall use is hugely reduced. Growing Underground's farm uses approximately 70 per cent less water than conventional farms. The water they use is pumped into the sewage system, preserving the quantity of water available overall as well as ensuring that biochemical nutrients can be removed as part of the standard sewage sanitisation process, rather than leaching into waterways. The United Arab Emirates, which imports 80 per cent of its food, has just invested US$100 million into vertical farming in an effort to establish resilient production of food in a desert, something that would have been unthinkable a generation ago.[45]

YOUR MOTHER WAS RIGHT

Science is only just beginning to figure out why fruit and vegetables are so important for health: but in the meantime, it's enough to know that eating a range of fruit and vegetables is extremely important for our health, whether because they give us tiny quantities of vitamins and minerals or huge amounts of fibre. But far from being a basic necessity, they are a luxury for many. Water, an essential requirement for growing fruit and vegetables, is also unequally distributed. We need to address the unequal distribution of both in societies worldwide. In the meantime, those of us who can afford to should eat as much fruit and as many vegetables as possible. One of the ways we can make this an affordable possibility for more people is by using less water to produce other, less sustainable foodstuffs. It's time to talk about the impact that meat has on the planet.

CHAPTER 6

ANIMAL PROTEIN

PLANETARY HEALTH DIET RECOMMENDATION:

ANIMAL PROTEIN (EXCLUDING FISH)

Weekly recommendations: one to two portions each of poultry and eggs every week, and one portion of red or processed meat every seven to ten days, depending on size.

Humans are omnivores: we can, and do, eat pretty much anything. But if alien observers were visiting earth for the first time, we'd have to forgive them for thinking that one of the main aims of all humanity was to grow and eat meat – and, looking at the numbers, we'd be forced to conclude that they had a point.

For a start, there is a reliable trend between a country getting richer and increasing meat consumption.[1] For example, in 1990 China had a GDP per person of US$1,500, and people ate an average of 25kg of meat per year. By 2013 the GDP per person had increased to US$12,000, and people were eating about 60kg of meat annually. Similarly, Trinidad and Tobago's GDP per person rose from US$12,300 in 1990 to US$31,400 in 2013, and its meat consumption followed suit, with average annual consumption rising from 31kg per person to 76kg. It seems to be that, all other things being equal, people will always choose to eat more meat when they can afford it.

Second, the aliens could not fail to notice that humans have transformed a lot of living matter on the planet to accommodate their bloodthirsty preferences. A recent paper undertook the heroic (and somewhat insane) task of assessing the world's biomass – the weight of all living creatures on the planet. Looking just at land animal biomass, people make up about 35 per cent. Wild animals (including birds) account for 5 per cent. And the rest? Fully 60 per cent of all land animal biomass on the planet is livestock: animals we farm to eat.[2]

Finally, the aliens could point to the fact that humanity seems to care more about growing animals as food than doing anything else on the planet. Of the 104 million square km of habitable land on earth which is not icebound or desert, only 1 per cent is occupied by urban spaces, whereas half is used for agriculture. Forty million square km of that – 77 per cent of all space used to produce food, and about 39 per cent of all habitable land on earth – is used for rearing livestock. That area is equivalent to devoting the whole of North, South and Central America solely to raising animals and the food they eat.[3]

Given the allocation of resources to rearing animals, the aliens might well assume that they form the bulk of our diet. Given how we prize eating meat, surely, the aliens might assume, every human meal consists of nothing but steak? In fact, despite the vast expanses of earth we use to rear animals, they provide only 18 per cent of the global calorie supply.[4] In short, we invest disproportionately in growing meat compared to all other food products.

Even if we were to sit the aliens down and explain that they've got it wrong, it would be hard not to acknowledge their puzzlement. They would have a point: what is it with us and eating meat?

It does appear true that eating meat is inextricably bound up with our evolution. Some evolutionary biologists have made the argument that it was only by eating meat, which provides a dense quantity of vital nutrients that are otherwise environmentally scarce, that we were able evolve into the social and brainy animals we are today.[5] Our nearest living primate relatives, orang-utans, gorillas and chimpanzees, are predominantly herbivores which eat meat only occasionally. But judging by the butchery marks left on bones, meat has been an important component of protohuman and human diets since the Stone Age. Although people initially hunted to obtain meat, data suggests that they started to domesticate pigs, sheep, goats and cattle about 12,000 years ago. This is roughly the same time period that we began to farm our first crops, such as wheat, barley and lentils – and significantly earlier than we began growing other staple crops such as rice and millet.[6]

So humans have been carnivorous for pretty much as long as we have been in existence. Strikingly though, over the last 50 years or so we appear to have been eating much more meat. The amount we produce has more than quadrupled from 71 million tonnes in 1961 to 318 million tonnes in 2014 (the last year for which we have data).[7] Part of the increase can be explained by the fact that our population has grown over the past 50 years: there were three billion people on earth in 1960 and seven billion in 2011.[8] While it makes sense to increase our meat production to feed more mouths, we're producing almost twice the quantity of meat you'd expect based on population growth alone.

Why are we eating so much more meat? And does it matter? The answers to these questions seem to be, respectively, 'because we can' and 'yes'. I will explore the complexity behind these annoyingly simple-sounding answers in this chapter and the next.

WHY YOU SHOULD EAT MEAT

In 2019, the Belgian Royal Academy of Medicine raised more than a few eyebrows by calling for the state to prosecute parents who raise their children as vegan. The academy put forward a legal opinion that it was unethical to subject children to veganism because of the diet's lack of essential proteins, fatty acids and micronutrients such as vitamin B12 which are required for healthy growth. They added that a vegan diet could only be made safe for growing children if they were given frequent medical supervision, blood tests and vitamin supplements, which most parents are not qualified to provide. The academy stated that the warning also applied to teenagers, as well as pregnant and lactating women.[9] 'We can no longer tolerate this endangerment,' said Professor Georges Casimir, who led the commission that wrote the report. *The Telegraph* reported that its warning was issued in response to the request of a regional government official who was concerned at the number of health incidents affecting vegan children in nurseries and schools, including some deaths.

As you can imagine this was not well received, to put it mildly. Scores of vegans in Belgium and abroad reacted with anger, pointing out that their children were perfectly healthy, thank you very much. The academy was forced to publish a clarification which emphasized that it was not critiquing a vegetarian diet, only a vegan diet, but that it stood by the fact that veganism could cause growth retardation in foetuses and infants, hypothyroidism, severe anaemia and vitamin B12 deficiency, among other problems. This, they added, 'causes exposure to the risk of developmental retardation, intellectual disability and an increased risk of disorders such as autism'.[10] Somewhat defensively, it pointed out that both the German Medical Association and the European Society for Paediatric Gastroenterology, Hepatology and Nutrition had issued similar recommendations, advising against veganism during pregnancy, lactation, childhood and even adolescence.

While many children are raised vegan and are absolutely healthy, not eating animal products, especially during pregnancy and the early years, requires careful nutritional planning. It's much easier to ensure that children have the proteins, fatty acids and micronutrients that they need through a diet which involves eating meat or other animal products. The reason for this is simple: meat (which for simplicity I am defining here to mean any protein, including eggs, from any animal, be it fish, fowl or farmyard) is very nutrient-dense, especially with nutrients which are required for growth. This is basically because the animals have done the hard work for us.

If you recall from Chapter Three (see page 63), all crops need reactive nitrogen to be able to create amino acids, which in turn make up proteins, in the same way that Lego building blocks combine to form huge intricate structures at Legoland. There are 21 amino acids, of which nine are classified as essential. This is an inadvertently misleading term. All amino acids are essential in the sense that we need them all to be able to build the full range of required proteins, but an essential amino acid is one that we are not capable of synthesizing ourselves. Instead, we have to eat foods which contain these essential amino acids, whereas our bodies can make the other 12 amino acids from other foods.

Other animals have the same amino acid requirements as us, and so they eat and/or synthesize all 21 amino acids. We then take up these essential amino acids from their protein when we eat it. So eating meat is the easiest way of getting the full complement of amino acids in one go. It is possible to get all essential amino acids from eating plant-based foods, but it takes more work. Simply put, imagine that eating only plant-based foods is a little like an essential amino acid Easter egg hunt which requires multiple stops to find them all, whereas eating meat is like finding a whole basket of eggs under a tree: meat is considered a 'complete' protein source. This is one of the reasons meat is considered by some medical professionals and nutritionists as so important for growth and development: if you eat meat there is no risk of inadvertently missing out on any of the essential amino acids, without which growth or development could be stunted.

All types of meat (as defined above) can be considered complete protein sources, but not all animal products have the same quantities of micronutrients. For example, seafood is a particularly rich source of nutrients compared with other proteins. Fish contain a large quantity of omega-3 fatty acids which, like essential amino acids, we cannot synthesize. Equally fish, red meat and other types of seafood (clams especially) contain extremely high levels of vitamin B12, which is vital for red blood cell formation, brain function and DNA synthesis. Deficiencies of B12 can cause anaemia, fatigue, weakness and neurological changes, among other symptoms. However, unlike the essential nutrients mentioned above,

B12 can be made synthetically, and is routinely added as a supplement to some food such as breakfast cereals.

Then there are dietary elements such as iron, which, despite being famously found in red meat, is also found in abundance in seafood such as mussels and clams, and in chicken liver. Iron is vital for transporting oxygen in our blood as a component part of the oxygen-carrying molecule haemoglobin. (This is also why we feel tired when we're iron-deficient; we are actually getting less oxygen.) Animals do the hard work of synthesizing haemoglobin for us, which means when we eat them the iron is in a readily absorbable form. Although iron is also found abundantly in many dark-green leafy vegetables, for example spinach, the iron is in a non-haem form and so is harder for us to absorb. Spinach also contains various factors which inhibit iron absorption, making it tricky to meet your iron needs from spinach alone. The difficulties of getting iron in our diets means that anaemia is one of the most common nutritional deficiencies in the world.

And, perhaps most famously of all the nutritional elements, dairy products can be important sources of calcium, which, as every school child in the West is told, is vital for healthy bones and teeth.

So while the Belgian Royal Academy of Medicine might have put their foot in it from a public relations point of view in the way they issued their advice, the science behind their statement makes sense. Meat products are ready sources of multiple nutritional components, and it is harder to ensure that eating a plant-based diet contains all of them. It is perfectly possible to be a healthy vegan: it just takes much more thought about what you eat.

But there is also a flip side which cannot be ignored. While there can be a benefit to eating a certain amount of meat, there can also be harms from eating too much of some types of meat. So it's important to define the different animal-derived protein food sources and approaches to eating (or not eating) them. We live in a society where people can be vegan, vegetarian, pescatarian or flexitarian, and each label denotes a specific attitude to consuming animal-derived products.

For my purpose here, red meat includes beef, lamb, pork or goat, and poultry includes chicken or turkey. There can be a difference between ruminant red meat (beef, lamb and goat) and pork, as the animals are raised in different agricultural settings. Seafood refers to fish as well as other marine animals (everything from the eight-legged octopus to the clam), but sometimes I refer specifically to fish alone. Dairy refers to both milk and milk-derived products such as cheese and yoghurt. Eggs are eggs. There are many more animal-based products which people around the world eat on a regular basis (such as rabbit, duck, camel, horse, and so on), but here I am considering the most common meat and animal products, which are also the ones for which we have the best data.

Eating any of the above categories can bring specific health benefits if they are eaten in moderation – or harms, if gorged on. Each is considered separately, and given a specific recommendation in the planetary health diet. In this first chapter on protein, I consider red meat and poultry specifically. I consider dairy and seafood in the next chapter.

A CHICKEN IN EVERY POT MEANS A LOT OF CHICKENS

In 2018 farmers raised 346 million tonnes of meat, which breaks down as 68.79 billion chickens, 1.48 billion pigs, 656.31 million turkeys, 573.81 million sheep, 479.14 million goats and 302.15 million cattle (these numbers only include animals raised solely for their meat, so exclude chickens raised to produce eggs and dairy cattle). In 2018 there were 7.6 billion people on the planet, so per person that's about nine chickens a head, a fifth of a pig and a quarter of a turkey, sheep, goat or cow, presumably depending on preference.[11]

Producing such numbers of animals for our plates has led to technological innovations in industrial farming techniques. We'd all prefer to think of the animals we eat leading a bucolic outdoor existence until they pass away peacefully in their sleep, but we also know that the reality is starkly different. While this issue has ethical implications in terms of animal welfare, it also has serious implications for human health.

The first problem is that the rising density of animals increases the risk of infection. Viruses and bacteria spread most efficiently within animals that are housed close together. The degree of proximity in some intensive farming systems is hard to comprehend. For example, EU regulations for chicken rearing stipulate that you can raise 42kg of chicken per square metre. If we assume that a chicken has an average slaughter weight of 2.2kg, this means that 19 chickens can be raised per square metre. That allows each chicken a space smaller than an A4 piece of paper. Even the highest welfare chickens are raised in a system we would find intensive, as they have on average a space the size of an A3 piece of paper.[12] When disease arises such intensive rearing systems allows it to spread quickly between animals.

For example, in 2019 China's pig population was hit by an epidemic of African swine fever. The disease wiped out between a quarter and a third of the country's pigs – about 100 million of them, although exact numbers are unclear – which had serious knock-on implications for the cost of meat. In China, which makes a huge effort to be entirely self-reliant in food production, there was concern that there might be social unrest when pork prices rose by 70 per cent. The disease subsequently spread to Vietnam and the Philippines, and the combined losses have raised the export prices of pork worldwide.[13]

A little longer ago the British beef industry was seriously affected in the 1980s and 1990s by an outbreak of BSE (bovine spongiform encephalopathy). As exemplified by BSE, when our livestock catches a cold – or any other virus – humanity tends to sneeze.

For example, 2020 saw the world overwhelmed by the spread of a new type of coronavirus, COVID-19. This virus is believed to have originated in China in a wild animal meat market in Wuhan, possibly through a pangolin. Many viruses can evolve to jump species barriers: in fact, almost all the major epidemic diseases in the past few centuries have evolved from the infectious diseases of animals, including smallpox, flu, tuberculosis, measles and cholera. While some diseases, such as COVID-19 and HIV, probably jumped the species barrier from human contact with wild animals, others have come from domesticated animals. For example, in 2013 a deadly strain of bird flu was believed to have been transmitted to humans from chickens at a wet poultry market.

In his prize-winning book *Guns, Germs and Steel*, the geographer Jared Diamond suggests that Europeans were able to conquer much of the world partly because their domestication of livestock meant they were exposed to far more endemic infectious disease.[14] When the Spanish conquistadors reached the new world of Latin America, far more indigenous peoples were killed by the viruses the Spanish brought with them than by the settlers. Although populations develop immunity over time, helped by vaccines and public health campaigns, an increasingly densely populated and globally-connected world in which people live alongside increasingly densely farmed and rising animal populations is at greater risk of new epidemics. The more meat we produce, the more we increase the risk.

As we increase the risk of new diseases arising, the way in which we rear meat is also hampering our chance of dealing with infections. Overuse of antibiotics in farming and agriculture is one of the main causes of rising antibiotic resistance. Current estimates of global antibiotic consumption in agriculture range between 63,000 and 240,000 tonnes, which is roughly equivalent to the quantity consumed by humans.[15] Overuse of antibiotics increases antimicrobial resistance, which has happened in the case of drug-resistant MRSA in British hospitals. Antimicrobial resistance already causes at least 700,000 deaths globally a year, and is forecast to rise.[16]

The widespread use of antibiotics in agriculture makes the risk worse in three different ways. First, if animals become drug resistant these resistant strains can be passed directly to humans via human-animal contact. Second, the resistant strains could potentially stay in the food chain, infecting those who prepare or eat infected meat. Finally, the resistant strains and/or the antibiotics used to treat them can be excreted by animals into the environment, allowing the possibility of further infection and also further increasing exposure to the antibiotics, risking the development of yet more drug resistance.

It makes sense to use antibiotics to treat sick animals, but only a tiny proportion of antimicrobials are used for this purpose. Most antibiotics are given to animals prophylactically, to guard against the possible development of an infection before it arises, or because of a quirky property of antibiotics: promoting growth. Giving antibiotics to livestock allows them to reach market weight faster, so increases farmers' profit margin. Prophylactic or growth-promoting use of antibiotics is especially common in intensive agricultural systems where animals are kept in confined conditions, creating a potential perfect storm for infection. However, if antibiotic supplements in animal's food are restricted their antibiotic-resistant bacteria is reduced by almost 40 per cent.[17]

So the industrial scale at which we grow most of the meat we eat increases the risk of new epidemics and simultaneously hampers our ability to cure them. But these intensive farming practices are a response to our increasing demand for meat – which, as it turns out, is probably harming us as well.

WHY YOU SHOULD EAT LESS RED MEAT 1

Spare a thought for the scientists of the International Agency for Research on Cancer (IARC). This specialized agency, part of the World Health Organization (WHO), is dedicated to figuring out what causes cancer. As part of this work they have an entire research wing systematically dedicated to assessing how likely a certain substance is to cause cancer in humans (its carcinogenicity). These scientists don't choose what they evaluate. The choice is made by an independent advisory group and the schedule published several months in advance. Once the substances have been picked, the IARC puts together an international group of experts, plus some interested observers, and everyone descends on the French city of Lyon for an intense week of debate and scientific literature assessment.

At the end of the week, the working group assesses all the data they used and publishes a monograph: a thick book outlining their thoughts and available information and providing a recommendation for the substance's carcinogenicity classification. There are four categories the group can put a substance into. The carcinogenicity to humans of group 3 substances is not classifiable: essentially there's insufficient data to make a call. Group 2B substances are those which are possibly carcinogenic to humans; group 2A are those which are probably carcinogenic. Whether a substance sits in group 2A or 2B depends on the nature of the studies and data available. And finally, group 1 substances are those which are classified as being carcinogenic: there is enough data on these to say with confidence that this substance causes cancer in humans.

Most of the time, the substances the IARC examine are the ones you'd expect: volume 107, for example, was on 'Polychlorinated Biphenyls and Polybrominated Biphenyls' (chemicals in dielectric fluid in capacitors and transformers, and fire extinguishers, if you were wondering); volume 119 was memorably entitled 'Some Chemicals That Cause Tumours of the Urinary Tract in Rodents'. These publications tend to be received with resounding silence around the world, except by the small number of people who deeply care about, for example, dielectric fluid in capacitors. They're not usually at the centre of a media storm.

But in 2015, when they published another otherwise routine volume 114, the IARC found themselves in the international public eye. Volume 114 was entitled 'Red Meat and Processed Meat' and the scientists delivered their verdict in exactly the same matter-of-fact manner with which they had dispatched polychlorinated biphenyls. Red meat (beef, lamb, pork) was classified as 'probably carcinogenic to humans' (group 2A), and processed meat (meat which has been cured, salted or otherwise preserved, such as bacon, salami, ham or sausages) was 'carcinogenic to humans' (group 1).

I inadvertently had a front-row view of the uproar this unleashed. I was then senior editor at *The Lancet Oncology*, which has a publishing arrangement with the IARC. As a clinical oncology journal aimed at medical professionals, we published abridged versions or summaries of their monographs as news items as soon as the working group had reached their conclusions. Publication of the monograph in full, with its detailed evidence and reasoning, followed several months later. This is intended to ensure that those who need to know the findings can begin to act on the recommendations as soon as possible.

The *Lancet* summaries come through every few months, and are edited on a rota system. Monograph 114 happened to be my turn. I remember reading the manuscript a few times before walking to my editor-in-chief's office, popping my head around the door and telling him that the monograph was a bit different this time round, and we should be prepared for a media reaction. However, none of us was prepared for the reaction we did get.

For a start, contrary to our expectations, *The Lancet Oncology* was not the first media outlet to publish the news. Instead, the findings were leaked to a British newspaper ahead of our publication date (we never did find out who leaked them). On the day before our expected publication we awoke to sensationalist headlines, which were just as nuanced as you would expect from a world which woke to find its bacon sandwiches under threat.

The *Daily Mail*, for example, suggested that we might see warning labels on packets of bacon, and pointed out that processed meats now had the same carcinogenicity ranking as asbestos and cigarettes. *The Sun* ran with 'Banger out of order: sausages and bacon top cancer list'. Even the normally staid *Guardian* got in on the act: its headline read 'Processed meats rank alongside smoking as cancer causes – WHO' with the subheading 'UN health body says bacon, sausages and ham among most carcinogenic substances along with cigarettes, alcohol, asbestos and arsenic'.

In short, reading the papers you got the strong impression that eating a bacon sandwich was as bad as developing a packet-a-day smoking habit. Certainly this seemed to be many people's response: sales of bacon dropped 11.3 per cent in December 2015 compared to the previous year, with sausage sales also falling.[18] *The Grocer*, a British magazine and website about the food industry, suggested that these changes could be due to the IARC classification.

So what should have been a routine assessment turned into a huge international scare, with a predictable backlash from both members of the public and meat lobbyists: scientists were being hysterical, they said (and how dare they spoil my sausage roll, they muttered to each other during their lunch break). The WHO was forced to issue a statement in response to 'a number of queries, expressions of concern and requests for clarification'. They stood by the findings but tried to clarify the implications, stating that the 'latest IARC review does not ask people to stop eating processed meats but indicates that reducing consumption of these products can reduce the risk of colorectal cancer'.[19] The subject of red and processed meat, and links with cancer, remains contentious and scientific investigations continue years later.

So do red and processed meat cause cancer? The answer generally appears to be a qualified yes – but that qualification is vital (this is also why leaking complex scientific findings under sensationalist headlines without proper clarification is irresponsible). The IARC classification identified processed meat as definitely being hazardous to human health, and red meat as probably being hazardous, in certain quantities and under certain conditions. A cancer hazard is defined as something which 'is capable of causing cancer under some circumstances'. But different hazards have different levels of risk: just because something can cause cancer doesn't mean it will. The likelihood of developing cancer after being exposed to a specific factor, or 'agent', determines how risky it is.

For example, both cigarettes and secondary cigarette smoke are group 1 carcinogens: known to be capable of causing cancer. However, the risk of developing cancer as a regular smoker is much, much higher than the risk of developing cancer as a result of inhaling second-hand smoke. This is due to frequency of exposure – if you pass someone's cigarette cloud once a month you're exposed to far fewer potential carcinogens than if you smoke a packet of cigarettes a day.

Different agents also have inherently different risks. Being exposed to ionizing radiation after nuclear fallout is a seriously bad idea: this is a strong carcinogen which greatly increases your risk of developing a range of blood cancers. Being exposed to second-hand smoke is not completely harmless, but the chances of going on to develop lung cancer are remote. Finally, exposure to a carcinogenic element does not mean you will develop cancer: many people have an octogenarian chain-smoker in their family who, between hacking coughs, explains that they owe their longevity to Marlboro Lights and daily vitamin tablets.

In the case of red and processed meat specifically, while there is enough data to suggest that the first is probably carcinogenic and that the second is carcinogenic, the risks associated with eating them are low. Cancer Research UK ran the numbers when this research was announced and came up with a useful way of understanding the relative risks. About 3 of every 100 cancers in the UK every year are probably due to eating excessive red and processed meat, which, given how many new cancers are diagnosed annually, means that about 8,800 cases of cancer can be attributed to meat-eating.[20] By contrast, around 64,500 new cases of cancer are caused by smoking.[21] So red and processed meat only make up a small proportion of all new cases – which seems insignificant, unless you're one of the people who are included in that.

But risk depends on the degree of exposure. And people worldwide are eating more meat generally, and eating much more processed red meat specifically. Between 1990 and 2013, the consumption of processed meat rose in every region of the world, and in Southeast Asia, Latin America and North America the intake rose by about 40 per cent.[22] So while there might be a low risk overall, the more red and processed meat we eat, the more we expose ourselves to that risk, increasing our chance of getting cancer.

A huge American study gave some concrete data on this: the researchers followed more than half a million people between the ages of 50 and 71 for 20 years. They assessed meat consumption at the beginning of the study using a questionnaire and validated this by asking the participants a day later what they had eaten. The researchers then waited more than two decades to discover the cause of people's deaths.

The results were strikingly dependent on the quantity and type of meat that people ate. The researchers divided the whole population into five equal groups ranging from those who ate the least meat (the bottom 20 per cent) to those who ate the most (the top 20 per cent). The study found that people in the top 20 per cent for processed meat consumption were significantly more likely to die of any cause compared with those who were in the bottom 20 per cent. They were also more likely to die of cancer, or of cardiovascular disease (for example a heart attack) specifically, than those in the bottom 20 per cent. The same was true of those who were among the top 20 per cent of eaters of red meat. By contrast, they found that those who ate the most white meat seemed to live longer than those who ate the least, as well as being less likely to die of cancer (although there was a slight association between men who ate more white meat and cardiovascular disease).[23]

The link between eating red and processed meat and developing cardiovascular disease has been established elsewhere. A meta-analysis which looked at 13 different studies involving more than a million people found similar outcomes, suggesting that people who ate the most processed meat had an 18 per cent higher risk of dying from cardiovascular disease compared with those who ate the least; those who ate the most red meat had a 16 per cent higher risk. But these researchers drilled down further and found that the risk of dying from cardiovascular disease directly correlated with how much meat people ate: eating 50g more of processed meat or

100g more of red meat daily were both associated with a greater risk of dying from cardiovascular disease.[24]

So the message seems clear that, at least from a health perspective, almost all meat-eaters should reduce their intake of red and processed meat. Based on these and other findings, the English National Health Service somewhat conservatively recommends that adults eat no more than 70g of red or processed meat a day. That's about the weight of a burger patty, or a couple of slices of ham or two sausages. By contrast, the planetary health diet recommends almost a quarter of that amount, approximately 14g of red or processed meat daily – about a third of a sausage.

What accounts for the difference between these two recommendations? The answer is that the planetary health diet also takes into account the harm that red meat does to the planet.

WHY YOU SHOULD EAT LESS RED MEAT 2

Not eating meat is the best-known and most widely adopted modification of our diets for environmental reasons in the Western world – and is also big business. For example, in 2019 in the UK, the popular bakery chain Greggs added a vegan sausage roll to its products and watched its like-for-like sales and share price skyrocket. Beyond Meat, a US-based company which makes vegetarian meat substitutes, had the most successful initial public offering of shares on the stock market of any company since 2000, and as of July 2020, was valued at more than $12 billion.[25] Alternative meat options have started to become mainstream, with vegan offerings that include an 'Impossible Whopper' being served at Burger King, which, the adverts proudly claim, is '100% Whopper, 0% beef' (although controversy surrounds the offering because it is cooked on the same grill as the meat products, making the finished product non-vegan). Research into alternative meat offerings has been growing for a while: the first lab-grown meat burger was produced and eaten in 2013, although it came in at a pretty hefty US$280,000 per burger (watch out McDonalds!). The company behind it, Mosa Meat, hope to reduce that to US$10 per patty by 2021.[26]

Many people are aware that meat – and red meat particularly – has a high environmental cost, but quite often they are unaware of exactly why. The planetary boundary (see Chapter Two, page 30) most people have heard of is climate change, so generally speaking people seem to have the idea that meat production increases greenhouse gas emissions. There is some truth to this, and in fact meat production affects more planetary boundaries than any other type of food. But the biggest planetary boundary that meat production is pushing us up against is land-use change – the conversion of natural wilderness space to land for human use. The increasing conversion of land to produce meat is the predominant cause of harms: changing land-use to rear meat leads to an increase in greenhouse gas emission and eutrophication. It also decreases biodiversity and natural landscape resistance (for example, deforestation increases the risk of soils being washed away by rains). This is a cluster-bomb of related complications, and once the implications sink in it's clear that we should begin approaching eating meat differently.

MEAT'S UNIQUE ENVIRONMENTAL HOOF AND CLAW PRINT

To fully understand the environmental impacts of meat, we need to consider all the components that go into rearing an animal for slaughter. For example, what does it take to raise a cow? First you need space – how much? Does that space exist already or do you need to cut down some trees to make a field? Then you have to feed it. Do you have access to pasture, or will you feed the cow grain or feed (and if so, what kind, in what proportions)? It needs water to drink; is there a ready source? Why are you raising the cow in the first place? Do you want to eventually eat its meat, or do you want it for its milk? If the latter, the cow needs to become pregnant in order to begin lactation, which in turn requires a bull at some stage and that brings further complications (doesn't it always?). Finally you need to think about other aspects of creating a cow: you'll either need to shovel the proverbial or accept the harmful consequences of manure running off into the water supply.

Measuring the environmental cost of everything required to produce a unit of food is known as a life-cycle assessment. So for example, to assess the environmental impact of producing 1kg of beef, a life-cycle assessment will take into consideration not just how much food and water an animal needs, but also other less obvious aspects such as its methane-producing farts, the environmental cost of producing the food needed to feed the cow, the potential of the cow's manure for eutrophication of the water, and so on. You'd think these life-cycle assessments would be hard to do, and you'd be right. But because they're so important, they have been painstakingly developed, methodologically fine-tuned and widely carried out. Assessments have been done for the majority of foodstuffs we eat. But farms and their impacts vary hugely around the world. There are about 570 million farms in the world, located everywhere from the equator to the extreme north and south. The smallest farm could be less than a hectare; the largest farms in the world (for instance in Australia) are bigger than some countries. How can these be comparable?

A truly heroic meta-analysis in 2018 attempted to answer this question by bringing together all the data the researchers could find and standardizing it to give an overall picture of the environmental impact of different foodstuffs. They assessed a total of 38,700 commercial farms in 119 countries, with farms ranging in size from half a hectare in Bangladesh to 3,000 hectares in Australia, to build up a picture of the true environmental costs of the food we eat. (And if this sounds familiar, well-remembered. I first mentioned this study in Chapter Two – see page 42).[27]

One of the questions the researchers attempted to answer is where we emit the most greenhouse gases in our food production system. (A side note: when I refer to greenhouse gas emissions, I present all data in terms of carbon dioxide equivalents. This is based on the potential of a unit of gas to warm the atmosphere, using carbon dioxide as a baseline, and is why people talk about some gases being more harmful than others: they have greater warming potential. When I refer to greenhouse gases these therefore include not only carbon dioxide, but also methane, nitrous oxide, and so on, to give a sense of their overall warming potential.)

Of all the greenhouse gas emissions in the world, agriculture is responsible for about a quarter of annual emissions, 26 per cent. More than half of these, 52 per cent, result from producing meat – and a huge amount of these emissions are caused by the way in which we use land to produce our meat.

In contrast to one of the concerns we often hear, comparatively few greenhouse gases are generated by transporting food ('food miles'): only 6 per cent of the total. In fact, the greenhouse gas emissions we produced by the entire supply chain (retail, transport, food packaging and processing) only accounts for 18 per cent of the total emissions created by our food system. Just by growing the crops for animals to eat, we produce the same quantity of greenhouse gases as is produced by all food transport systems (6 per cent).

A full 16 per cent of greenhouse gas emissions – almost as much as every emission produced in moving food around the world – comes from changing land-use to farm livestock. And a whopping 30 per cent comes just from livestock and fisheries farming. In other words, more than half of all greenhouse gas emissions generated by the food system (52 per cent, from growing crops, land-use change, and livestock and fisheries) comes from our desire to eat animals and their products.

Global greenhouse gas emissions from food production[28]

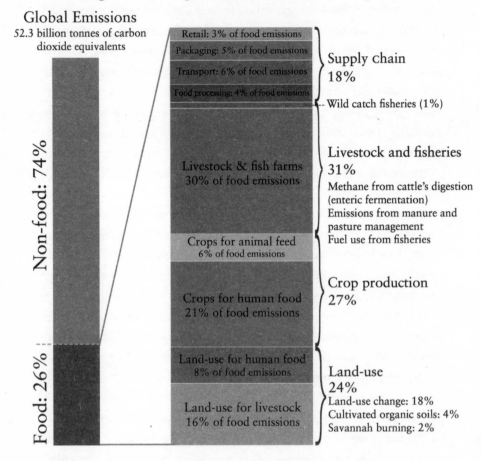

Global Emissions
52.3 billion tonnes of carbon dioxide equivalents

Non-food: 74%

Food: 26%

Retail: 3% of food emissions
Packaging: 5% of food emissions
Transport: 6% of food emissions
Food processing: 4% of food emissions

} Supply chain
18%

-- Wild catch fisheries (1%)

Livestock & fish farms
30% of food emissions

} Livestock and fisheries
31%
Methane from cattle's digestion
(enteric fermentation)
Emissions from manure and
pasture management
Fuel use from fisheries

Crops for animal feed
6% of food emissions

Crops for human food
21% of food emissions

} Crop production
27%

Land-use for human food
8% of food emissions

Land-use for livestock
16% of food emissions

} Land-use
24%
Land-use change: 18%
Cultivated organic soils: 4%
Savannah burning: 2%

So what causes these emissions? I'll look in more detail at fisheries later. Emissions from land animals come from a variety of sources and include what we put into raising animals, the food and land it takes to maintain them – and what we get out of them.

BULLSHIT – AND BULL BURPS AND FARTS...

As previously discussed, ruminant animals are those which have evolved a symbiotic relationship with certain types of bacteria that allows them to digest the complex carbohydrate cellulose in plant cell walls. This is what allows bulls and cows to eat only grass while growing hundreds of kilos of muscle: they can unlock nutrients in grass that we cannot. As part of this digestive process, some of the bacteria produce methane gas, which cows release either by burping or, as one paper puts it, from the opposite direction, into the atmosphere. Methane is a greenhouse gas which has a much greater warming potential than carbon dioxide and a single cow can release up to 320 litres a day.[29]

Serious scientific effort is going into figuring out how to reduce cow methane production. Even Bill Gates has weighed in on the issue. He talked on CNN in early 2019 about how we can't ignore bovine flatulence in our attempt to get the planet down to net zero greenhouse gas emissions.[30] There are many different possible solutions, each more outlandish than the last.

A research group in New Zealand is working on a vaccine which will target some of the bacteria in a cow's gut responsible for the methane-producing step of digestion. Others have discovered that including seaweed in cows' diets can reduce methane output by about 20 per cent (although scaling up seaweed production to feed the world's cattle would be a challenge, given that supplying just 10 per cent of Australia's cattle and dairy industry is estimated to require 300,000 tonnes of seaweed annually). Alternatively, a company called ZELP (Zero Emissions Livestock Project) has created a 'methane reduction wearable': a sort of cow Fitbit which fits over the animal's nose to convert the burped methane into carbon dioxide and water vapour.

The impact of livestock excretion on the environment is far more serious than the sum of their farts: as anyone who has gingerly tried to cross a field without standing in a cowpat knows, they also produce copious quantities of manure.

Why do we care about this? To understand, we need to go back to the nitrogen and phosphorus cycle (see Chapter Three, page 63). As you will recall, crops can take up these nutrients only in certain forms, which they then incorporate into various molecules essential for life. We can get these vital nutrients either by eating the crops directly or by feeding the crops to animals and then eating their meat. Unfortunately, the latter approach is wildly inefficient. A stunning 80 per cent of all nitrogen and phosphorus in the world goes into fertilizing grass and crops which end up as animal feed. Of these nutrients, only about 20 per cent ends up in human diets.[31]

One of the biggest losses from livestock is in the form of their manure. If you recall from Chapter Three (see page 66), one of the contributing causes to the eutrophication of our waterways is active nitrogen run-off from manure and human waste. Beef has by far the biggest eutrophication hoofprint. In order to produce 1kg of beef, we also produce 301kg of eutrophying emissions (this is the total of all nutrients which have the potential to cause eutrophication, as measured in phosphate equivalents, much as we used carbon dioxide equivalents to measure greenhouse gas emission). It's even worse if we're eating beef from a dairy herd, which produces 365kg of eutrophying emissions per 1kg of beef. Sheep are significantly lower, but still produce 97kg per 1kg of lamb. Poultry is far lower, but still high, producing 58kg of emissions per kilo of chicken.[32] Contrast all these numbers with the quantities required to produce a kilo of wheat: just 7kg of eutrophying emissions.

Unless reclaimed (a euphemism for shovelling the shit) this manure washes into waterways, eventually leading to the suffocation of fish and other types of aquatic life in rivers and oceans. However, reclaiming and reusing manure and so keeping the nutrient cycle unbroken not only prevents eutrophication, but also means that extra greenhouse gases are not generated to fix more nitrogen or dig out more phosphate. The combination of ruminants' excreted manure and methane has a huge impact on the environment. In the EU, 44 per cent of all greenhouse gas emissions come from manure management and methane from cattle (half each).[33] In the UK, livestock farming is estimated to produce 60 per cent of all nitrogen pollution and a quarter of all phosphate pollution in waterways.[34]

FOOD OR FEED?

Now let's consider what livestock eat. This is an extremely contentious topic known in academic agricultural circles as the food/feed debate. The question boils down to this: are we competing with livestock for food? Would it be a much more efficient use of resources to cut out the cow and just eat the grain we grow to feed animals ourselves?

The contentious nature of this question comes from the fact that there are multiple agricultural systems around the world which grow livestock, and so multiple different answers. Whether animals are taking food from human mouths and how much meat we obtain from them as a result depends on the animals we're considering, what they're fed and how efficient the agricultural system in question is. These are tricky technical points but they're important because they have a direct bearing on whether we should not eat meat for environmental reasons.

Let's continue to use cows as an example. Cows can be raised either on pasture (eating predominantly grass and leaves) or in an intensive feedlot system (eating predominantly grains). Feedlot and pasture systems start in the same way: calves are born on pasture and roam with their mothers, first drinking her milk and then being weaned on to grass. However, in a feedlot system, when cows reach a certain weight – generally when they are between 9 and 11 months old – they are transferred to a penned yard (feedlot) where they are given changing quantities of grain to help them gain muscle mass fast, ready to be sold to the beef industry (normally after 60 to 200 days).[35] Most cattle worldwide are raised on pasture, with the more intensive feedlot system only accounting for 7–13 per cent of the global population (although feedlot systems are increasing around the world).[36]

What animals eat makes a big difference to how efficient they are as sources of food for humans. (Incidentally, if you find these analyses of animals solely as walking hunks of meat a little distasteful, rest assured that I do too. However the distaste we feel is a luxury; most Western consumers do not think about these decisions, but the truth is that almost all the meat we eat has been subjected to this kind of thinking to ensure that those who produce it can make a living. So it's important, and anyone who eats meat can't pretend that they don't implicitly endorse it.) Agriculturalists talk about the feed conversion ratio, which describes the ratio of dry matter intake (animal feed) to kilogram of animal product (gain in animal weight). It's one of the key factors taken into account in selective breeding. The lower the ratio, the more efficient the animal is at converting their food into edible meat. For most animals the ratio is about 2 or above (for battery farmed chicken it's about 1.8; for beef cattle it's about 6).[37] The feed conversion ratio depends on a variety of factors, including the breed and how the animal is fed and raised.

Due to the huge variety of meats and ways that animals are farmed round the world, it's hard to know the exact proportion of human crops that animals eat. The most conservative global average estimate suggests that producing 1kg of boneless meat requires about 2.8kg of human-edible grain for ruminants (such as cattle or goats) or 3.2kg of human-edible grain for other animals.[38] If you include soybeans as part of this assessment (which for complicated reasons aren't considered a source of human grain for this analysis, but are grown in areas which would otherwise be used for human crops), that number jumps to 6.7kg per kilo of protein product for cattle or sheep and a stunning 20.3kg per kilo for other animals. Look only at feedlot systems and that number jumps even higher: it takes around 42.5kg of human-edible food (including soybeans) to produce one kilo of beef protein. To visualize the relative difference, that's equivalent to choosing between half a bathtub of rice – enough to feed you and 70 others – or just four hamburger patties.

Of course, the solution isn't as simple as elbowing cows out of the way when it comes to being first at the trough, or clearing livestock off pastures and converting them to rolling fields of wheat.

But it is important to consider the relative inefficiencies of raising animals on food that we could be eating ourselves. And this does not take into account how much space we use to produce all that food. It is this, more than anything else, which is damaging the world.

HUNGRY, HUNGRY COWS (AND PIGS AND CHICKENS)

In 1954 the naturalist and animal collector Gerald Durrell found himself in a pickle in Argentina. He had intended to arrive in Buenos Aires and then fly down to the tip of South America, Tierra del Fuego, to collect aquatic birds for the Severn Wildlife Trust. Unfortunately, once he and his team reached the Argentine capital, they discovered that they had forgotten to take into account the holiday season. All flights to the south of the country, to the stunning lakes of Patagonia and thence the southernmost tip, were completely full. One of his local friends suggested that the expedition should reverse direction and fly north to Paraguay, where they were sure to find some interesting animal specimens to collect and take back to Europe.

Durrell's subsequent adventures in the Chaco region of Paraguay were chronicled in his book *The Drunken Forest*, in which he describes a region of stunning natural beauty. The book's title was inspired by encountering floss silk trees, known locally as *palo borracho* – drunken sticks. These bizarre and beautiful trees store water throughout the dry season in the base of their trunks, making them look like serried ranks of pot-bellied drunks lounging about the landscape. To add to their strange appearance, their grey-green trunks are covered with thick thorny spines, presumably to discourage any enterprising thirsty animal which might be thoughtfully eyeing the trunk.

Durrell's description of the drunken forests of Chaco in 1954 is worth repeating here, because it is so beautifully evocative of a lush Eden-like landscape:

'The trees were not tall, but they grew so closely together that their branches interlinked; beneath them the ground was waterlogged and overgrown with a profusion of plants, thorny bushes, and, incredibly enough, cacti... In between the *autovia* lines [local railway tracks] there grew a small plant in great profusion; it was only a few inches high, and topped with a delicate cup-shaped flower of magenta red. So thickly had it spread in places along the track that I had the impression of travelling along an endless flower bed. Occasionally the forest would be broken by a great grassland, studded with tall, flame-coloured flowers that covered several acres, and neatly bisected by rows of palms, their curving fronds making them look like green rockets bursting against the sky.'[39]

Throughout the book, which recounts his escapades with wily armadillos and poisonous snakes, the overwhelming impression Durrell gives is of a vast, rich landscape, teeming with a profusion of life. The Chaco is the largest dry forest in South America, containing 3,500 bird species, 220 reptiles and amphibians, and 150 mammals – including 18 species of armadillo alone. Durrell's favourite was the three-banded armadillo, which he described as looking like a weird clockwork toy when walking and, when curled into a defensive ball, like a large plum pudding. The Chaco straddles Brazil, Argentina, Paraguay and Bolivia, along with the neighbouring Cerrado region, which is no less diverse. The Cerrado is enormous – it's South America's largest savannah, around the size of Western Europe, and contains 5 per cent of all species of animal on earth.

But whether Durrell would recognize the landscape he described only 70 years ago today is a different question. Since his visit in the 1950s, about half of the Cerrado's forests and savannahs have been converted to agriculture, as have about a quarter of the Chaco. Our seemingly insatiable hunger for all sorts of meat is driving these changes – but not because we're using the land to rear animals. When we see images of cleared fields next to pictures of teeming rainforest and are told that the land has been cleared for meat, we imagine that the fields are for farming Brazilian cows. In fact the land is being cleared to grow feed for Chinese pigs and European chickens – and indeed feed for almost all farmed animals around the world. We're clearing vast swathes of landscape to grow a single crop: the protein and carbohydrate-rich soybean. Almost all the soy grown in the world, about 80 per cent, is used to feed the world's increasing population of poultry, cattle and pigs.

In 2010, 114 million acres (461,342 square km) of South American land were devoted solely to growing soy.[40] That's an area of land about the size of Spain just growing one crop. Because of the increasing demand for meat, soy production is a lucrative business. Together, Brazil, Argentina and Paraguay now produce almost half the world's soy, an incredible expansion when just 50 years ago they produced only about 3 per cent. Brazil is the world's biggest exporter of soy, and soy is now Brazil's most valuable export, worth US$25.9 billion in 2018 – more than any other commodity.[41] Soybeans and their derivative products (meal and oil) make up three of Paraguay and Argentina's top five exports, constituting more than 50 per cent of Paraguay's total export value and 25 per cent of Argentina's.

The rising demand for soy products that is endangering the Chaco and Cerrado is caused by the growth in demand for meat. The EU demand for soy accounts for about 32 million acres (129,500 square km) in South America, just under a third of the total area, or 90 per cent of Germany's entire agricultural land. And as other countries grow richer they can afford to buy more meat products, further increasing demand. This is shown by the rising consumption of meat in China, which is the world's biggest importer of soy beans, taking 63 per cent of the world's crop in 2017 at an annual cost of US$36.6 billion. Just 20 years ago, in 1997, China bought only 5.4 per cent of the world's soy. This huge increase in soy consumption is mainly due to increasing production of pork. Annual pork production has increased 30 times in the past 50 years, to feed about 440 million pigs.[42][43] The US is the world's other biggest producer of soy, but as the trade war between China and the US hots up, the pressure on South America to produce more soy is intensifying.

We use an enormous amount of the world's land to grow crops to feed livestock. Looking just at the United States, a recent paper suggested that the country uses about 600,000 square km to produce the crops needed to feed all farmed animals (including eggs and dairy), which is about 40 per cent of all cropland in the country. When pasture for grass-fed animals is included, the total is about 3.7 million square km, or 40 per cent of the whole country.[44] Worldwide, of all the land suitable for growing crops, 40 per cent is used to grow crops that feed livestock.[45]

It's easy to imagine that as we aim to feed a globally increasing population we will have to continue to encroach onto wild land to provide food for ourselves and our livestock. But this fails to take into account the cost of such a move. Wild land does much more than simply provide inspirational images for our screensavers and a habitat for endemic species. Land-use change is one of the planetary boundaries that we are pushing against most – we are closer to the tipping point than we are with climate change (although the two are closely linked). We've changed enough of the earth's surface to be unsure of the future implications.

The planetary boundary for land-use change is expressed as the percentage of forest cover remaining on earth. Originally the measure was of cropland, but it was changed because forest – and plant cover generally – is the most critical element of land that acts to regulate climate by reflecting sunshine, regulating water cycles and absorbing carbon dioxide from the atmosphere. Globally, we need to preserve between 54 and 75 per cent of the world's original forest cover – a combination of temperate, tropical and boreal forests (forests in cold climates). At the moment, it is estimated that only 62 per cent remain: we are within the zone of uncertainty. It is unclear what impact this change will have. But by looking at the bittersweet story of soy in South America, we can get some idea of the harm land-use change can cause – as well as how this can be reversed.

LAND-USE CHANGE IN THEORY AND PRACTICE

The Chaco and Cerrado were not South American soy growers' first choice of location. For many years the Amazon rainforest was preferred. Using slash-and-burn agricultural methods, clearing a patch of rainforest was easy, and quickly resulted in a clear patch of land with highly fertile soil ready for planting. Between 2001 and 2006, an area of the Amazon forest the size of Jamaica was cut down for soybean fields.[46] But then in 2006 something remarkable happened. In response to pressure from retailers and non-governmental organizations (NGOs), major soybean traders signed a voluntary zero-deforestation agreement for the Amazon in Brazil. Known as the Soy Moratorium, soybean traders agreed not to buy any soy grown on lands that had been deforested after July 2006 in the Amazon to produce them. The aim was to reduce further deforestation by encouraging farmers to return to already cleared lands, rather than seeking new fertile soils through land-use change.[47]

Farms were monitored by air and satellite using technology developed by industry, governments and NGOs. Any farmers identified as violating the deforestation agreement were blocked from selling to the signatories of the moratorium (all large soy traders). These measures sound extreme – but they worked. Before the signing of the moratorium, about 30 per cent of soyfield expansion came from encroachment into virgin rainforest; afterwards, this dropped to less than 1 per cent. However, soy production from the Amazon area didn't drop: rather it increased by 400 per cent! Instead of expanding through deforestation, farmers returned to already open and degraded land. Deforestation decreased dramatically. The mortarium was a stunning success story which set the standard for voluntary agreements for supply-chain governance for other commodities such as palm oil.

But unfortunately it only covered the Amazon area. Other neighbouring areas had no such guarantees and that means deforestation continues unabated elsewhere. For example, in the Cerrado the area given over to growing soy beans expanded by 253 per cent between 2000 and 2014.[48] The Cerrado now represents the largest frontier of deforestation on earth, driven by land speculators cashing in on soy's profitability. It's easy enough to clear the land: a chain is slung between two tractors and forcibly driven through the native plant species, ripping up everything in its path. Cattle are then introduced as mobile clearance and fertilization units, eating the torn foliage and spreading manure. Compared to the prices that soy-ready land fetches, cattle in Brazil are extremely unprofitable per hectacre of land. Clearing land in this manner can increase its value by about 600 per cent: the combination of such a strong incentive and very little land protection means there's no barrier to further land clearance.

This is, to put it mildly, a pity: about 425,000 square km of land in the Cerrado is already cleared and suitable for soy production. Reusing this land has the potential to triple current soy production without any further deforestation. But without land protection or a change in economic incentives this is unlikely to happen. Consequently, those living in the Cerrado and surrounding areas – and potentially elsewhere in the world – will begin to experience the environmental consequences that result from further land-use change.

Changing the amount of vegetation in a region, especially through large-scale deforestation, has an immediate impact on the water cycle. Depending on local weather systems, reducing forest and plant cover can turn normal seasonal dry seasons into drought. For example, the Cerrado contains the headwaters of three of South America's largest river basins (Tocantins-Araguaia, Paraná-Prata and São Francisco). Together with the Amazon, the area is known as the water tank of Brazil; environmentalists are concerned that the tap of this tank risks being closed through deforestation.

This is not idle speculation. In 2014–2015, Southeastern Brazil experienced a record drought. Like Cape Town (see page 6) the area had a dry season with only half the expected rains falling compared with previous years. This was exacerbated by low reservoir supplies. In January 2015 the water levels of the main reservoir had fallen to 5 per cent: about a month's supply of water was left. The water crisis badly affected São Paulo, Brazil's largest city, which experienced lowered water pressure and taps running dry.[49] Dozens of smaller towns nearby declared states of emergency in order to receive federal and military assistance. The worst affected city, Itu, was overrun by fighting and emergency water trucks were looted.[50]

João Doria, São Paulo's mayor in 2017, was convinced that there was a link between deforestation and the droughts, saying, 'We need to preserve the rainforest to preserve the cycle of rain in central and southeast Brazil.' Brazilian environmentalists believed the drought to be directly related to both deforestation and global warming. The Amazon and surrounding areas release a huge amount of water vapour, which has been dubbed 'flying rivers': the humid air rises from the forests and travels south, bouncing off the Andes mountain range. Tree loss means that this huge quantity of humidity vanishes. Satellite images taken during the drought showed that for the first time in 2015, the flying rivers failed to arrive in the drought-stricken southeast.

Paradoxically, extensive deforestation can also lead to increased risk of flooding, depending on the area's local climate and the extent of tree loss. Lack of trees and vegetation to absorb rain mean that more water runs off into river systems, potentially overwhelming them. This has also happened in the Cerrado. Scientists have data dating back to 1955 for the river flows of the Tocantins and Araguaia rivers (which drain parts of the Cerrado and the Amazon). The data shows that river discharge has increased by about 25 per cent during this time period of expanding cropland and deforestation, despite no statistically significant changes in rainfall in the area.[51]

An increased risk of floods and drought are both intricately entangled with climate: both extremes depend to a large extent on rainfall, or lack of it. As noted above, our land-use change now places us in the 'uncertain' section of the boundary – the changes we have enacted on the earth are now too great for us to fully understand or model the consequences. But the catch-22 here is that land-use change also directly impacts climate change, which in turn changes the effects of land-use change. They're tied together. And again we can use the example of the Amazon and Cerrado region of Brazil to understand how.

All plant matter takes in carbon dioxide from the atmosphere. Trees, being the largest plants, take in more than most. They use the carbon to photosynthesize and, like us, to build their cells. So an area of forest stores a huge amount of carbon in its plant matter, and has the potential, as the plants grow, to absorb even more from the atmosphere. If you recall from Chapter Two (see page 34), one of the ways we can act on climate is to control the quantity of greenhouse gases in the atmosphere, carbon dioxide being the best-known of these. If we reduce the quantity of carbon dioxide in the atmosphere, we act to reduce global warming and hopefully reduce the extent to which our climate will change. The Amazon is famous for its ability to extract carbon from the atmosphere, with historical records from towards the end of the 20th century suggesting that it absorbed an estimated two billion tonnes of carbon dioxide a year – as much carbon dioxide as all the European counties combined emitted in 2017.[52]

The visible parts of the trees are not the only parts that store carbon. The soils and root systems of the forest also store an immense amount. For example, the Cerrado is known as 'the upside down forest' because it mainly comprises small, gnarly, twisted trees with immensely deep root systems – an adaptation that the trees have developed to find water sources during arid periods. Such an adaptation creates immensely rich carbon soils, storing an estimated 13.8 billion tonnes of carbon, a little less than China and the USA combined emitted in 2017.

Deforestation and ploughing the soil for agriculture leads to two kinds of carbon harm: first, it releases stored carbon back into the atmosphere, and second, it prevents the environment from acting as a natural sink. This double whammy of harms means that land-use change directly worsens climate change. And again, this is not idle speculation or forecasting: we can see it happening right now.

In 2020, for the first time in the decade since measurements began, data have emerged that show that a fifth of the Amazon has become a net emitter of carbon, rather than a carbon sink.[53] The area giving out carbon dioxide in the southeast of the forest is heavily deforested. This comes after 2019, which was an exceptionally bad year for Amazon deforestation as a result of illegal logging and forest fires. In August 2019, an estimated 76,000 individual fires were burning throughout the rainforest. The resultant blanket of smoke was so huge that it was visible from space, and caused a temporary blackout in São Paulo, almost 3,000km away. The fires were the worst in years, and by far the worst in a year which was not beset by drought – the normal trigger point for these catastrophes. Scientists believe that 2019 was so bad because deforestation has been unofficially allowed to continue in response to a relaxation in official oversight after years of rigorous enforcement of the Soy Moratorium.[54]

This means that the Amazon's capacity to alleviate climate change is rapidly diminishing as a result of deforestation, with recent estimates suggesting that the forest is capable of absorbing only about half the carbon dioxide of previous years. Scientists believe that a tipping point is approaching after which the entire ecosystem might switch to becoming a net carbon emitter. We don't know that might happen, or what might trigger this – more deforestation? An extra degree of warming? The recent data indicate that such a point might come sooner than we suspected.

Droughts, floods and worsening climatic conditions are just some of the potential consequences which widespread land-use change and deforestation can bring about. A study by the Amazon

Environmental Research Institute found that converting inland terrestrial forests to pasture increases local land temperatures by 4.3°C (7.74°F). Similarly, land-use change from natural forests to farmland generally leads to large-scale clearing of layers of vegetation, which normally keep the fertile topsoil intact. A recent report by the United Nation's Food and Agriculture Organization (FAO) estimates that rates of soil erosion in arable or intensively grazed pasture are about 100,000 times greater than natural background erosion rates; we have lost 20–200 gigatonnes of nutrient-rich topsoil in the last decade.[55] (A gigatonne is a billion tonnes, and the large range given is due to the inherent uncertainty of such estimates.) Together both these factors increase the risk of an area transforming from a fertile potential source of food into a desert.

It's almost impossible to predict exactly what will happen when we begin transforming wilderness into farmland: it depends on the extent and type of land-use change, what provisions are made in anticipation of change and the local environment. But it is certain that such actions have consequences. And our growing consumption of meat is one of the single biggest factors driving this change.

MEAT AND LAND-USE CHANGE

So just how much land does it take to make a meaty dinner? To return to life-cycle assessments, scientists have managed to quantify how much land it takes, on average, to produce a certain amount of different types of food, including all the land needed to grow animal feed. The results make painful reading for the carnivores among us. For a kilo of beef (from a cow raised to be eaten rather than as a by-product of the dairy industry) it takes 326 square metres of land. The average UK home is around 68 square metres. So to put that into perspective, producing just 1kg of beef – a small Sunday joint for a family of four – takes 4.8 times more land than the average British family lives on. Or to think of it another way, every time you eat a single burger patty (which weighs about 250g) it costs the world quite a bit more land than all the space in your house. By contrast, producing an equivalent weight of plant crops takes far less space. One kilo of wheat and rye takes about 4 square metres, a kilo of rice 3 square metres (32 square feet) and a kilo of potatoes less than 1 square metre.

Are these fair comparisons? It's valid to argue that while meat requires more space to produce, it is a worthwhile compromise because the end product is extremely nutrient-dense: less goes further. While it is true that meat is nutrient-dense, it's not sufficiently so to outweigh the extra costs that growing it entails. If we consider the area needed to grow 1,000 calories' worth of beef or lamb this comes to about 120 square metres, whereas wheat takes only 1.4 square metres and rice only two-thirds of a square metre to provide the same number of calories. To put it differently, if you look solely at calories, you could grow 85,000 calories worth of wheat in the area that it would take to grow a 1,000 calories worth of beef. One thousand calories is less than half the recommended energy intake for an adult in one day; 85,000 kilocalories is enough food for one person for 34 days (although they'd probably get rather bored of the meal).

You could argue that comparison remains unfair: if we are talking about meat, we're talking about protein. What about how much space it takes to produce equivalent quantities of protein from animal and vegetable sources?

A fair argument, but still one that's not going to end well for those of us who like eating meat. To produce 1kg of beef protein takes 1,640 square metres of land and to produce the same quantity of protein from wheat and rye takes 30 square metres. That is to say, it takes 55 times the area of land to produce the same quantity of protein from beef than from wheat. Lamb and mutton need an even larger area to deliver 1kg of protein: 1,840 square metres. Compare this with soybeans, the main constituent in tofu, which requires only 20 square metres. Arguing solely from the perspective of land-use efficiency in providing protein, soy is 94 times as efficient as lamb. Eating vegetable-based sources of protein is a more efficient way of getting the same amount of protein while taking up much less space on earth.

At the moment, human land-use for agricultural purposes has remained more or less constant since the 1970s but this hides a disturbing fact. While the area of land we are using to grow our food is constant, we are shifting from already cleared areas to wilderness. Just as the South American soy farmers move their area of focus from cleared, suitable land into virgin territory, we are leaving behind vast tracts of abandoned land. The World Wide Fund for Nature estimates that about 20 million square km of land worldwide have been used and abandoned, but remain suitable for farming.[56] That is an area of land the size of South America. In short, the world has plenty of land that we can use for agriculture, be that farming plants or livestock, without encroaching any further into wilderness. This is critical if we are to maintain the land-use planetary boundary, even in its present state of uncertainty. In order to make the best use of the land we have while feeding a growing population, eating less meat is probably the best decision that we can take.

Meat and dairy produce provide about 18 per cent of the world's calories, but the space needed to rear animals, including that required to grow their food, represents 83 per cent of farmland worldwide. And of all agriculture-related deforestation worldwide, 67 per cent is used to grow animal feed products (soy, maize and pasture).[57] We currently eat far more meat than we need: the average European citizen consumes 70 per cent more protein than needed for a healthy diet.[58]

The planetary health diet recommends that we aim to adopt a 'half earth policy', in which at least half the world remains wilderness, in order to halt the expansion of land-use change. We now have 51 per cent wilderness, which gives us very little leeway! So one of the easiest ways to reduce our environmental footprint would be to eat less meat.

There are some caveats to this recommendation. First, not all animal sources of protein have an equally large footprint. Chicken and pork farming, for example, use far less land and resources than beef (7 and 11 square metres/for 100g of protein from chicken and pork respectively). So eating less red meat will have a bigger impact than eating less chicken.

This leads to my second caveat. It is extremely important to emphasize that we cannot, nor should we, argue for worldwide conversion to veganism on the basis of animal-raising inefficiencies. There are other environmental considerations depending on the protein sources, but not all land grazed by animals is suitable for or even capable of crop production. One study estimates that 57 per cent of the land used globally to produce animal feed is not suitable for food production.[59] The rocky hillsides of Wales or Greek islands could not suddenly grow lush vegetation if we got rid of their native sheep and goats, and I am not advocating for an end to livestock farming. As I mentioned before, animal sources of protein are the only sources of complete protein containing all the required amino acids, and also contain many other micronutrients that we shouldn't aim to strip from our lives. Losing them would not bring about miraculous health benefits nor restore all ecosystems. But eating less meat overall would not only be healthier for the planet, it would probably be healthier for us as well.

The quantities of meat the planetary health diet recommends reflect all the considerations that I have covered in this chapter, and so are correspondingly small. It recommends 0–14g daily of beef and lamb and a further daily 0–14g of pork. More chicken and eggs are suggested: 0–58g and 0–25g daily. The reason these ranges start at 0 is because it is possible to have a healthy vegan diet, and so meat is not classed as an essential nutrient.

While these numbers look extremely small and make us think of an entirely new way of eating, the truth is that they reflect historic precedent. For much of human history, meat has been an expensive commodity. Think of traditional celebration meals, with a ham or turkey at Christmas or a special Sunday roast. It's only relatively recently with the advent of technology in the form of the green revolution, that we've been able to make meat more widely affordable. For example, a Sunday roast was a way of stretching a limited quantity of meat through the week: a roast chicken eaten on Sunday by a family of four would then constitute many meals later in the week. After roast meat on Sunday, cold cuts can be used for sandwiches, scraps turned into casseroles or pies, and finally the carcass can be boiled to make stock for soup.

Even if we find the quantities the planetary health diet recommends too small to stomach, many scientific assessments considering different environmental factors have found that simply transitioning towards eating less meat can make a real and tangible difference. For example, halving the quantity of meat we eat in Europe would still mean that the average European ate twice as much protein as necessary, but would reduce nitrogen and ammonia emissions by about 40 per cent, free up enough land to make Europe a net exporter of cereals, decrease demand for deforestation-driving soy by 76 per cent and could restore grass-lands throughout the area.[60]

Increasingly, people are beginning to talk about the cost of the services that nature provides for free. If we acknowledge that a forest indirectly contributes to our economy and stability through climate regulation, it is possible to put a price on its continued existence. This idea of pricing nature's services shows us that eating meat comes at great expense, but we extract that cost from natural resources which so far are not represented. When we begin to think of its real cost to the world, a cheeky chicken nugget is neither cheap nor inoffensive.

The way we currently eat meat is not sustainable. We need to embrace the idea that meat is a treat: a delicacy to be enjoyed, not the central component of our diet. Whether we manage to cut our intake down to the measures recommended by the planetary health diet, or simply halve what we eat, we need to begin to eat less, both for our health and that of the planet.

CHAPTER 7

OTHER SOURCES OF PROTEIN

> **PLANETARY HEALTH DIET RECOMMENDATION:**
>
> **OTHER PROTEIN SOURCES**
>
> Daily recommendation: three to four portions of vegetable-based protein (legumes, nuts, seeds, soy-based foods) and two portions of dairy foods (cheese, milk, yoghurt).
>
> Weekly recommendations: one to two portions of fish every week.

What's the difference between a tomato that costs 5 cents and a tomato that costs 35 cents? In early 2020, in the street markets of Nairobi in Kenya the answer was about three weeks.[1]

Kenya normally has two wet seasons annually. The rainfall in the later part of the year, normally between October and December, is known as the short rains (the long rains are between March and May). But in late 2019 East Africa was hit by abnormally heavy prolonged rainfall, affecting an estimated three million people. Hundreds of people died in the resulting flash flooding and landslides across the region, with thousands of others told to evacuate their homes for fear of dams collapsing. These disasters also devastated local agriculture; about 80 per cent of Kenya's farms were affected and some lost all their crops.[2] Market economics dictate that scarcity increases value, and so as tomato crops were lost, the price of a tomato increased sevenfold over a matter of weeks. By May 2020, further rains had fallen, with nearly 200 people losing their lives to overflowing rivers and 40,000 people displaced.[3]

The cause is believed to be a phenomenon known as the Indian Ocean Dipole. This refers to the difference in the sea's surface temperature between the western and eastern ends of the Indian Ocean. The different sides shift in natural cycles between being warmer than average at one end and cooler than average at the other. When the difference between the western and eastern end is positive, more water evaporates off the coast of East Africa and falls as rain. Normally the temperature differences are around 1°C (1.8°F) – but in late 2019 and early 2020 the difference rose above 2°C (3.6°F), which is believed to be the reason for the abnormally heavy rainy season. This difference is the widest it has been for 60 years, and while scientists are cautious about the cause, they acknowledge that such a difference in the Dipole is an attributable factor in the heavier-than-average rains.

While Kenyan farmers were watching their land drown, on the other side of the Indian Ocean Australian farmers were watching their lands burn. By March 2020 about 33 people had died and an area the size of Austria had been burned.[4] The same mechanism believed to underlie the floods in East Africa – a positive Indian Ocean Dipole – is thought to have contributed to the Australian bush fires by increasing the land's surface temperature and reducing rainfall, leading to chronically dry conditions. In December 2019 the all-time temperature record in Australia was broken twice. The previous record had been 40.3°C (104.5°F) recorded in 2013; then an average maximum of 40.9°C (105.6°F) was recorded on 27 December 2019, followed the next day by a new average maximum high of 41.9°C (107.4°F). By the end of the year, every state in Australia had recorded highs above 40°C (104°F). These high temperatures are strongly believed to be due to anthropogenic causes – the result of man-made climate change. High temperatures alone do not cause fires, but combined with record low levels of rain as at the end of 2019, the risk increases.[5]

Even before the impact of the fires could be assessed, the Australian government had issued a warning that ongoing drought conditions had led to 'a forecast unprecedented third consecutive year of falling production' in the country, with export earnings falling by 8 per cent. At the time of writing the full cost of the fires was unknown, but there is anecdotal evidence to suggest that cattle farmers were hit hardest. Many only just escaped from the inferno, and they were forced to leave their animals to die in the blaze. Despite models clearly predicting an earlier, hotter fire season as the global climate warms, analysis suggests that the impact of the fires was greater than anything scientific modelling had suggested. This shows two things: first the terrible extent of the recent fires, and second the complexity of accurately forecasting climatic models. However, a 2014 paper had predicted that extreme Indian Ocean Dipole events would begin to occur about three times more frequently than previously, about once every six years, instead of once every seventeen years.[6]

Torrential floods, annihilating fires. While the complexity of climate modelling makes it hard for scientists to say whether these two incidents were the direct result of global climate change or just aberrant spikes, all are agreed that there is no question that as our climate continues to change, there will be a rise in extreme weather incidents like these.

At the same time as East Africa was beset by floods and Australia by fire, the World Meteorological Organization (a specialized UN agency covering weather, climate and water resources) issued its state of the global climate report for the year 2019 looking back at change over the past decade.[7] It found that 2019 'concluded a decade of exceptional global heat, retreating ice and record sea levels driven by greenhouse gases from human activities', with average temperatures for the five-year period (2015–2019) and the ten-year period (2010–2019) almost certain to be the highest ever recorded. The year 2019 was declared the second hottest year on record – 2016 squeaked ahead by just 0.04°C (0.072°F) to hold the title. Between January and October 2019 the average global temperature was about 1°C (1.8°F) above pre-industrial levels. This is the baseline we compare anthropogenic climate change against; the Paris Agreement aims for a 1.5–2°C (2.7–3.6°F) increase compared to pre-industrial levels, giving us a maximum of 1°C (1.8°F) more to play with. Every decade has been warmer than the one preceding it since the 1980s. In short, there's a lot of data to tell us what we now know: that our planet is getting warmer.

Climate change, you will be unsurprised to learn, is one of the planetary boundaries (see Chapter Two, page 30) which we have already transgressed. It is measured through two metrics, one of which is rather complex and not directly related to food production and so I will not delve into it here. The other one is infamous: the concentration of carbon dioxide and equivalent greenhouse gases in the atmosphere. The boundary is set at about 350 parts per million; we are currently at over 415 parts per million. The quantities of greenhouse gases in the atmosphere affect how warm our planet is, which gave rise to the Paris Agreement's target that global temperatures should not rise more than 1.5–2°C (2.7–3.6°F). The zone of uncertainty extends between 350 and 450 parts per million: with carbon dioxide levels in this zone, what might happen next is unpredictable. However, unless you have been deliberately avoiding the news over recent years (and who would blame you?) you cannot help but notice that we have begun to experience the effects of pushing at this boundary.

A warmer planet changes the weather, increasing both extreme weather events such as floods and drought, but also abnormal, unreliable weather patterns. Farmers need to work in anticipation of the season to come, sowing seeds and adding nutrients at precise times. If weather patterns are skewed, they risk losing whole seasons of crops. We are already seeing this happening. For many decades, the number of people who went hungry every year declined. However, that trend stopped in 2015. Since then, the number of people going hungry each year has started to increase. By 2018, more than 820 million people in the world were still going hungry. Of the 33 countries which experienced a food crisis in 2018, climate variation and extreme weather was the main reason for the crisis in 12 of these, and a compounding factor in 14 more.[8]

So climate change can cause crops to be washed away by floods or landslides, or be burned to a crisp or simply fail due to unseasonal weather. As if that weren't enough, worrying research has suggested that changing the composition of gases in the atmosphere (by increasing the amount of carbon dioxide in the air) can also change how nutritious crops are. A meta-analysis showed that growing rice, wheat, maize, soybeans, peas and sorghum under conditions in which carbon dioxide is raised (designed to mimic the forecast carbon dioxide increase for the middle of this century) decreased the concentration of zinc and iron in some crops and the concentrations of protein in others. Two billion people already suffer from zinc and iron deficiencies, dramatically reducing life expectancy. Further reducing the nutritional quality of staple food crops can only lead to malnourishment and disease rising worldwide.[9]

So climate change risks affecting the world's food security. This is a political term which the United Nation's Food and Agriculture Organization (FAO) defines as 'a situation that exists when all people, at all times, have physical, social, and economic access to sufficient, safe, and nutritious food that meets their dietary needs and food preferences for an active and healthy life'. Food security means that there must be sufficient food and that people must be able to access it (overcoming economic and social barriers). It must also provide sufficient nutrition to enable a healthy life. That means that the available and accessible food should contain sufficient calories, but not too many, as well as essential micronutrients. Food security and social security are strongly tied together: nothing foments revolution like hungry bellies. Based on the risks posed by changing weather patterns, about a billion people are currently deemed 'food insecure': climate change is likely to directly affect their food supplies. For example, raised surface temperatures could reduce harvests of staple wholegrains such as rice and maize by 20 to 40 per cent in tropical and subtropical regions by 2100, irrespective of any potential catastrophic weather events.

In short, climate and food are intricately linked. Changes to our global climate and local weather patterns are going to make food production – especially in the quantities we need to produce it to feed ten billion mouths by 2050 – much harder. In Chapter Six, I touched on some of the ways in which raising livestock contributes to greenhouse gas production, which is partly through animal production itself, and partly the result of land-use changes to make space for them. In this chapter, I will look at other sources of protein to see how climate affects their production – and how producing them affects climate.

FISH AND OTHER SEAFOOD

There's nothing quite like your attitude to fish to help place the culture you come from. In Japan, seafood is a delicacy. The indoor fish market in Tokyo has become a tourist attraction, with visitors arriving before 5am for the chance to watch one of the world-famous tuna auctions. Over before most people get out of bed, these fierce auctions for the best specimens can raise the price of the prized fish to desperately expensive heights. For example, in early January 2019, Kiyoshi Kimura, the self-styled 'tuna king', paid over US$3 million for a single tuna in a tuna auction. It did weigh around 275kg, so it's still better value than an anchovy weight for weight, but it cost him US$11,000 per kilo of fish, including the bones, scales and organs. (When asked about the purchase, Mr Kimura said, 'It's an excellent tuna. However, I believe I did pay too much.')

However expensive the fish, Mr Kimura would not have had any trouble selling it: the Japanese are some of the biggest consumers of fish per person worldwide, an average of 45.5kg of fish per year.[10] Although fish consumption in Japan is high, the figures are dwarfed by Iceland's, where the average person eats about 90kg annually (that's equivalent to eating a portion of fish daily... except for the 85 days when you'd eat two portions). You might assume that Japan and Iceland eat a lot of fish because they're island nations but it's not quite that simple. For example, at the other end of the spectrum is Madagascar, where people eat an average of only 5.3kg of fish a year. Even Britain, traditionally a seafaring nation, has comparatively low figures, eating about half of what Japan gets through (19.7kg per person per year). Attitudes to seafood are determined by our culinary and cultural traditions, but research suggests that eating seafood – and especially fish rich in omega-3 oils – is one of the most important changes we can make to improve the quality of our diet.

Fish, like livestock, are complete protein sources, which provide all the health benefits discussed in the previous chapter. However, unlike land-based animals, many types of seafood also contain omega-3 fatty acids, which are extremely important for good health. There are three main omega-3 fatty acids: alpha-linolenic acid (ALA), eicosapentaenoic acid (EPA) and docosahexaenoic acid (DHA). ALA is mainly found in plant oils, but EPA and DHA are found in fish and other seafood. Of the three, ALA is an essential fatty acid: as with essential amino acids, there is no way our bodies can synthesize ALA, so we have to eat food containing it. However, we can convert ALA to EPA and DHA, although only in extremely small quantities. While ALA is the only truly essential fatty acid, the main source of all three is dietary.

The best dietary sources of omega-3 fatty acids are fatty fish such as tuna, trout or salmon, but they're also naturally present at much lower levels in meat such as beef, pork and poultry. In most Western countries meat supplies far more omega-3 fatty acids than fish, despite the difference in relative quantities contained in meat and fish, simply because we eat so much more meat than fish.[11]

So what are omega-3 fatty acids and why are they so crucial? If you cast your mind back to school biology, you might recall that every cell in the body is surrounded by a cell membrane, which is made of something called a phospholipid bilayer. The phospholipid bilayer is made up of phospholipid molecules which look like little two-tailed sperm. The head of a molecule is the phosphate group, which is hydrophilic (water-loving) and the two tails are the hydrophobic (water-hating) fatty acids. If you invert one of these molecules and place it below another you have the basis of a phospholipid bilayer, where the fatty, oily tails form a double barrier between the watery interior of the cell and the outside world (where, by contrast, the hydrophilic heads of the molecules can sit happily). In this rather ingenious way, the cell has control over what it can take in or out: no molecules can come into the cell by osmosis without meeting the fatty barrier and being repelled.

Omega-3 fatty acids are part of the cell membranes in all the tissues in the body, with especially high proportions in the brain, heart and the eyes' retinal cells. The body responds extremely fast to eating omega-3 fatty acids: there's a measurable change in the cell membranes a few days after eating them, which indicates the important role they play. Omega-3 fatty acids have also been shown to be extremely important in regulating cardiac rhythm, probably by enabling better control of the signalling molecules that can pass in and out of heart muscle cells via channels in the cell's membrane. Eating about two servings of fish containing omega-3 every week (about 2g of omega-3 fatty acids) is estimated to reduce the chance of dying from heart disease by around a third.[12] However, typical Western diets include far less than this – about 150mg daily, or one serving of fish every ten days. So fish is one of the food groups which the planetary health diet recommends that most of us (though perhaps not people in Iceland) consume more of, recommending that we eat up to 100g of fish daily. The Global Burden of Disease study which estimated the harms of a diet low in wholegrain carbohydrate also found that a diet low in seafood containing omega-3 fatty acids was responsible for almost two million deaths annually, predominantly due to cardiovascular disease.[13] Fish is a bit of a one-hit wonder, nutritionally speaking: it provides both essential fat and protein. It's no surprise that societies which traditionally eat a lot of fish are among the longest-lived in the world.

But if we want to eat more fish, we run into a difficulty. The familiar saying, 'there's plenty more fish in the sea', has become a bit outdated.

THERE'S NOT SO MUCH FISH IN THE SEA

If you had been an inmate in an American prison in the 1800s, you could have expected to be fed on lobster. This is not because 19th-century prisons were kinder compared to their latter-day counterparts – far from it – but because there were so many lobsters that they were one of the cheapest foods available. In fact some early American colonies had laws against feeding lobster to prisoners more than once a week, seeing it as cruel and unusual punishment. Lobster fishing did not require traps: one simply waded in and grabbed however many one wanted; a contemporary account describes the situation as one of 'unbelievable abundance'.[14]

A sea teeming with fish is what we have historically expected of our ocean waters. Take for example the Canadian Grand Banks fishery off the coast of Newfoundland. A fishery is an area of ocean where fish are caught, not where they're farmed: the Grand Banks fishery is the name of an area of ocean where fish were caught in abundance. In 1497 the Italian explorer Giovanni Caboto (also known by his Anglicized name John Cabot) wrote that the sea there was so full of cod that a man 'could walk across their backs'. Catching cod was a simple matter of scooping them from the water with baskets. A century later English fishermen wrote testily about how difficult it was to row to the shore through the thick shoals of fish. Even as recently as the 1950s marine researchers published a book entitled *The Inexhaustible Sea*, saying that the ocean was a resource 'beyond the limits of our imagination'.[15]

Unfortunately, we know how this story ends. Lobster is now a luxury, served at white-tableclothed restaurants for more than £40. The Grand Banks fishery was so depleted by overfishing that it closed in 1992, putting 40,000 people out of work. And estimates of current fish stocks show that the oceans are far emptier than they used to be. A recent report by a UN agency found that about a third of the marine fish stocks in the world are being harvested at unsustainable levels, and 60 per cent were at maximum capacity (which means that no more can be caught if the fish population is to remain stable). In the whole world, only 7 per cent of oceans were underfished.[16]

Thanks in large part to technological advances, we are catching vast quantities of fish every year. In 2015, that came to around 94 million tonnes of seafood annually,[17] enough for just under 19 billion meals of fish and chips (as long as you don't mind a lot of variation in what you count as fish). This is mainly because of the ways we're catching fish. One of the most efficient and harmful fishing techniques is trawl fishing. When trawling, boats throw a huge, heavy net overboard weighted down with a chain. The net hits the seabed and is dragged along it by the slowly moving boat above, engulfing everything in its path. Not only is this type of fishing unselective, it also damages the ocean floor and marine environment: it has been likened to hunting for squirrels with a bulldozer.

Wild fisheries are managed by target catches, which give fishermen quotas for the number of fish of a particular size and species they can catch. The problem is that the fish involved don't know about this, and do not come forward in an orderly queue. So any fishing net is likely to catch more than one species, with the rest of the fish being known as bycatch (or, if the unwanted fish are thrown overboard rather than taken back to land, discard). Some fishing methods accrue more bycatch than others.

A 2019 report by the FAO estimated that about 9.1 million tonnes of fish were discarded – about 10 per cent of the world's total catch (although because of the difficulty of assessing the weight of fish thrown away, the number ranges between 6.7 and 16.1 million tonnes).[18] While it's not exactly accurate because of the number of species and their variable weight, it's helpful to think of one in every ten fish caught being discarded as the 'wrong' species – either illegal (because it's protected, endangered or exceeds the quota) or unsellable. Unsurprisingly, those fisheries which target bottom-feeding fish such as crustaceans had the highest discard rates, compared with those which aim to catch open-water fish such as tuna: there's simply more on the bottom of the ocean to catch accidentally. Of the discarded species, about 20 million individual animals were estimated to be endangered, threatened or protected (although again exact numbers are hard to come by). Estimates suggest that these included a million seabirds, 650,000 marine mammals such as porpoises and dolphins, 8.5 million turtles and ten million sharks. And this is the best-case estimate: other researchers suggest that about a third of the world's fish catch is illegal, unreported or unregulated. So it is extremely difficult to estimate the damage already done by the industry.

Such indiscriminate fishing damages everything, including the long-term sustainability of the industry, because it prevents the natural regeneration of fish stocks. If too many fish are taken, or too many young fish are removed, the population won't be able to recover. Indiscriminate harvesting also affects the regeneration of the marine environment. All the animals and plants living there contribute to a thriving and healthy ecosystem, which in turn increases the ecosystem's resilience and ability to regenerate. In short, such fishing methods are lose-lose for both the fish and the long-term viability of the fishing industry.

The good news is that many initiatives are now under way to change large-scale trawl fishing, based on innovations and zoological research. To take one example, cod and haddock often swim in the same areas and and at the same depth of the ocean. Indiscriminate fishing catches both but discards any fish not within a specific quota, leading to great waste. Fortunately, research into the behaviours of different species of fish when they're tired have resulted in a variety of ingenious trawl net adaptations.

Trawl nets effectively chase fish across the ocean, catching them when they're exhausted and unable to escape the net's confines. But haddock and cod behave differently when they're tired. Haddock swim up towards the surface, whereas cod go deeper. By designing a trawl net with two tails, one at the top of the net and one at the bottom, fishermen can effectively segregate the catch, as the tired haddock accumulate in the top portion and the tired cod in the bottom. If their fishing quota is for cod, they can leave a hole in the top portion of the net, allowing the haddock to pass through the top portion, but continuing to accumulate cod in the bottom. While not perfect, it's an easy way of reducing bycatch, especially as it requires no work by the fishermen. Other methods involve inserting square metal grilles into the net which hold their shape underwater, allowing fish segregation by size (and also releasing juveniles), or adding 'dark panels' of mesh which trigger some species' natural flight responses.

Changing the way in which we catch fish has been proven to work. In 2017 the Marine Stewardship Council (MSC) certified that the North Sea cod fishery was sustainable, after local fishermen implemented changes such as these. This revived the fishery from near collapse, after the stocks plummeted by 84 per cent between the 1970s and 2006. So with careful management improvements can and have been made. Along with multiple resources showing which fish are sustainable when caught in certain regions, and certification programmes such as the MSC blue tick (which indicates that the fish has been caught sustainably), we can continue to enjoy the fish we need for our health without further depleting the world's wild fisheries. It is worth noting, however, that the North Sea cod fishery lost its MSC certification in 2019, just two years after its recovery. Sustainable fishing practices are not just a means to an end; they are the way in which we must fish in the future in order to continue to enjoy eating fish.

FARMING OR HARMING?

The other option is to eat farmed fish. Fish farming, or aquaculture, is a rapidly growing industry. In 2013, aquaculture overtook wild fish catches as a means of providing seafood for the first time, and since then the proportion of farmed fish has expanded. The most recent data shows that we farmed a stunning 106 million tonnes of seafood in 2015 – and that number has probably risen since. It's hard to imagine how much this is, especially because seafood varies in size so much, so let's think of it in terms of an animal whose size we can understand more easily: elephants. We farmed the biomass equivalent of about 18 million elephants in the oceans in 2015. Fish farming is a growing and profitable industry. Including the farming of aquatic plants, aquaculture is the fastest growing industry in agriculture – in 2016 it was valued at around US$243.5 billion, about the same value as the entire GDP of Finland at the time.[19]

But farming fish does not address the problem of declining wild fish stocks. There are several challenges, most of which are potentially surmountable by technological innovations – and one which is much harder to solve.

The less difficult problems are similar to those of rearing livestock. First, fish farming, like animal farming, brings together high densities of animals in close proximity, which allows the spread of disease. Infectious microbial disease spreads rampantly through aquaculture, resulting in losses of about US$6 billion a year. The problem is worse for some species: for example disease is believed to kill a staggering 40 per cent of farmed shrimp, with Shrimp Early Mortality Syndrome threatening to collapse production in Asian countries.[20]

The answer to the rise of disease cannot simply be the widespread use of preventative antibiotics, as this encourages the rise of antibiotic-resistant bacterial strains with terrible implications for both human and animal health. Instead we need to find healthier ways to farm these species. Caring for sick fish is also much harder than caring for sick land-based animals. Say you have a certain number of sick fish in a tank: do you add a medication to the water and hope it's at the right concentration to heal the fish that are ill, while not harming those that are healthy? And how do you prevent illness through preventative measures such as vaccines? While this raises some bizarre mental images, the answer to the latter question is that manual fish vaccines are one means of preventing disease. It's a slow, difficult, expensive and – one imagines – frustratingly slippery process. And of course it only works with large fin fish (can you imagine trying to individually vaccinate crayfish or mussels?). The problem of disease, both its prevention and cure, is believed to be the main barrier we need to overcome if we are to scale up aquaculture to meet the rising demand.

The second problem is what to feed the fish. At the moment aquaculture is a cannibalistic process, heavily reliant on fishmeal and fish oil as food for farming fish. Fishmeal is described as a 'brown flour' which is made from the inedible offcuts of fish as well as dried whole fish. These products provide all the nutrients that fish need to grow and thrive in the perfect proportions, and hence are extremely efficient as feed. While most of the fish used for making fishmeal and fish oil is described by the FAO as 'not marketable' as human food, this very much depends on where in the world you live. In Western countries the fish is not saleable and so is turned into these by-products, whereas in low- and middle-income countries the same fish is eaten by humans. There are widespread concerns that we are depleting wild fish stocks in order to farm fish.

Again there are possible solutions to this problem on the horizon, but they come with certain challenges. For example, new companies are trying to establish farmed insects as a high-protein, low-impact replacement for fish feed: after all, as anyone who's seen a stereotyped picture of a fisherman knows, fish can't resist a worm on the end of a hook.[21] However, there are some concerns about introducing insects into a food chain which ends up feeding us, especially those insects which feed on decaying organic matter.[22] There are also doubts about whether producing insects on the huge scale needed to make them viable sources of protein can ever be sustainable. Giving fish plant-based food is another option, but as with soybeans, scaling up vegetable protein production comes with a price tag.

A third problem is that farming some species of fish causes far more harm than good. Farming prawns and other crustaceans has one of the highest environmental footprints of any food. It has the second highest level of carbon emissions per 1,000 calories of any food: producing 1,000 calories of prawns emits 26kg of carbon dioxide and equivalent gases (lower than producing beef, which leads with 36kg produced per 1,000 calories).[23] This is because such calculations take into account the whole life cycle of the food, including clearing habitats. Crustacean farming is one of the main drivers of mangrove deforestation and it has been likened to slash-and-burn Amazonian destruction. This does not mean that prawn farming can never be sustainable, but it does mean that such farms need to be closely monitored and regulated to ensure that they are run in a sustainable way.

None of the problems facing fish farming are insurmountable, especially as solutions are likely be a mixture of different approaches. What is problematic is what we do about the effects of climate change on our oceans. We do not have a solution to this yet because as oceans begin to change, we risk making them inhospitable for any fish, whether they are farmed or wild.

UNCHARTED WATERS: THE EFFECTS OF CLIMATE CHANGE ON OUR OCEANS

Oscar Wilde once quipped that to lose one parent may be regarded as misfortune, but to lose both looks like carelessness. Similarly, for a fisherman to not be able to find one fish is unlucky; to not be able to find any fish looks like carelessness. But this is what is happening all round the world, and it is a function of warming waters.

The ocean absorbs more than 90 per cent of the excess heat produced as climate change warms the world. At the same time, the oceans' temperatures rise too. These were recorded at their highest ever levels in 2019.[24] And as the waters warm, fish migrate in search of cooler climes: some of the world's first climate refugees. Generally speaking marine life has been observed to be travelling towards higher latitudes – in the direction of the north and south poles – where waters are cooler.

This has given rise to some surprising catches; for example, in Portugal fishing fleets found 18 new species between 2011 and 2016, of which 12 are normally found only in the subtropics or tropical waters.[25] However, while the Portuguese might have been pleased to be landing fish such as bullet tuna, they are likely to be dismayed by the decline in their traditional catches of mackerel, pilchard, cuttlefish, octopus and crustaceans. Some of these were caught in different places, for example, there was a significant rise in octopi caught in traps close to the shore, although trawlers caught them less often. But changing types and distribution of fish can have economic consequences for fishermen: if they have invested in buying a boat and managing a mackerel fishing operation, then they are not equipped for landing other species. And if they catch them they may find that no one will buy them. It is not only animals who struggle to adapt to some of the implications of climate change – this is just one example of the type of food insecurity which climate change brings with it.

There are similar stories all round the world. For example, in Greenland, fish accounts for a staggering 96 per cent of its total exports, with prawns alone making up 45 per cent of all exports.[26] The prawn fisheries were traditionally off the south west corner of Greenland, but have in recent years been moving steadily north. While they can be tracked, the prawns are starting to reach areas which have never been fished before, meaning both that catching them is trickier in unknown waters but doing so may also be potentially more damaging for the virgin marine environment. However, the economic consequences of losing the prawn fishery are inconceivable for the country. Greenland is working with the MSC to address these issues. Other countries are not so responsible, or will not be able to afford to take such considered measures.

Migrating fish and strange new catches are part of a larger problem. When oceans warm this changes the waters' chemistry, making it act in strange and unpredictable new ways. To understand the extent of this fully, I will have to delve into some natural science which is critical for understanding the threat that climate change poses to how the world fits together as a single earth system.

The oceans are by far the largest feature of earth. They cover about 70 per cent of the surface. As well as being home to many animals, larders for us and others, a means of transport and the inspiration behind a million holiday daydreams, they also play a vital role in regulating the earth system. For example, oceans store more carbon than anything else on the planet: 95 per cent to be precise. That's 38,000 gigatonnes of carbon, or about 70 times more carbon than is contained in all living organisms on the planet.[27] By way of comparison, there are only about 700 gigatonnes of carbon in the atmosphere.

As we have increased the amount of carbon dioxide we emit into the atmosphere as a result of our various activities, the ocean has systematically absorbed it. It's estimated that our seas have absorbed about half of all human emissions for the past 200 years. But the seas cannot absorb an infinitely increasing quantity of carbon dioxide without there being some chemical consequences. Increasing quantities of dissolved carbon dioxide in the ocean change it: the waters become more acidic. And this has many serious consequences, both for marine life and for our fight against global warming. Ocean acidification is in fact another planetary boundary; as it's not directly affected by our food production, I haven't mentioned it earlier. But it is directly tied to global warming via the quantity of carbon dioxide in the atmosphere.

First things first: why does a high concentration of carbon dioxide in the atmosphere make our waters more acidic – and what does that mean? First, it does not mean that you will emerge from your sea dip in 2050 as a gleaming, grinning skeleton. Bear with me for some simple chemistry to understand this. Hydrogen, the most abundant element in the universe, is also the simplest. As an atom, its nucleus consists of a single proton (which has a charge of +1) and a single electron (a charge of −1). As an atom it is stable and has a charge of 0, with the two charges balancing each other out. When it loses its electron it becomes unbalanced. In this state it is known as a hydrogen ion, and has a charge of +1. Acidity, also known as pH, is a chemical measure of how many hydrogen ions there are in a solution. The more hydrogen ions there are, the more acidic the solution is. Acidity is therefore a sliding scale, based on how many hydrogen ions there are in a solution, ranging from weak acids such as vinegar, which you can spill on your hands without hurting them, to strong acids such as hydrochloric acid, which you really can't.

At the opposite end of the scale from strongly acidic solutions are strongly alkali solutions. These solutions have a high concentration of hydroxide ions, which is an oxygen and hydrogen atom bound together. Hydroxide ions carry a single negative charge, and so are written OH^-. So it shouldn't surprise you that the product of a hydroxide ion and hydrogen ion, otherwise known as water (H_2O), is neutral: the single positive H^+ and single negative OH^- cancel each other out.

The strongest acids have a pH of 0 and the strongest alkalis have a pH of 14; the level depends on the relative ratios of the different ions. More H^+ means more acidic, more OH^- means more alkaline. However, it's important to note that this is a logarithmic scale: simply put that means that the number of hydrogen ions between pH1 and 2 are not doubled; instead they differ by a magnitude of 10. So the difference in hydrogen ion concentration between pH0 and 7 is huge: there are 10x10x10x10x10x10x10 (10 million) times more hydrogen ions at pH0 than there are pH7 (this matters later on, I promise). Many different substances which we encounter routinely have different levels of acidity. For example, lemon juice is a weak acid, with a pH of around 2; black coffee has a pH of around 5. Water and blood are neutral at 7; bleach is a strong alkali at around 13.

Seawater is a weak alkali, with a pH of around 8, although this varies between areas of ocean and depends on depth. Because there is no barrier between the ocean and the atmosphere, the waters of the sea are free to absorb whatever is in the air, which includes carbon dioxide. When carbon dioxide dissolves in the water, it forms a weak acid (carbonic acid). Under normal circumstances, because seawater is usually mildly alkaline, the weak carbonic acid is neutralized.

However, because there is now such a high concentration of carbon dioxide in the air, the oceans' ability to neutralize this acidity is declining. In total, marine biologists estimate that the ocean's pH has dropped by about 0.1. This sounds almost laughably small until you consider that pH is measured on a different scale. In reality this means there are about 30 per cent more acidic hydrogen ions in the ocean than there were in pre-industrial times. If our atmosphere's carbon dioxide levels continue to rise as forecast, the oceans will continue to become more acidic, with the pH potentially dropping by as much as 0.5 by 2100: this is a 300 per cent increase in hydrogen ions – or the difference in acidity between vinegar and honey.

As with climate change, it's hard to predict exactly what effect increasing acidification will have on our oceans, but there's no doubt that it will set off a series of chain reactions that will have widespread implications for marine life. For a start, all the animals that make hard shells in the oceans, from corals to cockles, will be affected. This is because these shells are made of alkaline calcium carbonate. Studies have shown that increasingly acidic waters will make it much harder for those animals with shells to build them.[28]

This will have a huge impact on the marine environment. Let's take coral reefs as an example. Coral reefs are unique ecosystems which house thousands of species. From just a human perspective they're economically extremely important. About 500 million people worldwide depend on reefs for work, food and coastal defences, and the value of this worldwide is estimated at about US$7 trillion.[29] They're made from colonies of hundreds of thousands of individual coral polyps. In tropical and subtropical waters these

tiny animals build calcium carbonate exoskeletons to form spec-
tacularly colourful reefs. Acidifying water slows or stops the coral
building their skeletons to make reefs. Worse, some research has
shown that waters are already so acidic that corals in some parts
of the ocean are actively being dissolved. The acidity combined
with warming waters, which also have an impact on reefs, means
that we may lose them altogether. Depressing research suggests
that if the world's temperature increases by only 1.5°C (2.7°F) –
the best-case scenario – we may lose up to 90 per cent of our coral
reefs; if the temperature increases by 2°C (3.6°F) – still considered
a good outcome, according to the Paris Agreement – we'll probably lose 99 per cent of them.[30] In short, reefs look set to become
extinct in our lifetime.

And increasing acidity doesn't just affect corals. Sea butterflies
are a type of swimming snail. Unlike their earth-bound counterparts, these molluscs flap around the ocean using the feet which
protrude from the base of their shells as wings. As you'd expect
from the name, they're delicate and attractive animals. Experiments
predicted that acidifying waters might affect the resilience of their
shells, but scientists were unsure (oceanic chemistry is complex)
until they found specimens in the Southern Ocean, near Antarctica,
which had far weaker, partly dissolved shells.[31] Water samples taken
at the same time as the butterflies were found show that that part of
the ocean was especially acidic at the time. Researchers have called
these findings the canary in the coal mine of ocean acidification:
one of the authors of the study that discovered this effect wrote: 'we
did not expect to see [sea butterflies] being affected to this extent'.

In short, the effects of ocean acidification are coming faster and
harder than we expected and this has knock-on implications for our
food systems. Coral reefs and microorganisms are the basis of many
of the ocean's food chains. Like the world itself, no single change in
the ocean happens without consequences reflected elsewhere.

But there's also not much we can do about it. A Royal Society
report cheerfully notes that 'ocean acidification is essentially irreversible during our lifetimes'.[32] We don't know exactly what effect

this will have on the marine environment, but we do know that it has serious implications for global warming.

The quantity of carbon dioxide water can absorb depends on its temperature and acidity. Warmer waters absorb carbon dioxide at a slower rate than colder waters. So polar regions can take up more carbon dioxide than tropical regions. This means two things. First, polar regions are becoming more acidic faster than warmer regions elsewhere in the world, and tropical waters are now releasing carbon dioxide into the atmosphere instead of absorbing it.[33]

The planetary boundary for ocean acidification uses ion concentration as a measure; the boundary is set at an acidity equal to or more than 80 per cent of the pre-industrial concentration of carbonite ions, and we're currently estimated to be at 84 per cent. So far, this is one boundary we have not exceeded. But it is almost certainly one we will exceed, because it is directly tied to atmospheric carbon dioxide levels. Several components dictate how much carbon dioxide waters can absorb. The biggest is temperature – warmer waters absorb more carbon dioxide than colder waters – and the others are ocean currents, biological activity and acidity. All these factors can differ in the same area of ocean, depending on depth, so we can't predict for certain exactly how the oceans will respond. But warming, acidifying oceans that stop being carbon sinks and instead start adding to the quantity of carbon dioxide in the atmosphere, along with changing, vanishing or dissolving marine life, is yet another compelling reason (as if we needed one) we need to get climate change under control. And one of the ways we can do that is by looking at which foods contribute directly to climate change.

NEW NORMALS

Anyone who has travelled out of their comfort zone in another country can attest to just how relative the concept of normal is. My personal revelation came in the large city of Xiamen in southern China, where I was giving a talk at a conference. After it ended, my hosts took me on a tour of the city, finishing at a beautiful rooftop restaurant overlooking the sparkling waters of the South China Sea. The restaurant served an extremely fancy buffet. Not only did I have no idea what most of the dishes were, as I don't speak Chinese I had no way of asking. Instead, I asked my hosts to pick their favourites for me to try. They returned to the table with plates piled high with mainly unrecognizable delicacies – and one dish which I instantly recognized. I had always thought that eating chicken's feet was something of a stereotype; I certainly did not expect that they would be served to me in a swanky restaurant by proud hosts. I nibbled gingerly on a jellied claw – the nail was still attached – as visions of crippled British pigeons came unbidden to mind, trying not to gag. I can't remember anything about the taste or texture – it could well have been very nice – but I just couldn't get over my strong preconceived inhibitions.

Cultural preconceptions are at their most evident in the foods we consider normal. Often taking an alternative perspective in the same way as a foreigner to the culture, makes us see them differently. Dairy products are considered normal by the Western world but are alien to vast swathes of the rest of the world's population.

People in many cultures don't eat dairy products and many people can't digest them – about 68 per cent of adults. The ability to digest milk and milk-derived products is a function of your genetic background, so lactose intolerance varies around the world: about 4 per cent of Danish people are lactose intolerant compared to almost 100 per cent of Chinese people.[34] As babies and young children, we all have the ability to digest milk, thanks to an enzyme called lactase which neatly snips lactose – the sugar in milk – into two further sugars, glucose and galactose, which we can digest. This is vital for us get the nutrition we need from our mother's milk. However, as we grow older, our bodies make less and less of this enzyme. This makes sense: given that we biologically need to drink milk only while feeding as an infant, what's the point of expending costly energy on building an enzyme that we don't use?

However, around 7,500 years ago, a single genetic mutation in Hungary changed that. This mutation enabled the enzyme lactase to continue being made throughout life and so allowed the adults who carried it to digest milk. For people whose cultures developed alongside domesticated cattle, this mutation offered a huge benefit: suddenly they could drink milk and receive all the nutritional benefits of dairy products rather than stomachache. The mutation conferred such an advantage that it's possible to track global human migration using the lactase gene signature. It spread to become predominant in northern Europe and the parts of the world populated from this region. This ability to drink milk as an adult is known as lactase persistence, and the term is perhaps more useful in the Western world than referring to the inability to digest milk as lactose intolerance.

So why did lactase persistence persist? It's because dairy produce is such a good source of so many vital nutrients – protein, fat and calcium. I've already discussed the importance of protein for our health, as well as the fact that fats are a vital component of our diet (see Chapter Four, page 79). Calcium, as every school child knows, is vital for building healthy teeth and bones: there is more calcium in your body than any other mineral. Insufficient quantities of calcium can cause rickets in children or osteomalacia in adults – poor growth of soft bones that can lead to bone deformities. Calcium is also vital for regulating muscle contractions (which are extremely important when, for example, the muscle that is contracting makes your heart beat), and for ensuring that our blood forms a neat clot on our skin when we cut ourselves. In addition to all this, dairy produce gives us an additional nutritional benefit by supplying our gut with tons of interesting bacteria from its fermented forms, yoghurt and cheese. I covered the importance of bacteria for our health in much greater detail in Chapter Five (see page 123), but it's worth noting here that yoghurt adverts which stress the importance of friendly bacteria are right: our health depends, in part, on hosting a thriving community of bacterial cells. Because yoghurt and cheese rely on bacteria for fermentation, they are an important source of dietary bacteria.

Assuming that you can digest dairy products, many Western nutritional guidelines suggest you eat about three servings a day, a serving being about a cup of milk (approximately 240ml) or 40g of cheese (many guidelines use an index finger's length of cheese as a guide, although it depends on how thickly you cut the slice). Most of these guidelines are informed by the need to consume the recommended daily allowance of calcium, although the optimum daily calcium intake varies depending on who you consult. The USA recommends 1,200mg per day, whereas the World Health Organization recommends 500mg per day. The UK comes in between, with a recommended 700mg daily, which the planetary health diet supports: if the diet is followed fully then it provides about 718mg of calcium daily.

The key here is to note that the planetary health diet does not assume that dairy is your only source of calcium. It recommends that about 153 calories a day come from dairy produce – about 250ml a day of whole milk or 40g of Cheddar cheese. This would give you about 300mg of calcium from dairy sources. The remaining 400mg or so comes from eating the rest of the diet, because although dairy produce provides many nutritional benefits, none of them are irreplaceable: we can get all the nutritional contributions we need from other sources. This is easy to grasp for the macronutrients such as fat and protein, as we don't think of dairy produce as being the primary source of these, but less so for a micronutrient such as calcium. But calcium is found in many different foods: good sources include green, leafy vegetables such as broccoli and cabbage, legumes (especially soy and calcium-set tofu), nuts and some kinds of fish, especially when eaten with their bones as with tinned salmon. If we eat a varied diet in the proportions recommended by the planetary health diet we will get at least the required amounts of calcium that we need, if not more.

To put it differently, dairy produce is a 'nice to have', not a 'must have'. While this is evident from the fact that dairy products are indigestible for almost two-thirds of the people in the world, it's harder to grasp in countries where eating them is standard. But like me when faced with a steaming pile of chicken feet and proud, happy hosts, we need to learn that normal is a relative concept.

Embracing new versions of normal is key to the planetary health diet. Although it does not require a big adjustment, the diet still represents a change from 'normal' Western eating. The change is most evident in the recommendations for quantities of animal-derived foods, both meat and other products. This change might seem daunting at first, but there are two important points to consider. First, it's important to realize that the adjustments aren't as hard as they might initially seem to be. For example, 250g of dairy produce a day would allow you to have milk in your coffee or tea (5ml) and a bowl of cereal with milk (125ml) for breakfast, a sandwich with cheese in it (40g) for lunch and even a burrito for dinner (25g grated cheese), with 55g left over as an allowance for buttering bread, or milk for extra coffees throughout the day. This is not an especially restrictive eating plan: it just means being aware of your choices throughout the day. There are also compromises you can make to ensure you still eat your favourite things: if you love ice cream but you're not fussed about what goes in your coffee, you can choose a plant-based alternative milk and pick a different sandwich at lunch. I will examine this in more detail in Chapter Eight (see page 215), which gives specific dietary suggestions.

The second reason it's important to make small adjustments to create a dietary new normal is that we really do not want to have to adjust to a new normal that does not lie within our control. The latter would be what climate change represents. While humans are almost infinitely adaptable creatures – witness how dramatically ways of living changed during the COVID-19 pandemic – we cannot experience continuous extremes of weather, failed crops and dried up water tables without there being conflict, starvation and drought. Reducing our consumption of animal-based products is one of the single biggest changes we can make in a personal effort to stave off an uncertain future marked by environmental change. Making this change has an impact on a multitude of planetary boundaries at once: for example, it reduces both greenhouse gas emissions and land-use change, and in so doing allows more resources to go into the production of other foods which contain the same nutrients but use far fewer resources. Nowhere is this clearer than if we move from getting our protein predominantly from animal-based products to a mixture of animal and vegetable sources. Let's look at why the change matters so much.

NOT ALL PROTEIN IS CREATED EQUAL

In the previous chapter, I looked at how much land it takes to get equivalent amounts of protein in grams from meat and vegetable-based sources. I also looked at the huge quantities of greenhouse gases which result from raising livestock. Animal-based products in all their forms have a far larger impact on the earth than vegetable-based protein.

By way of illustration, think about the 100ml of milk you pour over your cereal every morning. Taking into account every aspect of producing that milk (land needed for production, by-products of farming, providing nutrients, processing, packaging, transport and retail costs), it generated 300g of carbon dioxide equivalents (if all greenhouse gases normalized to carbon dioxide). But if you had decided to drink soy milk instead, even taking into account the land-use change of soy plantations, that 100ml of milk would have produced just under 100g of carbon dioxide equivalents. Dairy milk produces approximately three times the greenhouse gas emissions of soy milk, mainly due to the methane emissions of cows.[35] You could argue that comparing soy milk to dairy milk is a narrow, specific comparison – and you'd be right. There are a plethora of other milk alternatives – oat, almond, coconut, rice, hemp – and for each of these many brands which all use varying quantities of the base plant in question. But while the exact numbers differ, growing all the base plants produces fewer carbon dioxide equivalent emissions than dairy produce. (As a side note: picking exactly which plant-based milk is the best is a tricky, contested subject, as it depends very much on the metric you use to define best – including nutritional contributions. Soy milk is generally held to have the most similar nutritional profile to dairy milk which is why I chose it for this comparison.)

The problem with comparing plant- and animal-based foods is that all plant-based foods produce dramatically fewer emissions than animal-based foods, even when you consider different foods as a source of protein. As discussed in the last two chapters, eating meat and fish bring their own health benefits, but when just based on getting the requisite amount of protein in our diets, it is hard to make a case for the sheer quantities of animal-based foods we eat.

Take for example, tofu, made from the protein-containing legume soy, and compare its relative production harms to that of, for example, chicken. Producing 100g of protein from chicken leads to an average production of 4.3kg of greenhouse gas emissions (these figures account for the entire lifecycle of the chicken production, including emissions caused by land-use change for growing feed and housing the birds, and so they vary depending on how the chicken is reared). Producing an equivalent quantity of protein from tofu (so as to not include soy which is used as cattle feed), only creates 1.6kg of carbon dioxide equivalent. And that number keeps getting lower for other types of plant-based protein: it's only 650 *grams* for beans, and due to how they're produced, nuts actually absorb greenhouse gas emissions, making their total greenhouse gas emissions a negative number, –800g. (This is because nut trees are often grown on former cropland – the nut trees remove and store carbon dioxide from the air, and displace whatever carbon-dioxide-emitting crops grew there previously.)

I have not cherry-picked these comparisons. In fact, chicken is one of the least greenhouse gas-emitting animal sources of protein. Beef tops the chart, producing 25kg of carbon dioxide equivalent gases per 100g of protein. (Depending on how the cattle are raised, beef has one of the widest ranges of emissions – from as high as 105kg of gas produced per 100g of protein to merely 9kg.) Lamb comes second, producing an average of 20kg of carbon dioxide equivalents per 100g of protein.

How does the carbon footprint of protein-rich foods compare?[36]

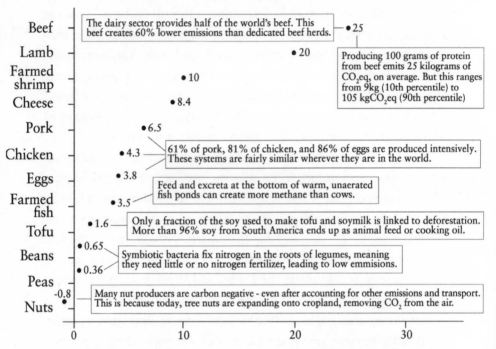

The dairy sector provides half of the world's beef. This beef creates 60% lower emissions than dedicated beef herds.

Producing 100 grams of protein from beef emits 25 kilograms of CO_2eq, on average. But this ranges from 9kg (10th percentile) to 105 kgCO_2eq (90th percentile)

61% of pork, 81% of chicken, and 86% of eggs are produced intensively. These systems are fairly similar wherever they are in the world.

Feed and excreta at the bottom of warm, unaerated fish ponds can create more methane than cows.

Only a fraction of the soy used to make tofu and soymilk is linked to deforestation. More than 96% soy from South America ends up as animal feed or cooking oil.

Symbiotic bacteria fix nitrogen in the roots of legumes, meaning they need little or no nitrogen fertilizer, leading to low emmisions.

Many nut producers are carbon negative - even after accounting for other emissions and transport. This is because today, tree nuts are expanding onto cropland, removing CO_2 from the air.

Beef – • 25
Lamb – • 20
Farmed shrimp – • 10
Cheese – • 8.4
Pork – • 6.5
Chicken – • 4.3
Eggs – • 3.8
Farmed fish – • 3.5
Tofu – • 1.6
Beans – • 0.65
Peas – • 0.36
-0.8
Nuts •–

Median greenhouse gas emissions per 100 grams of protein
(kilograms of carbon dioxide equivalents; kgCO_2eq)

This graph shows the median greenhouse gas emissions from protein-rich foods per 100g of protein across a global sample of 38,700 commercially viable farms in 119 countries. 75 per cent of protein production creates between -3 and 11kgCO_2eq per 100g protein, while the remaining 25 per cent (between 11 and 250kgCO_2eq) generates 70 per cent of emissions from protein. In total, this is equivalent to 5 billion tonnes of CO_2eq – this is more than the EU's *total* emissions.

Every animal-based source of protein, including fish, cheese and eggs, contributes a larger quantity of greenhouse gas emissions than an equivalent quantity of vegetable-based protein. And so when it comes to meeting our nutritional needs, it is starkly clear that we can get as much protein as we need without eating as many animal-based products as we do.

And it's not just greenhouse gases that eating fewer animal-based products affect. A 2015 European analysis found that total protein intake per person from meat, eggs and dairy produce in the EU has increased by 50 per cent since 1961 (and is 70 per cent higher than we need). The analysis found that if Europeans ate just half of the meat that they currently do, they would still be eating more protein than they actually need. This would lower greenhouse gas emissions from agriculture by up to 40 per cent, reduce soy imports to Europe by 76 per cent, increase the area of land available for growing cereal crops or reforestation, and reduce nitrogen pollution by about 40 per cent. In short, eating fewer animal products brings about many benefits across a range of planetary boundaries.[37]

BETTER FOR EVERYTHING

Thinking of the world as a single interconnected system, it should be clear that reducing the quantity of finite resources we use to produce one type of food frees those resources to produce another food – one which could potentially provide equivalent or more calories with less impact. In the European example above, the authors calculated that the area of land that could be freed up if we reduced meat consumption in Europe by 50 per cent would allow Europe to raise its grain exports from five million tonnes to 170 million tonnes, if all the land was used to grow cereal crops.

In another example, one of the recommendations of the planetary health diet is that we should all eat more fruit and vegetables. However, growing more fruit and vegetables is water-intensive. We'd need to increase the water available to allow everyone on earth to eat their (minimum) five a day. That can only be done if we free up some water globally by eating fewer water-demanding foods such as red meat and cheese, and divert that water to growing fruit and vegetables.

Climate change is already beginning to have an impact on our lives in ways that we can witness – extremes of weather around the world – and ways we can't, for example, dissolving marine life. In a complex interconnected system, pushing these boundaries has many unexpected effects, and some of them are harmful. If we can make a difference to these by eating fewer animal-based sources of protein, it seems pretty clear that we should. Not only would that be better for the planet, it would also be better for us. And that would free up resources which would allow us to feed more people, which we need to do as the world's population increases. This would be a win-win situation. Now let's see how we can do it.

CHAPTER 8

THE WORLD ON YOUR PLATE

This is a transition. Let us be patient and impatient with ourselves.

CHRISTIANA FIGUERES

London is a city of around nine million people, and at peak rush hour, it can feel like they're all in the same train as you. The underground transport system originally built in the mid-1800s has grown to accommodate a staggering number of passengers passing through it every day. Transport for London (TfL), the authority in charge of the city's public transport network, estimates that around five million journeys are taken on the underground every day. And that's just the underground. TfL's network extends across the whole city, encompassing buses, trains, trams, cabs – even the city's singular cable car (which serves more as amusement for commuters than transport).

Any advertising campaign that TfL carries across its many different forms of transport reaches a huge audience of many millions a day. TfL has been able to use this gigantic reach to its advantage in dictating advertising terms. For example, the network no longer allows adverts which it believes will lead to body shaming – those in which an advertiser presents an unrealistic body image in an attempt to sell their product. A protein powder advert which featured a slim, toned woman in perhaps the original itsy-bitsy teeny-weeny yellow bikini standing next to the words 'ARE YOU BEACH BODY READY?' was banned in 2016 on the grounds that it promoted an unhealthy or unrealistic body image. And TfL extended its policy guidelines in February 2019 to clamp down on unhealthy food and drink advertising.

Using an assessment tool developed by the government's Food Standards Agency, any advert that 'promotes (directly or indirectly) food or non-alcoholic drink which is high in fat, salt and/or sugar' is unacceptable, and will not be approved to run on the TfL network. In banning these adverts, London acted autonomously ahead of the national government (the UK government public consultation on banning junk food advertising on TV before 9pm only launched in 2019). TfL began the scheme after extensive consultation with London residents, who were overwhelmingly in favour of the ban, despite (understandably) hostile responses from industry. Although the ban generated some silly headlines about Wimbledon tennis being unable to advertise its iconic strawberries and cream under new rules, most manufacturers have been able to find solutions by placing less unhealthy foods in their adverts, allowing everyone to walk away feeling more or less satisfied.

But what is most striking about the change is that the main driver behind the decision was the need to target rising childhood obesity in the capital. The decision to act via an advertising ban was based on a growing body of evidence that shows that the more advertising for unhealthy foods children are exposed to, the higher the risk that they will eat such foods and consequently become overweight or obese.[1] The study found that adverts which portrayed unhealthy food appealed to 87 per cent of young people, and that about 75 per cent were tempted to eat the products after seeing the advert.[2] Those children who recalled seeing unhealthy food being advertised every day were twice as likely to be obese as those who did not. These findings have serious implications for anyone who tries to follow the planetary health diet's recommendation to eat in a more sustainable way.

Whether we like it or not, the advertising we are exposed to on a daily basis has the power to influence our food choices. Advertisers clearly bank on this, and the research is strong enough to shape public policy. Despite these findings, many people find it hard to believe that advertising has such power. I certainly believed that such advertising was unlikely to influence my eating habits until I received a sharp wake-up call while writing this book.

One of the most surprising – and at times embarrassing – revelations was finding that I craved whichever food I was writing about at the time, irrespective of whether I was describing its positive or negative effects. So I developed a rapacious craving for biltong – a South African snack of dried, cured strips of meat, a bit like beef jerky – while writing the meat chapters, despite spending my days writing about why increasing our red meat intake was a bad idea. I bought a 5l tin of olive oil while writing the fats and oils chapter, and for a while my dinners were more or less pools of olive oil in which various foodstuffs floated decoratively. And during the writing of the fruit and vegetables chapter, I suffered a whole range of exciting bowel problems as I gorged on fibrous foods to excess. And this was just the result of spending a disproportionate amount of time thinking about a specific food – not even being exposed to advertising carefully crafted to make me crave something.

In other words, consciously or not, it seems that what we're exposed to in our local environment has a huge capacity to shape our diet choices. This makes sense in the context of food deserts, which I wrote about in Chapter Five (see page 129). If you can't buy fresh fruit or vegetables locally and you don't have the means to travel easily, you're unlikely to eat a diet full of fresh produce, but it is striking that even just passing an advertising hoarding can dramatically change our food choices. And it should come as no surprise that the foods which are advertised are disproportionately likely to be those in the ultra-processed category.

Studies looking at advertising trends in countries as diverse and wide-ranging as Sweden, Mexico, Australia and the USA have found that the majority of food and drink advertisements are for ultra-processed or otherwise unhealthy foods.[3] The two largest global companies selling sugary drinks spent a combined sum of more than US$8 billion on advertising in 2018 alone. (If you want more proof of the insidious effect of adverts, think of what the sales revenue must be to justify spending that much on product promotion.) This is especially important in a world where far fewer of us cook for ourselves on a daily basis than in the past. This decline in home cooking – partly related to changing lifestyles, partly related to cost – has been shown to decrease healthy eating and is associated with increased weight gain.[4] Knowing that no home cook could replicate the techniques needed to create ultra-processed foods and understanding ultra-processed food's terrible impact on our health, this makes sense.

Many people live in an environment where it's cheaper and easier to buy ready-made food than it is to access and cook fresh produce, and where advertising nudges them into buying unhealthy food irrespective of what they know about healthy eating. Scientists love to create a complex word to describe something when three simple ones will do, and the word that describes such an environment is obesogenic, which means an environment likely to lead to weight gain. An environment can be obesogenic because it promotes unhealthy eating habits (through the ready accessibility of cheap, highly caloric foods or because of a lack of alternative healthy options), or through reduced access to recreational or sports facilities. If that situation sounds familiar, it's because many local environments (especially in cities) could be classified as obesogenic. For example, in Tower Hamlets, one of the most deprived boroughs of East London, there are 42 fried chicken shops per secondary school. For £2 – well within most children's budget – you can buy a piece of fried chicken, fries and a high-sugar soft drink, and still get a penny change. This high density of fried chicken shops is being suggested as one of the reasons the borough has the sixth-highest rate of childhood obesity in the country – in 2016 more than one in four children over the age of eleven in Tower Hamlets was obese.[5]

If obesogenic environments exist everywhere, then TfL's decision to ban advertising might have some impact. But even if the adverts are banned TfL can't close down the fried chicken shops which stimulate people's appetites in much the same way. Nor can anyone point an accusatory finger at those running the chicken shops or those farming and distributing the chickens. They are simply supplying a demand which we, the consumers, are making. This is not to say that regulation has no influence. For example, there have been multiple examples of government regulators working with fast-food chains and the manufacturers of ultra-processed foods to tweak their recipes towards healthier options. In 2016 the British government announced its sugar-reduction programme, Childhood Obesity: A Plan for Action, which asked manufacturers to reduce sugar by 20 per cent by 2020 in each of the food categories that contributed the most sugar to children's diets (such as cakes, breakfast goods, biscuits).[6] But there was a catch because the regulations were formulated by sales-weighted average rather than recipe. This allowed manufacturers to simply reduce their sugar percentages by product category. So instead of changing their recipes, manufacturers simply reduced the portion sizes of a product, or promoted lower-sugar options so that within a category less sugar is consumed overall.

In short, regulation is not as easy as straightforwardly asking manufacturers to make their products healthier – or perhaps it is, but governments are not asking them to do so. Sugar taxes imposed by governments worldwide on sugary drinks are another means through which they can encourage healthier eating, but we just need to look at smoking to see that taxing something highly does not mean that people partake of it less.

To sum up all this: eating well is hard. The deck is stacked against almost all of us – considerably more so for some of us than others. Making changes will require some work, at least initially, as we try to reform some of our more ingrained habits. I am not going to underestimate your intelligence by pretending that you didn't know that eating more fruit and vegetables is healthier than eating two cheeseburgers. Yet it's entirely possible that you picked the cheeseburgers anyway for many possible reasons: you were tired and you didn't need to cook them; they were cheaper; they were more satisfying; you've been craving them. Even if I have convinced you – and I hope I have – that the way we eat now is leading us down the wrong path by making us sicker and causing unsustainable and damaging changes to the planet, turning away from cheeseburgers and facing the pile of vegetables will initially take willpower.

I hope I have shown you why this is worthwhile. As I discussed in Chapter Two (see page 29), right at the beginning, consumer choice has the potential to outweigh producers' decisions because of the power of our accumulated decisions. Making better decisions about what we eat alone is not going to save the world – but it is a critical and necessary step that we need to take. (It is necessary, if not sufficient.) So most of this chapter is dedicated not only to telling you about the recommendations of the planetary health diet, but also to explaining how we can move towards putting them into practice. The diet is not an entirely alien way of eating to some, but it is likely to be sufficiently different to need some readjustment in our ingrained habits. I hope that by the end of this chapter you will come away armed with ways of thinking that will help you to move your diet closer to these recommendations.

HOW TO FOLLOW THE PLANETARY HEALTH DIET

First things first. The planetary health diet (PHD) is not a diet in the traditional sense. It doesn't dictate exactly what you should eat every day, nor does it exclude any specific food. It's worth quoting the EAT Forum's description of the planetary health diet in full here to be clear about what exactly it offers:

'Although the planetary health diet, which is based on health considerations, is consistent with many traditional eating patterns, it does not imply that the global population should eat exactly the same food, nor does it prescribe an exact diet. Instead, the planetary health diet outlines empirical food groups and ranges of food intakes, which combined in a diet, would optimize human health. Local interpretation and adaptation of the universally-applicable planetary health diet is necessary and should reflect the culture, geography and demography of the population and individuals.'[7]

The diet was designed as an outline of food groups, with a range of food intakes, so that it can be adapted to whichever foods and cuisines are locally available – and personalized to individual need. In this sense it is more a blueprint than a diet in the traditional sense. Although it might be easier if I gave you a menu to follow, as you will have hopefully gathered by now, everything to do with changing how we eat is filled with nuance and this is no different. If it dictated that we should all eat exactly the same things at the same time the diet would be worthless: the recommendations need to be flexible and pragmatic in a world filled with variety. This may require a little more mental effort in the short term, but in the long run the likelihood of our sticking to the diet is much higher. As you will see, eating the PHD is mainly about consistently making better choices, rather than eating within restrictive confines.

In this section I set out the recommendations of the PHD by food group, and then break down each set of recommendations in terms of origin and frequency and provide a guide to what to eat and how often to eat it. The PHD food pyramid is below (see page 224) with a summary of the daily and weekly recommendations. The detailed full set of daily and weekly recommendations, calculated for the slightly different nutritional needs of men and women, are in an appendix at the back of the book, along with recommended portion sizes (see page 255). All the recommendations are given as portions. To standardize this I have taken the portion sizing recommendations from the British Nutrition Foundation (BNF). However, not all portions are interchangeable:

a portion of bacon is a lot smaller than a portion of steak, for example. So where portion sizes matter (mainly in how often to eat animal-based foods) I have given examples of what the BNF considers a portion to be.

Finally, you should be aware of some important caveats in this section. These recommendations are my interpretations of the science, and have been reviewed by a qualified nutritionist as an illustrative interpretation of the PHD's recommendations – but there is always potential for misinterpretation. So I urge you to check the recommendations on page 258 for full details, where they are given in grams and calories. The recommendations do not incorporate micronutrient distribution – as the best rule of thumb, dietary variety is encouraged to ensure that you get a full range of micronutrients.

These recommendations are made for healthy, moderately active, mid-life adults (aged 18 to 65). So they are average recommendations, not personalized ones. Growing children and adolescents, older people and pregnant or breast-feeding women have different nutritional needs which these recommendations do not take into consideration. Anyone with underlying health conditions that might be affected by diet (such as diabetes or high blood pressure) and those on medication which may interfere with nutrient absorption should bear this in mind when considering the recommendations.

Almost all the PHD recommendations are given in ranges to accommodate the different availability of certain foods, varying nutritional needs, and so on. For simplicity's sake when giving a snapshot of portion recommendations I have used the average value in these ranges, but it's worth looking at the recommendations at the back to see the flexibility around each one (although where it's especially important, I flag them below).

The table opposite gives a snapshot of how the PHD's recommendations for men and women differ nutritionally from the daily recommended portions suggested by the BNF. I chose the BNF's suggestions here because of their clear portion sizing recommendations. Each country's recommendations will vary to some degree because there is no gold-standard diet; this just illustrates the difference between one reference guide and the planetary health recommendations.

Macronutrient	BNF portions	PHD portions (male)	PHD portions (female)	PHD difference
Carbohydrates	3 or 4	4	3 or 4	Almost all wholegrain
Fruit and veg	5+	6 or 7	5	
Protein foods	2 or 3	4	3	More vegetable sources
Dairy and alternatives	2 or 3	2 or 3	2	
Fats and oils	Small amounts	4	3	All unsaturated vegetable

How BNF and recommendations compare

As you see, the suggestions for daily portions are broadly similar. There are three main differences, two of origin and one of quantity. The PHD suggests that your carbohydrate intake should come from a predominantly wholegrain source, which the BNF encourages but does not make explicit. Second, the PHD would prefer your regular source of protein to be vegetable-based, rather than animal-based; the BNF doesn't stipulate. Finally, the BNF doesn't recommend eating as much fat as the PHD does. So broadly speaking, the PHD does not depart significantly from normal food group recommendations for healthy eating: its main difference is to consider the sources of the food we eat in order to take their environmental consequences into account.

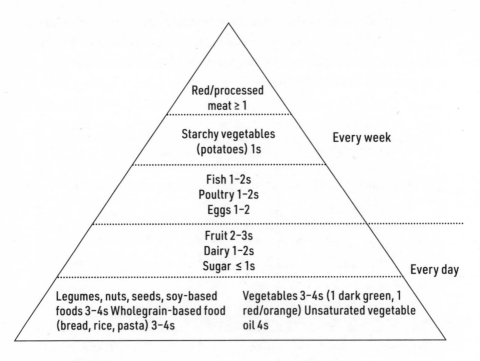

The PHD food pyramid (s = serving)

Carbohydrates

> **Daily recommendation:** three to four portions of wholegrain carbohydrates, substituting one portion of starchy root vegetables such as potatoes every two to four days. Sweeteners (added sugars) should be restricted to one portion a day, and are not included in the daily recommendation.

As starchy root vegetables are high in readily-absorbed simple carbohydrates, the PHD recommends limiting the amount of carbohydrate we get from eating these. Eating at the maximum end of this range would mean eating the equivalent of a small baked potato every two days; eating the average would mean eating a small baked potato or

equivalent about every five days. In the West we eat a lot more potatoes than this, so even though they are not a huge source of vitamin
C they provide a high proportion of our vitamin C intake. Reducing
our intake of potatoes means we'll need to eat more vitamin C-rich
fruit and vegetables as discussed in Chapter Five (see page 115).

Wholegrain carbohydrates

- Wholewheat in the form of wholewheat (brown) bread, pasta,
  crackers or couscous
- Brown, red or black rice
- Oatmeal/porridge
- Any whole grain as a base, including barley, bulgur wheat,
  quinoa, freekeh
- Whole rye bread and buckwheat foods such as pancakes
- Popcorn
- Wholegrain breakfast cereal such as muesli, granola, flaked
  wheat biscuits and bran flakes
- Starchy vegetables including potatoes and cassava

Added sugars

Sugar, or food with added sugars, should be restricted to one
portion a day or fewer. The UK Eatwell Guide suggests: 'These
foods are not needed in the diet and so, if included, should only
be consumed infrequently and in small amounts.'[8] This includes
chocolates, sweets and sweetened drinks such as soft drinks. The
BNF and PHD agree that a portion of food with added sugar is
equivalent to four small squares of chocolate, two small biscuits
or a mini muffin: in other words, an average-sized chocolate bar
would count as two portions of sugar-added food. A 330ml can
of sugar-sweetened drink slightly exceeds the recommended daily
calorie intake of food with added caloric sweeteners.

Fruit and vegetables

> **Daily recommendation:** between three and four portions of vegetables, with at least one dark-green vegetable and one red or orange vegetable, and two or three portions of fruit.

The PHD breaks vegetable recommendations down by colour, as this is a useful indicator of the different micronutrients (such as the colourful carotenoids) each has to offer. Only one portion of vegetables should be a legume. Legumes provide protein, which most other vegetables don't, but do not contain the same beneficial micronutrients as other vegetables. Both the PHD and the BNF recommend eating a high number of fruit and vegetable portions a day, but the PHD goes into more specific detail.

Vegetables

The PHD recommends at least one portion (about 80g) daily from each category.

DARK-GREEN VEGETABLES
- Cruciferous dark-green vegetables (named because their flowers have four petals that often form a shape of a cross): broccoli, bok choy (pak choi), turnips, collard and mustard greens, kale, rocket, swedes, kohlrabi, radishes, all types of cabbage
- Dark-green leafy vegetables: all types of lettuce and salad leaf, spinach, chard
- Dark-green legumes: green beans, soybeans (also known as edamame)

RED OR ORANGE VEGETABLES
- Peppers
- Beetroot
- Carrots

- Red cabbage
- Tomatoes
- Red salad leaves
- Red onions
- All members of the gourd family (including pumpkins and squashes)

OTHER VEGETABLES

- Fennel
- Courgettes (zucchinis)
- Cucumbers
- Onions, leeks and spring onions (scallions)
- Artichokes
- Aubergines
- Mushrooms
- Celery
- Sweet potatoes

NON-STARCHY ROOT VEGETABLES

- Celeriac
- Parsnips

Fruit

One portion of fresh fruit weighs about 80g and one portion of dried fruit weighs about 30g. Fresh, dried and juice all count towards your portions, although a maximum of one portion (150ml) of fruit juice or smoothie is recommended because processing the fruit increases the free sugar content.

FRESH FRUIT

- 2 plums
- 3 apricots
- 7 strawberries
- 14 cherries

- 1 apple, banana, pear, orange, nectarine, peach
- Half a grapefruit
- 5-cm slice of melon
- 1 large pineapple slice
- 2 slices of mango

DRIED FRUIT

- 1 heaped tablespoon of raisins
- 2 dried figs
- Handful of banana chips

FRUIT JUICE OR SMOOTHIE

- 150ml (small glass) of juice or smoothie

Protein foods

Daily recommendation: three to four portions of vegetable-based protein (legumes, nuts, seeds, soy-based foods) and two portions of dairy foods (cheese, milk, yoghurt).

Weekly recommendations: one to two portions each of poultry, eggs and fish and one portion of red or processed meat every seven to ten days.

Unless you are already vegetarian or vegan, these recommendations are likely to be one of the biggest changes to how you eat now. I have several suggestions to help you move towards eating as the recommendations advise while ensuring that you get all the essential fats and amino acids you need.

First and most important: do not exclude animal products from your diet unless you carefully plan this change. Nutritionally, swapping plant for animal protein sources is not a like-for-like swap.

Plant-based proteins are not complete proteins and lack key nutrients such as vitamin B12, iron (in its readily absorbed haem form), and so on. So it's important that you continue to eat the recommended quantities of animal products unless you plan carefully how to source these vital micronutrients from vegetable sources. If you want to transition to a vegetarian or vegan diet, there are many resources available to help you plan this, for example the Vegan Eatwell Guide which has been adapted and is available from the UK Vegan Society.[9]

Second, to get more of our protein from vegetarian sources we need to eat a wider range of food than we probably do currently. We can't simply swap burgers for a three-tins-a-day kidney bean habit. While it's always vital to eat a wide range of food for good health, it now becomes especially important.

Vegetable sources of protein

Vegetable sources of protein include nuts, seeds, legumes and pulses. Legumes are plants that grow seeds in pods and pulses are part of the legume family, the pulse being the dry edible seeds within the pod. A portion of pulses is about half a handful; a portion of nuts is about a cupped-palmful (around the size of a golf ball) and a portion of nut butter is about a tablespoon.

PULSES

Beans, lentils, chickpeas and split peas are the most common types of pulses. They include the following:

- Kidney beans
- Cannellini beans
- Black beans
- Broad beans (fava)
- Haricot beans (like those in baked beans)
- Pinto beans
- Brown, green and puy lentils

LEGUMES

- Peas including mangetout (snow peas) and sugar snaps
- Fresh beans such as runner, round, fine beans, soybeans and peanuts

SOY-BASED FOODS

- Soybeans (edamame) on their own or set into tofu

NUTS

- Almonds
- Cashews
- Brazil nuts
- Walnuts
- Pistachios
- Pecan
- Macadamia nuts
- Hazelnuts
- Nut butters (check that there is no added oil, sugar or salt)

SEEDS

- Flaxseed
- Chia
- Hemp
- Sesame
- Pumpkin
- Sunflower
- Poppy

The PHD does not make any recommendations about plant-based meat substitutes. Often foods made from vegetable proteins that aim to mimic the appearance of meat will have undergone a lot of processing to change their properties. It's too early to judge the health benefits of such foods, but my recommendation would be that they should be eaten sparingly and treated as ultra-processed food and that most portions of vegetable-based protein should come from unprocessed sources.

Red and processed meat (beef, lamb, pork)

The PHD allocates a small allowance of meat every day and so you need to build up to eating a full-size portion. The size of your meal will affect how often you can eat it. A portion of red meat can be eaten about once every week to ten days, depending on the size of the portion. Smaller portions can be eaten weekly, larger portions every ten days or so. A small portion of red meat would be three rashers of bacon, several slices of ham, a sausage or a small portion of mince cooked in a sauce as part of a wider meal. A large portion would be a (small) steak or a hamburger (see appendix page 258 for fuller lists of portions). UK government guidance recommends a maximum of 500g of red or processed meat a week; the PHD recommends around a fifth of that – less than 100g weekly.

Poultry, eggs and fish

The PHD classifies all three of these protein sources as interchangeable, although it's important to note that they are not exactly alike (an egg contains less protein than a chicken breast; mackerel more omega-3 fatty acids than chicken, and so on). So it's vital to eat the full range of these three protein sources unless you have carefully planned your diet. Depending on portion size, the PHD recommends eating one to two portions of poultry, eggs and fish each a week (between three and six portions a week, depending on portion size). A portion of poultry would be a chicken breast about half the size of your hand or two and half slices of white roast turkey meat. One egg counts as a portion. A fillet of white fish about the size of your hand, a medium tin (160g) of tuna or four tablespoons of prawns all count as a portion. Fish includes oily fish such as salmon, mackerel, trout, sardines, herring and pilchards. White fish includes cod, haddock, plaice, monkfish, mullet and tilapia. Shellfish includes prawns, mussels, oysters, squid and crab.

Dairy foods

The PHD suggests eating about two portions of whole dairy produce daily. In this instance, whole means not low- or reduced-fat cheese or yoghurt, and full-fat milk. Portion examples include 30g of cheese (about the size of two thumbs), four tablespoons of plain Greek yoghurt, 200ml whole milk (about a glass) or two teaspoons of butter.

If you substitute a plant-based milk alternative, bear in mind that not all alternative milks are nutritionally similar to cow's milk. All plant-based milks are far lower in protein than dairy milk. Soy milk has the closest comparable protein profile of all the plant milks, although it is still lower. Vegans and those on restricted diets should look for fortified versions of plant-based milks to ensure they get comparable amounts of calcium and vitamin D. It's also important to note that fish and dairy are important sources of iodine, and this should to be considered if opting for a vegan diet.

Fats and oils

Daily recommendation: four portions of unsaturated vegetable oil a day, and small quantities of animal-derived lard or tallow and palm oil, as part of meat intake or processed foods.

The PHD recommends an equal mix of unsaturated vegetable oils including olive, soy, rapeseed, sunflower and peanut oil. This is not feasible worldwide, as not all these sources are available in every country (or practical for every person; for example I am allergic to peanuts). Rather it reflects the range of oils in processed and/or preprepared foods. The large quantities of oil and fat in the diet are not intended to be taken as spoonfuls that you hold your nose to swallow; rather they reflect oil as the basis of all cookery (and a switch to vegetable-based oils away from fats such as butter). Lard or tallow is optional as it is derived from red meat; some palm oil consumption is inevitable.

It's important to flag that the intake of fats in the PHD is significantly higher than current UK guidelines recommend: four portions of unsaturated oils is equivalent to about four table-spoons a day. Add to that whole dairy sources and more nuts, which also contain a large amount of fat (about 10 per cent of which is saturated, although this varies depending on nut) and the PHD recommends a fairly high-fat diet. As previously discussed (see page 77), fat is an important part of a balanced diet and the most recent research shows the benefits of including increased quantities of unsaturated vegetable oils in our diets – but if you have any underlying health conditions that might be exacerbated by eating more fats (such as cardiovascular disease) this change could be harmful and should be discussed with your doctor. It's also important to note that not all oils are equal – good-quality cold-pressed olive and rapeseed oils are the highest in omega-3 fatty acids.

CAN WE DO IT? SHOULD WE?

Depending on your current eating habits, the recommenda-tions above might leave you slack-jawed in horror, or vaguely wondering what all the fuss is about. This is because although the PHD differs quite extensively from a modern American or British diet, it wouldn't be considered exceptional in other parts of the world. Specifically, it's very similar to the Mediterranean diet.

When you compare the planetary health and Mediterranean diets, there are many similarities between them. The most striking is that the bulk of both diets comes from plant-based foods. Both recommend three or more servings of cereal-based foods a day and lots of vegetables. The Mediterranean diet has more fruit – about three or four servings a day compared with the PHD's two or three.

The other striking similarity between the diets is the very low quantity of animal products they include. In short these diets, while not being identical, are similar enough to be comparable. This is important for several reasons. First it shows that eating in the way that the PHD recommends is not an impossible ask from scientists locked in their ivory towers. It is the way that millions of people have always eaten and continue to eat. Second, eating as Mediterranean people do is strongly associated with striking health benefits. I discussed these in Chapter Four: Fats and Oils (see page 77) but one is worth mentioning once again – longer life.

Many different factors affect how we age – genetic, socio-economic, environmental, and so on – and these affect our risk of developing different diseases, but one of the most important has been shown to be the food that we eat. Scientists and anthropologists have scoured the globe to find the longest living groups of people – communities where people regularly live to be a healthy 100 years or older (called blue zones). And what they have found is that, among other factors, these groups of people tend to share a similar diet. The shared features of these healthy diets include eating a lot of unrefined carbohydrates and vegetables, moderate amounts of protein including proportionally large quantities of legumes, fish and lean meats, as well as more unsaturated than saturated fats. If this pattern sounds familiar, it should: this description fits not only the PHD, but also the Mediterranean diet. And, perhaps not unexpectedly, two of the blue zones are in Mediterranean countries.

I hope I've established that the PHD is not a totally alien concept that is impossible to put into practice. Another equally good question is: are these foods really the least environmentally harmful? In other words, how do you know that making these changes will make the difference that we need to see? You may remember a paper I first discussed in Chapter Two (see page 43) which assessed 15 types of food for their health and environmental impacts. This paper, which was published after the PHD by an entirely separate group of scientists, found the following (I quote verbatim to emphasize the independent nature of the findings, although the emphasis is mine):

'We find that while there is substantial variation in the health outcomes of different foods, foods associated with a larger reduction in disease risk for one health outcome are often associated with larger reductions in disease risk for other health outcomes. Likewise, foods with lower impacts on one metric of environmental harm tend to have lower impacts on others. Additionally, of the foods associated with improved health (*wholegrain cereals, fruits, vegetables, legumes, nuts, olive oil, and fish*), all except fish have among the lowest environmental impacts, and fish has markedly lower impacts than red meats and processed meats. *Foods associated with the largest negative environmental impacts – unprocessed and processed red meat – are consistently associated with the largest increases in disease risk.* Thus, dietary transitions toward greater consumption of healthier foods would generally improve environmental sustainability, although processed foods high in sugars harm health but can have relatively low environmental impacts.'[10]

In other words, independent research confirms that the PHD's suggestions help to change our diets towards healthier, more environmentally friendly choices. Taking this and the Mediterranean diet into consideration, you can see that eating as the PHD suggests is not impossible. But it would be disingenuous to suggest that it would be an easy transition. In the UK, we eat an average of five servings of red meat a week,[11] and in other parts of the world this number is even higher. How can we cut our consumption to a fifth, or even less?

THE THREE RULES RULE
(OR THE CONFESSIONS OF A CARNIVORE)

Despite growing up surrounded by nature in all its glory, having pets throughout my childhood and being that irritating person in the park who wants to continue patting your puppy even when you clearly have somewhere else to be, I am not a vegetarian. I love animals, but I also love eating meat. One of my favourite meals is a steak that has been cooked just to the rare side of blue, extremely salty thin fries and a big glass of red wine. While I feel this makes me something of a hypocrite, I suspect I am not alone in both loving animals and eating them. I tell you this not to air my moral inadequacies but to point out that I do not have a hidden agenda. I am not a vegetarian – and definitely not a vegan – nor do I plan on converting to become either. Nonetheless, I still believe it is possible to follow the PHD's recommendations. As I have been writing this book, I have been working not only on the science of the recommendations, but also on putting them into practice.

We're all busy with many demands on our time. When considering what to cook and eat, our choice is often constrained by many factors: price, time, our preferences, others' preferences. Adding yet another factor can seem daunting. Here is the key: I want to change how you weight the decisions you make every day. We all constantly make choices about what we eat: when we're staring at rows of prepacked sandwiches; when we're in a restaurant; when we're staring into a fridge or cupboard wondering what to cook that evening. Instead of all the options being weighted equally, the PHD nudges us to lean towards plant-based foods much more frequently. As I have worked to change how I think about my daily eating habits, I have come up with a few rules of thumb which make daily decisions easier, and lead to following most of the recommendations without needing to sit down and consider how many portions of a food group I have left.

First is what I have called the three rules rule. I can sum up the main recommendations of the PHD as three rules. If you take nothing else away from this book, following these on a daily basis will ensure that you get it right almost all the time. They are:

1. Eat less meat, and especially less red meat.
2. Eat less processed food, especially ultra-processed food.
3. Eat more fibre in any form (fruit, vegetables, vegetable-based protein such as legumes, wholegrains).

Applying these three rules to all meals makes it much easier to decide what to pick at any given moment. To make them easy to remember and apply, I've come up with some quick strategies to guide my thinking and make food decisions easy. These are by no means the only way to think about your eating habits but I share them as an example of what has worked for me.

My suggestion for how to easily eat less meat is to reframe the way you think about shopping. I used to plan meals based around portions of meat, with vegetables and carbohydrates coming in as a supporting act. I have changed two aspects of this. First, I now try to think about vegetables without having a specific meal in mind. By this I mean that I try to buy a range of vegetables (fresh, tinned and frozen) when doing a big shop and consider what I can do with them when I get home, much as I used to pick up packets of mince or chicken thighs. I call this the veg-first approach. It makes the vegetables the centre of whatever I cook, a position previously occupied by meat. For example, a new staple meal has become black bean tortillas. The tortillas I used to cook have changed very little except that I use black beans instead of meat to make the filling (and pick wholegrain tortilla wraps). I now don't consider cooking meat-based tortillas: I'd rather savour the meat on its own than as a texture in a dish that doesn't need it.

Following on from this is adjusting to the idea of meat as a treat. Rather than thinking of meat as just another ingredient, I now try to enjoy the meat I eat as a treat in its own right. So, for example, I've almost entirely stopped buying minced meat: I can replicate this very effectively in most dishes using coarsely chopped vegetables such as aubergines and mushrooms. When I buy meat now, I do so with the idea of making an occasion out of that meal. So I buy sausages and savour them in toad-in-the-hole, or roast a whole chicken on Sunday, use the leftover meat in stews and salads over the course of the week, and boil the carcass for stock. I also feel better about eating meat in this way. I feel that I am showing the animal more respect. (A side note: I can afford to buy higher welfare meat so I do; I strongly suggest that you do this if you can afford it, as higher welfare meat is also less likely to have been reared intensively, making it environmentally friendlier. However, this decision is based on personal circumstance.)

For the second rule, in aiming to eat less processed food I think about whether I could attempt to make something at home. This doesn't mean that I *could* make it at home, but, rather, I ask myself whether there is a recipe I could attempt to follow, even if I fail in the execution. So bread passes this rule – we all know people who bake their own bread, even if my own attempt ends up as more rock than loaf. However, a lot of snack foods fail this test: how would you begin to make Pringles or Haribo sweets? It's not a perfect rule but it's an easy way of quickly checking if you're unsure about a purchase.

Snack foods are probably the hardest habit to kick when trying to eat less processed food – but I have discovered some great alternatives. As a result of having a severe peanut allergy, when I started writing this book I had spent my life avoiding all nuts, just in case my reaction to them was as deadly as it is to peanuts. But as I read more about the many health benefits of nuts, I bit the bullet and submitted myself for allergy testing. To get a sense of how your body might react without feeding you the allergen and risking potentially life-threatening anaphylactic shock, you undergo a skin-prick test. This is exactly what it sounds like: a smiling nurse carefully takes a small needle, jabs it into the allergen of choice and then scrapes open a small wound on your arm, making sure to really smear the allergen into it. You're also scraped with a positive and negative control, all annotated on your arm with ballpoint pen, and then sent to sit in the waiting room to watch your arm and see what happens. If large, itchy, unsightly welts emerge from the scratch then it's a sign of allergy; no reaction means you move on to the next stage, known as the oral challenge (I didn't laugh at this because the waiting room was full of children, but I wanted to). This means eating an increasingly large quantity of, in my case, different types of nuts over six months or so. By the end of the allergy testing, I had discovered that I was able to eat all nuts except peanuts – I only have hazelnuts to try.

This means that I have spent the past six months eating nuts with the joy of a child. Who needs crisps when you have a handful of roasted almonds or pistachios? They are much more satisfying and tasty, and fill you up in a way that a packet of crisps does not. My other discovery in searching for crisp replacements are roasted pumpkin or sunflower seeds in their shell: they have the same moreish quality as crisps but are more substantial, and the ritual deshelling is satisfying and slows you down so they're harder to binge on. Other options I have discovered (can you tell I love crisps?) is the joy of home-made popcorn and oven-roasted chickpeas – when sprinkled with a lot of spices both make fantastic large bowlfuls for guilt-free eating.

For the third rule – eating more fibre – I suggest aiming to make your carbohydrates brown and everything else as colour-ful as possible. This means that you'll be eating wholegrain-based carbohydrates and also a wide variety of fruit, vegetable and vege-table-based protein sources. Choosing brown over white has been the adjustment I found easiest to make. For example, my local take-away pizza place offers a wholewheat base option, which I chose semi-reluctantly. While I'm aware that what I'm about to say will bar me from entry into Italy, I actually preferred it. It had more flavour and gave the pizza more substance. I filled up faster and so didn't gorge by eating the whole thing, meaning that I had plenty of pizza for breakfast the next day (breakfast of kings); I now always pick this option. I find brown and red rice more interesting and

flavourful than white as a base for stews, have developed something of an obsession with black rice noodles in soups and stir-fries
and think that brown bread makes everything, especially honey,
taste better. (Be sure to check the back of the packet when buying
brown bread: sometimes dark sugars are added to make the bread
look brown – choose options that state that they're wholewheat.)

Eating a lot of colourful fruit and veg follows on naturally from
shopping veg first. One of my other discoveries is that veg-heavy
eating doesn't always mean having a focal point in a meal. Think
about tapas or mezze; they consist of a lot of small dishes, often
vegetable-based, which could be too heavy if eaten in quantity but
are perfect for a few bites. So I have been experimenting with a meal
consisting of vegetable fritters and dips such as the aubergine-based
baba ganoush. Another way of including a lot of fruit and veg in
your diet is to cook without really thinking about it. For example,
soffritto is the Italian word for fried slowly and refers to the near-
ubiquitous base of diced onion, carrot and celery which forms the
beginning of many Italian dishes – these count as a helping or two
of vegetables.

Here are some suggested swaps which I have found useful as a
way of transitioning towards eating as the PHD recommends:

- Instead of white bread products, choose either wholewheat
  (brown) bread or rye bread (checking for unnecessary additives
  such as sugar).

- When eating a refined grain product such as white rice, make a
  straight swap for black, red or brown rice instead (you can do
  this with many items, for example, wholegrain couscous or
  pasta instead of white couscous or pasta).

- Buy oats and make porridge from scratch rather than buying it
  prepacked; it's cheaper and contains significantly less sugar.

- Instead of eating cornflakes, which are made by refining the
  grains and stripping them of fibre, buy wholegrain cereals such
  as granola (checking for added sugar) or wholewheat biscuits.

- Add fibrous wholegrains to meals, for example, put pearl barley in soups. This is barley which has been polished, or pearled, to remove some or all of the outer bran layer along with the hull. Although it is technically a refined grain, it's much healthier than other refined grains because some of the bran may still be present and the fibre in barley is distributed throughout the kernel, and not just in the outer bran layer. Pearl barley cooks more quickly than wholegrain barley.

- If you want to make pancakes for a lazy Sunday breakfast, you can be like the French and make them with buckwheat rather than white flour (buckwheat is technically a berry, but it shares the same healthy fibre and carbohydrate-containing properties as a grain).

- Instead of thinking of bread, potatoes or pasta as the carbohydrate base for a meal, experiment with other grains which add new and interesting textures, such as freekeh.

- When looking for a crunchy, salty snack eat wholegrain popcorn instead of crisps (popping it yourself on the stove with a bit of oil is healthier, cheaper and more fun than buying ready-made microwave bags).

- If you fancy potatoes, either have a small quantity or try sweet potato for its high nutrient content. Don't bother peeling them: the fibre is in the skin!

- You can kill two birds with one stone by making vegetarian mince to go into a chilli, lasagne or other mince and tomato-based dish. Coarsely chopped aubergines, mushrooms and carrots work well, but there are many recipes to experiment with.

- Fruit is the best answer to a sweet craving when you're trying to ease off added sugar and up your fibre intake. Berries require no prep and are very moreish; they fit nicely into a sweet-shaped hole!

- Carrot sticks and hummus are a great mid-afternoon snack which, unlike crisps, don't leave you hungry again an hour later.

Another excellent mid-afternoon snack is a nut and seed parfait: bulk-buy large bags of different nuts and seeds, and then combine them in small amounts. This gives you all the different nutrients they offer without overdosing (made in a small glass this looks like a layered pudding, hence the term).

- Dishes such as stir-fries and curries can easily become vegetarian by substituting beans or meaty vegetables such as aubergines for the meat, or by excluding meat altogether. A favourite in our house is a vegetarian stir-fry; the trick is to chop the vegetables yourself rather than buying a packet ready-chopped. Cut the vegetables more thickly and they won't cook away to nothing, making them more satisfying.

- It's easy to add vegetarian sources of protein and fibre to soup by adding beans to a minestrone.

- Slow-cooking vegetables is an amazing way of bringing out their character; for example, caramelizing and then slow-roasting butternut squash into a stew base is just as satisfying as eating a hearty meat-based dish.

- Think about ways of making meat go further. Don't buy a single cooked chicken breast to make a sandwich (I used to do this all the time). Instead, buy a whole chicken and make it last the week for your family by using the breast for sandwiches, the thigh meat in a pie or stew, and the carcass and wings in a soup.

- When you're hungover, have a bacon and egg sandwich. Enjoy it and then make sure you avoid eating a burger that week. Alternatively, eat a burger and then make the sandwich just from egg! Be conscious of the meat you eat – and make sure you enjoy it when you do.

- Experiment with different dishes. Variety is the key to good food health. Look up new recipes based on vegetables you haven't cooked before. You'll be amazed at how many ways there are of making delicious food.

- Ensure that you eat sustainably caught or farmed fish by checking with the international Marine Stewardship Council.[12] The
council has an app you can use to check whether the fish you're
considering buying is sustainable while you're at the shops.

A TIME OF TRANSITION

It is important to state that the PHD has not been without
critique. Science progresses through debate and the PHD is no
exception to this (nor should it be). It has been noted that there
will be significant variation in micronutrients depending on, for
example, if you pick chicken liver as your meat of choice rather
than chicken breast. Given the variety of foods that the PHD is
designed to encompass around the world, it's impossible to predict
exactly which micronutrients any person's choice will deliver. But
the important issue to emphasize is that eating a wide variety of
foods is the best way towards a balanced diet. If you are planning
to use the PHD as a path towards a vegetarian or vegan diet, then
you need be conscious of the possible dietary deficiencies to avoid,
and plan what you eat more carefully than you would otherwise.

Other criticisms of the practicality of following the diet have
raised the unaffordability or inaccessibility of fresh fruit and
vegetables for many people. This is a serious concern, and should
be addressed through government policy and subsidies – the cost
saving in terms of healthcare alone should cover the subsidies – but
should not deter anyone from attempting to eat in a healthier, more
sustainable way if they can afford to. Increasing demand for fresh
produce might also act as an incentive for some producers to change
what they choose to grow in response, and could lower costs.

Finally, some have taken the PHD as an attack on the meat
industry. While I believe that the recommendations are entirely
evidence-based, I can understand the hostility with which some
have received them. The meat industry provides meat that consumers demand, and it works to provide it efficiently and affordably.

I do not believe that rearing animals for meat should be halted: it is part of almost all cultures on earth. In some cultures, cattle are sources of wealth, status, livelihood and labour. And yet it is easy to interpret a call for a change in how we eat as an attack on the work of farmers and farming communities. People whose farm has been in their family for generations suddenly find themselves accused of destroying the planet. This is quite a charge to level at someone who is simply in the business of raising cattle or farming wheat. In particular, calls for people around the world to eat less meat have had a huge impact on farmers' mental health, according to the president of the National Farmers Union,[13] which has understandably left farmers feeling undervalued and demoralized.

This is not something to gloss over. The PHD asks us to make choices which will have an impact on people's livelihoods. To pretend that it does not would be disingenuous: if enough consumers make decisions which alter demand for certain products, as I am advocating, then at the other end of the line there will be someone who loses their job or has to make difficult decisions about their future. I stand by the science of my recommendations, but this doesn't mean I am blind to the impacts that they may have. I acknowledge that some of the people who work hard to produce the food that societies demand of them are being held up to blame, or will face uncertain futures. But equally, rearing animals on the vast, industrial scale that we currently do globally in order to create meat products which are actively damaging our environment cannot continue.

One of the wisest things I have ever heard was a throwaway comment after a lecture given by Christiana Figueres, then executive secretary of the UN Framework Convention on Climate Change, when she was talking in London in 2016 about the steps needed to tackle climate change. In response to a question about the impact of the USA's intention of leaving the Paris Agreement, she replied: 'This is a transition. Let us be patient and impatient with ourselves.'

I feel that this is a useful mantra as we start to try to move our eating habits towards the PHD's recommendations. As we try to change our daily habits to eat in a healthier, more sustainable way we will inevitably slip up, not want to continue, have good days and bad days. What matters is the direction of travel: adhering as much as possible to the three rules rule and forgiving ourselves and others when we do not succeed. The perfect should not be the enemy of the good when it comes to adjusting your eating habits. If everyone who read this book went on to follow the recommendations about half the time, it would make far more difference than if only 5 per cent of readers followed it to the letter while the other 95 per cent ignored it.

And I believe that Ms Figueres' words have value for our society. That there will be a backlash in such polarized times is more or less inevitable. When the PHD was published, it was amusing to see the range of headlines it generated. Some outlets hailed it as a scientific vindication of extreme veganism; others decried it as communism by the back door. I believe it is neither. Instead, it seems to me to be a rather rare thing: a pragmatic solution to two separate problems. If changing our eating habits can improve both our health and our environment's health, then it seems to me that doing it is a relatively obvious course of action to follow. But in so doing we must be mindful of all the people whose livelihoods would be affected by such a transition. Their lives and work matter too. We cannot ever hope to make societal shifts without impacting some people adversely, but it is disingenuous to dismiss their concerns; the effects on their lives cannot be discounted. So as we begin to move towards a more sustainable future, we must be mindful both of those who would rush us there impatiently, and those who resist. We must be patient and impatient with ourselves as we learn how to eat for all the tomorrows.

CHAPTER 9

ENOUGH

My guess is that the kind of thinking we are, at last, beginning to do about how to change the goals of human domination and unlimited growth to those of human adaptability and long-term survival...involves acceptance of impermanence and imperfection, a patience with uncertainty and the makeshift, a friendship with water, darkness, and the earth.

URSULA K LE GUIN, 'UTOPIYIN, UTOPIYANG' FROM
NO TIME TO SPARE[1]

In a characteristically grandiose painting King Charles II of England stands atop some steps in front of his mansion, manicured gardens and water feature, gazing somewhat smugly at the viewer. Kneeling at the king's feet as a supplicant is his gardener, John Rose, who offers something to the king with eyes respectfully downcast. It could be just another heavy oil portrait of the monarch until you look carefully and see what Rose is reverentially presenting to Charles: a pineapple.

The pineapple was first brought to Europe by Christopher Columbus in 1496 and presented to King Ferdinand II of Spain, who found that 'its flavour excels all other fruits'. People also fell in love with its striking shape and the French priest Father Du Tertre dubbed it 'the king of fruits' for both its taste and appearance. The French physician Pierre Pomet explains that its title is justified '...because it is much the finest and best of all that are upon the Face of the Earth. It is for this Reason that the King of

Kings has plac'd a Crown upon the Head of it, which is an essential mark of its Royalty.'

The picture described above (creatively named *Charles II Presented With A Pineapple*) is believed to have been painted around 1675. It is in fact a work of fiction, or at the very least, clever public relations. European gardeners only worked out the tricks of growing pineapples in cold northern climes in the early 18th century, but pineapples had become such an important symbol of wealth and prestige that it suited Charles to have a painting commissioned that indicated otherwise. Not only were pineapples symbols of prosperity, they occasionally did double duty as the symbol of the divine right of kings. By having his portrait painted with a pineapple, Charles was broadcasting a clear message of political power. 'Witness my greatness' is his unwritten message to the viewer, 'for I have a pineapple.'

I too have a pineapple. I bought it yesterday from a supermarket, and it is sitting on my table while I wait for it to ripen. It bears a label, impaled with a small piece of plastic through what Pomet referred to as its crown, announcing that it was grown in Costa Rica and declaring its tropical sweetness. I have never been to Costa Rica – it looks beautiful, but to go would be one of those once-in-a-lifetime trips. Yet every day thousands of pineapples arrive from that country's shores to be bought by masses of consumers who are partial to them. What would King Charles have made of it?

Well, he'd be furious probably. At least at first. And then perhaps bemused and then impressed by what is available to almost everyone in society for a tiny fraction of what we earn. The difference between what is available to almost everyone in modern affluent societies and what was available to him as King of England at the height of his reign is almost comically skewed in our favour. To dispute what the global food production system has achieved is to wilfully ignore history and the stunning successes of modern agricultural practice. Thanks to millions of people's research and dedication and the back-breaking hard work of farmers around the world, diseases of malnutrition in affluent societies are now curiosities, not endemic public health problems. We dismiss these achievements at our peril. But it has become clear that the ease of life and the luxuries to which we have become accustomed come at too high a price. Global agricultural systems are contributing to the way we are pushing the world out of a safe operating space for humanity and into an uncertain and unstable future. Things must change.

SUSTAINABLE TOMORROWS

As well as the planetary health diet, the EAT-*Lancet* Commission discussed other ways to move towards a sustainable and healthy global food production system, which are beyond the scope of this book.

The first is changing production systems towards sustainable intensification, which I discussed briefly in the carbohydrate and fruit and vegetables chapters (see pages 71 and 140). For example, we cannot use any new land without affecting the land-change boundaries or risking ecosystem services: the short-term gain in food production would ultimately be outweighed, rather quickly, by the overall environmental harms. Such large-scale sustainable intensification would mean assessing yield not just in terms of the quantity of crops grown per square unit of land, but would also take into account its environmental effects, such as greenhouse gas emissions, biodiversity impacts, and so on. To feed more mouths with fewer resources we will need a combination of new technologies and farming techniques. There is no one-size-fits-all solution to sustainable intensification because it varies from crop to crop, country to country, soil to soil.

But there are ways of helping the process along. Many farmers are already taking the lead on this. One style of farming is known as regenerative or conservation agriculture which involves growing cover crops (these are often nitrogen-fixing, non-edible crops such as legumes) so that bare soil is never exposed. This prevents soil erosion and provides food for animals to graze. It also increases the fertility of the soil, reduces the need for fertilizer and animal feed, and sequesters (removes) carbon in huge amounts. This doesn't provide huge quantities of meat, but it does provide high-quality meat. It wouldn't sustain our current eating habits, but could sustain them if they shifted towards the planetary health diet's recommendations, and farmers worldwide are turning to it as one way of ensuring the health of their land.[23]

Second, governments can take regulatory measures which offer financial cushioning and incentives to help farmers to make changes which might initially be costly but are ultimately better for the planet and provide more reliable sources of food in the future. These are backed by international policy. In 2015, The United Nations launched the 17 Sustainable Development Goals (SDGs), which recognize that economic considerations go hand-in-hand with natural ones.[4] We cannot talk about ending poverty or improving living conditions without considering the natural world in which these changes are to happen. So economic and environmental considerations are given equal billing in the SDGs. Their message is simple: there can be no economic growth without environmental consideration. This ties in with my explanation of ecosystem services in Chapter Four (see page 99). We must recognize that the planetary resources we access free do come at a price, and there are now too many of us to take these for granted. To begin or continue to prosper, societies need to place a value on their air, water, land and forests.

Third is a general reduction in food waste throughout the food supply chain. Food is wasted at every step of the way in the fields or in stores – or our fridges and cupboards. The commission calls for food waste to be halved, which is again supported by the SDGs. About a third of all the food in the world does not make it from the farm or factory to our plates. Apart from wasting nutrients, this represents a waste of all the resources needed to produce and process the food, whether that is fertilizer, energy, land or water. About 8 per cent of global greenhouse gas emissions are caused by food waste.[5] Food waste often occurs in low-income countries because of a lack of resources (for example, food rots on farms because there aren't enough pickers, or spoils because it is poorly stored). In high-income countries waste is the result of retailers and consumers rejecting food based on its appearance, or because we buy more than we can eat.[6]

So there are other aspects of the global food supply chain which also need to be addressed. A separate analysis has suggested that staying within the planetary boundaries might not be achieved by changing our dietary habits alone. It will require a combination of changing agricultural techniques, policies, greener energy generation, and so on.[7]

But as has been made abundantly clear by the policy inertia that continues, we cannot wait for governments or industry to initiate all these changes. And we don't have to. Just by changing what we eat, we have the power to change the world. Every single conscious choice we make to move our own diets towards the recommendations of the planetary health diet will allow us to improve our own health and will work towards keeping the planet safely within the planetary boundaries. We cannot fix every problem by changing our food choices. But just by starting to eat as the planetary health diet recommends will have an enormous, real impact. Just that will be *enough*.

ACKNOWLEDGEMENTS

If no man is an island, certainly no person could ever hope to have an intimate understanding of the range of topics covered in this book. I am indebted beyond measure to the many kind-hearted researchers who let me ask them obvious questions about their hard-won expertise. In no particular order, huge thanks are due to the following. At the Zoological Society of London, Emma Ackerley (now at MSC), Dr Alexa Varah, Louise McRae and Kirsty Kemp educated me on the importance of biodiversity. At NIAB, Ros Lloyd, Dr Stephanie Swarbreck and Bill Clark painstakingly explained crop sciences and the importance of fertilizers to me, as did Prof Mark Sutton at the UK Centre for Ecology & Hydrology. At WWF, Sarah Brown and Dr Emma Keller educated me on soy and palm oil plantations, and the impact they have on the environment. Prof Mark Maslin at UCL was a sounding board throughout the book, beginning with a fangirl email and ending with help on orbital forcing. Dr Hannah Ritchie from the superb resource Our World in Data shared work on land-use change for food use and other mind-blowing statistics. Richard Ballard and Bethany Thurston painted a visual picture of Growing Underground and the joys of vertical farming. Henry Dimbleby, Leon founder and now lead non-exec board member at DEFRA, helped me in untangling the many complexities this undertaking produced, as did Martin Bowman, food waste consultant. Prof Dean Ornish at UCFS helped me grasp that the whole is more than the sum of its parts. The entire *Lancet* family has been nothing but supportive and encouraging, even when I left them for several years to go down this path: enormous thanks are due especially to Richard Horton and David Collingridge for fielding my questions and many emails, and Gavin Cleaver for interviewing me on the inaugural *Lancet Voice* podcast.

This book would never have come into being were it not for two people: Dr Max Pemberton and my agent, Elly James. I can't thank you both enough for your unwavering support and kindness. It has meant more to me than I can express. I've been so lucky in my choice of publishers at Octopus. Denise Bates and Ella Parsons have guided me through the whole editing process from conception to end with insight and patience. Huge thanks are also due to the publicity and marketing team of Megan Brown, Matthew Grindon and Caroline Brown who with great patience and good humour tolerated my delays and social media ineptitudes. Thank you all very much.

Special thanks are due to Herr Professor Dr Rachel Warnock, Victoria Young, Rav Panesear, Barbara Probst, Soroush Pourhashemi, Olly Topping, James Couceiro, Liz Marozzi, Leila Vibert-Stokes, Maggie Gray and Luke Connoley, for keeping me – variously – fed, drunk, cheerful and sane over the years. Huge props to Tim Henshaw who read and commented on the entire manuscript and remains my friend despite my use of 'infinites'. My international adopted families of Eleni, Petros, Ioanna Koryzis, Jose Forero, Joy Glavani, and my beloved godparents Eileen and Davey Thayser, have supported me from near and far. And finally, Stefanos Koryzis, my *favourite* Greek, thank you for telling me I could do it when I wasn't sure I could. I love you all very much.

APPENDICES

In the following pages, I provide the planetary health guidelines to help you follow their recommendations. The first table outlines how many portions of food the diet recommends for men and women, presented by day and week (as some foods, for example red meat, are not recommended to be eaten on a daily basis). The second table provides examples of what a 'portion' looks like for each different type of food within each category. The subsequent pages are broken down specifically by food group, with the exact recommendations from the diet given in calories and grams, and further examples of different portion and food options. Sometimes you will see daily amounts of foods given in grams even when daily portions are 0. This is because the recommended quantity of food per day is too small to realistically count as a portion of food. These instead 'accumulate' over days towards a whole portion.

It's important to stress that these are for guidance only, especially as food weight and calorie content will vary, even when they're within the same category. However, sticking to the proportions of different foods outlined here (and the three rules rule – see page 236) will allow you to eat as the diet recommends. All of these recommendations are general: people's exact dietary needs will vary. If you have any underlying health conditions, please consult your doctor before changing your diet.

DAILY AND WEEKLY PORTIONS BY GENDER

		FOOD
Carbohydrates		Wholegrains (dry, raw)
		Starchy vegetables
Vegetables		Dark green
		Red and orange
		Other
		All vegetables combined
Fruit		Fruit
Protein	Dairy	Milk, cheese, yoghurt, butter
	Red meat	Beef, lamb, pork
	Poultry	Chicken, turkey
		Eggs
	Fish	All seafood, including all fish and shellfish
	Legumes	Pulses (dry beans, lentils, peas)
		Soy-based foods (soybeans, tofu)
		Peanuts
		Tree nuts (almonds, cashews, hazelnu
		Seeds
		All legumes combined
Fats and oils	Vegetable oils	Palm
		Unsaturated vegetable oils
	Animal	Lard, tallow
Added sweeteners	Sugar	Sugar

	DAILY		WEEKLY		
Men (2,500 kcal daily) portions	**Women** (2,000 kcal daily) portions	**Men** (2,500 kcal daily) portions	**Women** (2,000 kcal daily) portions		
4	3–4	28	21–28		
0	0	1	1		
4	3	28	21		
2–3	2	14–17	14		
2	2	14	14		
0	0	1*	1*	*depends on the portion
0	0	2	1		
0	0	1–2	1		
0	0	1–2	1–2		
4	3	28	21		
X	X	X	X	palm oil intake is assumed in packaged foods
4	3	28	21	assuming 1 portion oil = 1 tablespoon
X	X	X	X	optional
1	1	7	7	1 portion = 31g sugar, approximately a handful

EXAMPLE PORTION SIZES

Macronutrient

	Food	Example
Carbohydrates	Wholegrains	Dried rice/pasta
		Dry porridge oats
		Breakfast cereal
		Popcorn
		Cooked rice/pasta
	Starchy vegetables	Potatoes, cassava
Vegetables	Dark green	Kale, broccoli, spinach
	Red and orange	Tomatoes, peppers, carrots
	Other	Onions, aubergines, asparagus
Fruit		Apples, bananas, grapes
Protein	Dairy	Milk
		Cheese
		Yoghurt
	Red meat	Beef, lamb, pork
	Poultry	Chicken, turkey
		Eggs
	Fish	All seafood, including all fish and shellfish
		Tinned fish
	Legumes	Dry beans, lentils, peas
	Soy-based foods	Soya beans, tofu
	Peanuts	
	Tree nuts	Almonds, cashews, hazelnuts
Fats	Vegetable oil	Palm
		Unsaturated vegetable oils (20% each of olive, soybean, rapeseed, sunflower and peanut)
	Animal fat	Lard, tallow
Added sweeteners		Sugar

Portion size	Spoon/hand size
70g	2 handfuls
40g	1.5 handfuls
40g	3 handfuls
20g	3 handfuls
180g	2 hands cupped together
see page 260	see page 260
80g	3 tablespoons
80g	3 tablespoons
80g	3 tablespoons
80g	handful
200ml	medium glass
30g	size of 2 thumbs together
120g	4 tablespoons
130g	half the size of your hand
120g	half the size of your hand
1 egg	
120g	half the size of your hand
160g net	1 tin
120g	6 tablespoons
120g	half a handful
25g	small handful
20g	small handful
5g	1 teaspoon
5g	1 teaspoon
	eaten as part of meat intake
31g	4 small squares of chocolate or 2 biscuits

CARBOHYDRATES

DAILY

Food	Men (2,500 kcal daily)			Women (2,000 kcal daily)		
	weight (g)	kcal	portions	weight (g)	kcal	portions
Wholegrains (dry, raw)	232	811	4	186	649	3–4
Starchy vegetables	50	39		40	31	

WEEKLY

Food	Men (2,500 kcal daily)			Women (2,000 kcal daily)		
	weight (g)	kcal	portions	weight (g)	kcal	portions
Wholegrains (dry, raw)	1,624	5,677	28	1,299	4542	21–28
Starchy vegetables	350	273	1	280	218	1

		Weight (g)	Kcals		Handfuls
Wholegrains	**4 per day**				
Grains	Brown rice (dry)	65	236		2
	Couscous (dry)	90	328		2 cupped hands
	Popcorn	20	94		3
Cereals	Flaked breakfast cereal	40	140		3
	Muesli	50	183		3
	Porridge	40	171		1.5
Pasta	Wholemeal pasta (dry)	75	247		2
	Noodles	65	253		1 nest
Breads	2 slices wholemeal medium	80	180		
	2 slices wholemeal thick	110	239		
	Bagel	85	232		
Tubers	**every 5 days**				
Potatoes	Mashed	180	184		4 tablespoons
	New	180	122		6 small potatoes
	Oven chips	165	312		depends on brand
	Roast	200	322		4 small potatoes
	Baked	220	213		1 fist-size

FRUIT AND VEGETABLES

DAILY

	Food	Men (2,500 kcal daily)			Women (2,000 kcal daily)		
		weight (g)	kcal	portions	weight (g)	kcal	portions
Vegetables	Dark green	100	23	4	80	18	3
	Red and orange	100	30		80	24	
	Other	100	25		80	20	
Fruit	Fruit	200	126	2–3	160	101	2

WEEKLY

	Food	Men (2,500 kcal daily)			Women (2,000 kcal daily)		
		weight (g)	kcal	portions	weight (g)	kcal	portions
Vegetables	Dark green	700	161	28	560	129	21
	Red and orange	700	210		560	168	
	Other	700	175		560	140	
Fruit	Fruit	1,400	882	14–17	1,120	706	14

1 portion fruit or vegetable = 80g

1 portion dried fruit = 30g

I portion fruit juice or smoothie = 150ml max

Small fruit: 2 plums, 3 apricots, 7 strawberries, 14 cherries

Medium fruit: 1 apple, 1 banana, 1 pear, 1 orange, 1 nectarine

Large fruit: half grapefruit, 5cm slice melon, large slice pineapple, 2 slices mango

Dried fruit: 1 heaped tablespoon raisins, 2 figs, handful banana chips

Green vegetables: 2 broccoli spears or 8 florets, 4 heaped tablespoons cooked kale, spinach, green beans

Other vegetables: 3 heaped tablespoons carrots, peas, sweetcorn

Salad vegetables: 3 sticks celery, 5cm piece cucumber, 1 medium tomato, 7 cherry tomatoes

PROTEIN

DAILY

Food		Men (2,500 kcal daily)		
		weight (g)	kcal	portions
Dairy products	Milk, cheese, yoghurt	250	153	2
Red meat	Beef, lamb, pork	14	30	0
Poultry	Chicken, turkey	29	62	0
	Eggs	13	19	0
Fish	All seafood, including all fish and shellfish	28	40	0
Pulses	Dry beans, lentils, peas	50	172	
Soy-based foods	Soybeans, tofu	25	112	
Peanuts		25	142	
Tree nuts	Almonds, cashews, hazelnuts	25	149	
All legumes		125	575	4

Protein values in grams are for raw foods, and calories for cooked foods.
* depends on what it is

		Weight (g)	Kcal
Dairy	Cheese	30	100 (75–125 depending on type)
	Yoghurt	125	110
	Plain yoghurt	100	93
	Whole milk (quantity for cereal)	125	80
	Whole milk (drink)	200	126
Red meat beef/lamb pork	Bacon (2 rashers)	75	144
	Raw beef mince	125	157
	Beefburger	120– 150	261 –326
	Pork sausages	114	265
	Steak	175	310
	Ham	30	32
	Cocktail sausages	45	100
Poultry	Chicken breast	160	178
	Roast chicken	100	153
	Eggs	120	172
Fish	White fish (not battered)	140–195	100–140
	Canned tuna	120	131
	Salmon fillet	120–165	239–400
	Breaded frozen white fish	125	234
	Fish fingers	90	164
	Prawns	80	54N
Legumes	Beans, lentils, pulses	120	178
	Tofu	80	58
	Quorn mince	100	103
	Unsalted nuts	20	120

264

Women (2,000 kcal daily)			Men (2,500 kcal daily)			Women (2,000 kcal daily)		
weight (g)	kcal	portions	weight (g)	kcal	portions	weight (g)	kcal	portions
200	122	2	1,750	1,071	14	1400	857	14
11	24	0	98	210	1*	78	168	1*
23	50	0	203	434	2	162	347	1
10	15	0	91	133	1–2	73	106	1
22	32	0	196	280	1–2	157	224	1–2
40	138		350	1,204		280	963	
20	90		175	784		140	627	
20	114		175	994		140	795	
20	119		175	1,043		140	834	
100	460	3	875	4,025	28	700	3220	21

Spoon/hand size

size of 2 thumbs
small yoghurt pot
4 tablespoons
1 glass
half a glass
half size of hand
2 slices
4 sausages
half size of hand
2.5 slices of white meat
2 eggs
half to whole handful
medium can (160g)
half size of hand
3 fish fingers
4 tablespoons
half a handful
small handful

Daily recommendation: 3–4 portions of vegetable-based protein (legumes, nuts, seeds, soy-based foods) and 2 portions of dairy foods (cheese, milk, yoghurt).

Weekly recommendations: 1–2 portions each of poultry, eggs or fish every week, and less than 1 portion of red or processed meat (lamb, beef or pork).

It's possible to substitute all animal-based protein foods with vegetarian alternatives, but this must be done with care because vegetarian proteins are not whole protein sources.

FATS

DAILY

	Food	Men (2,500 kcal daily)			Women (2,000 kcal daily)		
		weight (g)	kcal	portions	weight (g)	kcal	portions
Vegetable oil	Palm	X	X		X	X	
	Unsaturated vegetable oils*	40	354	4	32	283	3
Animal fat	Lard, tallow	X	X		X	X	

*20% each olive, soybean, rapeseed, sunflower and peanut

WEEKLY

	Food	Men (2,500 kcal daily)			Women (2,000 kcal daily)		
		weight (g)	kcal	portions	weight (g)	kcal	portions
Vegetable oil	Palm	47.6	420		38	336	
	Unsaturated vegetable oils*	280	2,478	28	224	1,982	21
Animal fat	Lard, tallow	35	252		28	202	

*20% each olive, soybean, rapeseed, sunflower and peanut

Weight conversions

5g	⅛oz
10g	¼oz
15g	½oz
25g	1oz
40g	1½oz
50g	1¾oz
60g	2¼oz
70g	2½oz
85g	3oz
90g	3¼oz
100g	3½oz
125g	4½oz
150g	5½oz
175g	6oz
200g	7oz
250g	9oz
300g	10½oz
400g	14oz
500g	1lb 2oz
1 kg	2lb 4oz
5kg	11lb
10kg	22lb
25kg	55lb
50kg	110lb
100kg	220lb
200kg	440lb
500kg	880lb
1 tonne	157½ stone

Other conversions

1cm	½in
1m	3ft 3in
1km	0.6 miles
1 litre	¼ gallon

ENDNOTES

Chapter 1: The Global Syndemic

1. World Health Organization, 'Noncommunicable diseases country profiles 2018', 2018.
2. Bennett, J. E. et al., 'NCD Countdown 2030: Worldwide trends in non-communicable disease mortality and progress towards Sustainable Development Goal target 3.4', *The Lancet*, 392(10152), pp.1072–88, 2018.
3. Taubes, G., *The Case Against Sugar*, Portobello Books, 2018.
4. Global Panel on Agriculture and Food Systems for Nutrition, 'Food systems and diets: Facing the challenges of the 21st century', 2016.
5. Ibid.
6. Swinburn, B. A. et al., 'The global syndemic of obesity, undernutrition, and climate change: The Lancet Commission report', *The Lancet*, 393(10173), pp. 791–846, 2019.
7. https://www.unenvironment.org/news-and-stories/story/crisis-cape-town-3-months-until-taps-run-dry [accessed 12 September 2020].
8. Parks, R. et al., 'Experiences and lessons in managing water from Cape Town', Imperial College London Grantham Institute Briefing Paper No 29, 2019.
9. IPBES, 'Summary for policymakers of the global assessment report on biodiversity and ecosystem services of the Intergovernmental Science-Policy Platform on Biodiversity and Ecosystem Services', 2019.
10. Ritchie, H. and Roser, M., 'Environmental impacts of food production', Our World in Data, 2020, https://ourworldindata.org/environmental-impacts-of-food [accessed 10 Jun. 2020].
11. IPBES, cited note 9.
12. Myers, S. S. et al., 'Increasing CO2 threatens human nutrition', *Nature*, 510(7503), pp. 139–42, 2014.
13. Swinburn et al., cited note 6.
14. Willett, W., 'Food in the Anthropocene: The EAT–Lancet Commission on healthy diets from sustainable food systems', *The Lancet*, 393(10170), pp. 447–92, 2019.
15. Lucas, T. and Horton, R., 'The 21st-century great food transformation', *The Lancet*, 393(10170), pp. 386–7, 2019.

Chapter 2: Our Interconnected Earth

1. Lewis, S. and Maslin, M., *The Human Planet: How We Created the Anthropocene*, Pelican, 2018.
2. Mummert, A. et al., 'Stature and robusticity during the agricultural transition: Evidence from the bioarchaeological record', *Economics & Human Biology*, 9(3), pp. 284–301, 2011.
3. Lewis and Maslin, cited note 1.
4. Ruddiman, W., *Plows, Plagues and Petroleum: How Humans Took Control of Climate*, Princeton University Press, 2005.
5. Willett, W., 'Food in the Anthropocene: The EAT–Lancet Commission on healthy diets from sustainable food systems', *The Lancet*, 393(10170), pp. 447–92, 2019.
6. Lenton, T., *Earth System Science: A Very Short Introduction*, Oxford University Press, 2016.
7. Rockström, J. et al., 'A safe operating space for humanity', *Nature*, 461(7263), pp. 472–5, 2009.
8. Steffen, W. et al., 'Sustainability. Planetary boundaries: Guiding human development on a changing planet', *Science*, 347(6223), p. 1259855, 2015.
9. Ibid.
10. FAO, 'Water for sustainable food and agriculture: A report produced for the G20 Presidency of Germany', 2017.
11. Farinosi, F. et al., 'An innovative approach to the assessment of hydro-political risk: A spatially explicit, data driven indicator of hydro-political issues', *Global Environmental Change*, 52, pp. 286–313, 2018.
12. IPBES, 'Summary for policymakers of the global assessment report on biodiversity and ecosystem services of the Intergovernmental Science-Policy Platform on Biodiversity and Ecosystem Services', 2019.
13. Willett, cited note 5.
14. Ceballos, G. et al., 'Biological annihilation via the ongoing sixth mass extinction signaled by vertebrate population losses and declines', *PNAS*, 114(30), pp. e6089–96, 2017.
15. Ibid.
16. IPBES, cited note 12.
17. Springmann, M. et al., 'Options for keeping the food system within environmental limits', *Nature*, 562(7728), pp. 519–25, 2018.
18. Poore, J. and Nemecek, T., 'Reducing food's environmental impacts through producers and consumers', *Science*, 360(6392), pp. 987–92, 2018.
19. Ritchie, H. and Roser, M., 'Environmental impacts of food production', Our World in Data, 2020, https://ourworldindata.org/environmental-impacts-of-food [accessed 10 Jun. 2020].

20. Poore and Nemecek, cited note 18.
21. Clark, M. A. et al., 'Multiple health and environmental impacts of foods', *PNAS*, *116*(46), pp. 23357–62, 2019.

Chapter 3: Carbohydrates and Added Sugars

1. Monteiro, C. A. et al., 'The UN decade of nutrition, the NOVA food classification and the trouble with ultra-processing', *Public Health Nutrition*, *21*(1), pp. 5–17, 2018.
2. Monteiro, C. A. et al., 'Household availability of ultra-processed foods and obesity in nineteen European countries', *Public Health Nutrition*, *21*(1), pp. 18–26, 2018.
3. Ibid.
4. Rauber, F. et al., 'Ultra-processed food consumption and chronic non-communicable diseases-related dietary nutrient profile in the UK (2008–2014)', *Nutrients*, *10*(5), 2018.
5. Monteiro et al., cited note 2.
6. Baldridge, A. S. et al., 'The healthfulness of the US packaged food and beverage supply: A cross-sectional study', *Nutrients*, *11*(8), 2019.
7. Popkin, B. M. et al., 'Dynamics of the double burden of malnutrition and the changing nutrition reality', *The Lancet*, *395*(10217), pp. 65–74, 2020.
8. Hall, K. D. et al., 'Ultra-processed diets cause excess calorie intake and weight gain: An inpatient randomized controlled trial of ad libitum food intake', *Cell Metabolism*, *30*(1), pp. 67–77 e3, 2019.
9. Monteiro, C. A. et al., 'Ultra-processed foods, diet quality, and health using the NOVA classification system', FAO, 2019.
10. Development Initiatives, '2018 Global nutrition report: Shining a light to spur action on nutrition', 2018.
11. UNICEF, WHO and World Bank, 'Levels and trends in child malnutrition: UNICEF-WHO-World Bank joint child malnutrition estimates', 2015.
12. Popkin et al., cited note 7.
13. Monteiro et al., cited note 9.
14. https://www.nationalgeographic.org/encyclopedia/food-staple/ [accessed 22 Jul. 2020].
15. Aller, E. E. et al., 'Starches, sugars and obesity', *Nutrients*, *3*(3), pp. 341–69, 2011.
16. Reynolds, A. et al., 'Carbohydrate quality and human health: A series of systematic reviews and meta-analyses', *The Lancet*, *393*(10170), pp. 434–45, 2019.
17. Afshin, A. et al., 'Health effects of dietary risks in 195 countries, 1990–2017. A systematic analysis for the Global Burden of Disease Study 2017',

The Lancet, *393*(10184), pp. 1958–72, 2019.

18. Dehghan, M. et al., 'Associations of fats and carbohydrate intake with cardiovascular disease and mortality in 18 countries from five continents (PURE): A prospective cohort study', *The Lancet*, *390*(10107), pp. 2050–2062, 2017.

19. 'Subway rolls ruled too sugary to be bread in Ireland', BBC News, 2020, www.bbc.co.uk/news/business-54370056 [accessed 3 Nov. 2020].

20. Lustig, R. H., *Fat Chance: the Hidden Truth about Sugar, Obesity and Disease*, Fourth Estate Ltd, 2014.

21. Willett, W., 'Food in the Anthropocene: The EAT–Lancet Commission on healthy diets from sustainable food systems', *The Lancet*, *393*(10170), pp. 447–92, 2019.

22. Hashem, K. M., et al. 'Cross-sectional survey of the amount of sugar and energy in cakes and biscuits on sale in the UK for the evaluation of the sugar-reduction programme', *BMJ Open*, *8*(7), p. e019075, 2018.

23. Ibid.

24. Action on Sugar, 'Festive hot drinks loaded with sugar & calories reveals lack of progress in achieving sugar reduction targets', 2019, http://www.actiononsugar.org/news-centre/press-releases/2019/festive-hot-drinks-loaded-with-sugar--calories-reveals-lack-of-progress-inachieving-sugar-reduction-targets-.html [accessed 31 Dec. 2019].

25. 'Sweet success: Will sugar taxes improve health?' *The Lancet Diabetes & Endocrinology*, *5*(4), p. 235, 2017.

26. Sánchez-Romero, L. M. et al., 'Projected impact of Mexico's sugar-sweetened beverage tax policy on diabetes and cardiovascular disease: A modeling study', *PLoS Medicine*, *13*(11), p. e1002158, 2016.

27. Swarbreck, S. M. et al., 'A roadmap for lowering crop nitrogen requirement', *Trends in Plant Science*, *24*(10), pp. 892–904, 2019.

28. Sutton, M. A. and Ayyappan, S., 'Our nutrient world: The challenge to produce more food and energy with less pollution', UK Centre for Ecology & Hydrology, 2013.

29. Ibid.

30. Laffoley, D. and Baxter, J., 'Ocean deoxygenation: Everyone's problem', International Union for Conservation of Nature, 2019.

31. Queste, B. Y. et al., 'Physical controls on oxygen distribution and denitrification potential in the North West Arabian Sea', *Geophysical Research Letters*, *45*(9), pp. 4143–52, 2018.

32. National Oceanic and Atmospheric Administration, 'Large "dead zone" measured in Gulf of Mexico', 2019.

33. UNEP, 'Emerging issues of environmental concern', 2019.

34. Sutton, M. A. and Ayyappan, S., 'Our nutrient world: The challenge to produce more food and energy with less pollution', UK Centre for Ecology & Hydrology, 2013.

35. UNEP, cited note 33.
36. Willett, cited note 21.
37. Swarbreck, S. M. et al., 'A roadmap for lowering crop nitrogen requirement', *Trends in Plant Science*, 24(10), pp. 892–904, 2019.
38. Ibid.

Chapter 4: Fats and Oils

1. Menotti, A. and Puddu, P. E., 'Historic origins of the Mediterranean diet: The seven countries study of cardiovascular diseases', *Epidemiologia & Prevenzione*, 39(5–6), pp. 285–8, 2015.
2. https://www.sevencountriesstudy.com/ [accessed 3 Sep. 2020].
3. Spector, T. D., *The Diet Myth: The Real Science Behind What We Eat*, Weidenfeld & Nicolson, 2016.
4. Trichopoulou, A. et al., 'Adherence to a Mediterranean diet and survival in a Greek population', *New England Journal of Medicine*, 348(26), pp. 2599–2608, 2003.
5. Spector, cited note 3.
6. Estruch, R. et al., 'Primary prevention of cardiovascular disease with a Mediterranean diet', *New England Journal of Medicine*, 368(14), pp. 1279–90, 2013.
7. Ibid.
8. Willett, W., 'Food in the Anthropocene: The EAT–Lancet Commission on healthy diets from sustainable food systems', *The Lancet*, 393(10170), pp. 447–92, 2019.
9. Wang, Q. et al., 'Impact of nonoptimal intakes of saturated, polyunsaturated, and trans fat on global burdens of coronary heart disease', *Journal of the American Heart Association*, 5(1), 2016.
10. Hallock, B., 'Rise and fall of trans fat: A history of partially hydrogenated oil', *Los Angeles Times*, 7 Nov. 2013.
11. Mozaffarian, D. et al., 'Trans fatty acids and cardiovascular disease', *New England Journal of Medicine*, 354(15), pp. 1601–13, 2006.
12. Ibid.
13. Lemaitre, R. N. et al., 'Cell membrane trans-fatty acids and the risk of primary cardiac arrest', *Circulation*, 105(6), pp. 697–701, 2002.
14. World Health Organization, 'Denmark, trans fat ban pioneer: Lessons for other countries', 2018.
15. Food and Drug Administration, 'Trans fat', 2018.
16. https://www.who.int/news/item/14-05-2018-who-plan-to-eliminate-industrially-produced-trans-fatty-acids-from-global-food-supply [accessed 22 Jul. 2020].

17. Majid A., 'Ministers urged to ban deadly trans fats from foods', *The Telegraph*, 14 May 2018.
18. Wang, Q. et al., 'Impact of nonoptimal intakes of saturated, polyunsaturated, and trans fat on global burdens of coronary heart disease', *Journal of the American Heart Association*, 5(1), 2016.
19. Spector, cited note 3.
20. https://oec.world/en/profile/hs92/palm-oil [accessed 16 Mar. 2020].
21. Tullis, P., 'How the world got hooked on palm oil', *The Guardian* 19 Feb. 2019.
22. WWF, '8 Things to know about palm oil', https://www.wwf.org.uk/updates/8-things-know-about-palm-oil [accessed 10 Jun. 2020].
23. WWF, 'Palm oil buyers scorecard', palmoilscorecard.panda.org [accessed 10 Jun 2020].
24. Willett, cited note 8.
25. Wang et al., cited note 9.
26. Vijay, V. et al., 'The impacts of oil palm on recent deforestation and biodiversity loss', *PLoS One*, 11(7), e0159668, 2016.
27. IPBES, 'Summary for policymakers of the global assessment report on biodiversity and ecosystem services of the Intergovernmental Science-Policy Platform on Biodiversity and Ecosystem Services', 2019.
28. https://www.worldwildlife.org/stories/endangered-species-threatened-by-unsustainable-palm-oil-production [accessed 20 Mar. 2020].
29. WWF, cited note 22.
30. WWF, cited note 23.
31. Raup, D. M. and Sepkoski, J. J., 'Mass extinctions in the marine fossil record', *Science*, 215(4539), pp. 1501–3, 1982.
32. Sahney, S. and Benton, M. J., 'Recovery from the most profound mass extinction of all time', *Proceedings of the Royal Biological Society B: Biological Sciences*, 275(1636), pp. 759–65, 2008.
33. Ceballos, G. et al., 'Accelerated modern human-induced species losses: Entering the sixth mass extinction', *Science Advances*, 1(5), p. e1400253, 2015.
34. Diamond, J. M., *Guns, Germs and Steel: A Short History of Everybody for the Last 13,000 Years*, W. W. Norton & Company, 2005 [revised edition].
35. Ceballos et al, cited note 33.
36. Sánchez-Bayo, F. and Wyckhuys, K. A. G., 'Worldwide decline of the entomofauna: A review of its drivers', *Biological Conservation*, 232, pp. 8–27, 2019.
37. Ibid.
38. Ibid.
39. Hallmann, C. A. et al., 'More than 75 percent decline over 27 years in total flying insect biomass in protected areas', *PLoS One*, 12(10), p. e0185809, 2017.

40. Lister, B. C. and Garcia, A., 'Climate-driven declines in arthropod abundance restructure a rainforest food web', *PNAS*, *115*(44), pp. e10397–406, 2018.

41. IPBES, 'Summary for policymakers of the global assessment report on biodiversity and ecosystem services of the Intergovernmental Science-Policy Platform on Biodiversity and Ecosystem Services', 2019.

42. Cardinale, B. J. et al., 'Biodiversity loss and its impact on humanity', *Nature*, *486*(7401), pp. 59–67, 2012.

43. WWF, 'Living planet report – 2018. Aiming higher', *26*(4), 2018.

44. Steffen, W. et al., 'Sustainability. Planetary boundaries: Guiding human development on a changing planet', *Science*, *347*(6223), p. 1259855, 2015.

45. IPBES, cited note 41.

46. Pimm, S. L. et al., 'The biodiversity of species and their rates of extinction, distribution, and protection', *Science*, *344*(6187), 1246752, 2014.

47. Cardinale et al., cited note 42.

48. J. P., 'We have no bananas today', *The Economist*, 27 Feb. 2014.

49. Stokstad, E., 'Devastating banana disease may have reached Latin America, could drive up global prices', *Science*, 2019.

50. Bélanger, J. and Pilling, D. [eds.], 'The state of the world's biodiversity for food and agriculture', FAO Commission on Genetic Resources for Food and Agriculture Assessments, 2019.

51. Wetzel, W. C. et al., 'Variability in plant nutrients reduces insect herbivore performance', *Nature*, *539*(7629), pp. 425–7, 2016.

52. Torralba, M., 'Do European agroforestry systems enhance biodiversity and ecosystem services? A meta-analysis', *Agriculture, Ecosystems and Environment*, *230*, 2016.

53. Bélanger and Pilling, cited note 50.

54. Khasanah, N. et al., 'Oil palm agroforestry can achieve economic and environmental gains as indicated by multifunctional land equivalent ratios', *Frontiers in Sustainable Food Systems*, *3*, pp. 1–13, 2020.

55. Pimm et al., cited note 46.

56. Beck, M. W. and Lange, G. M., 'Managing coasts with natural solutions: Guidelines for measuring and valuing the coastal protection services of mangroves and coral reefs: Wealth Accounting and the Valuation of Ecosystem Services Partnership (WAVES) technical report', 2016.

57. Danielsen, F. et al., 'The Asian tsunami: A protective role for coastal vegetation', *Science*, *310*(5748), p. 643, 2005.

58. Das, S. and Vincent, J. R., 'Mangroves protected villages and reduced death toll during Indian super cyclone', *PNAS*, *106*(18), pp. 7357–60, 2009.

59. Beck and Lange, cited note 56.

60. IPBES, cited note 41.

61. Richards, D. R. and Friess, D. A., 'Rates and drivers of mangrove deforestation in Southeast Asia, 2000–2012', *PNAS*, *113*(2), pp. 344–9, 2016.

62. Hutchison, J. et al., 'The role of mangroves in fisheries enhancement', The Nature Conservancy and Wetlands International, 2014.
63. Aburto-Oropeza, O. et al., 'Mangroves in the Gulf of California increase fishery', *PNAS*, *105*(30), pp. 10456–9, 2008.
64. Capaldi, C. A. et al., 'The relationship between nature connectedness and happiness: A meta-analysis', *Frontiers in Psychology*, *5*, p. 976, 2014.

Chapter 5: Fruit and Vegetables

1. Lipner, S., 'A classic case of scurvy', *The Lancet*, *392*(10145), p. 431, 2018.
2. Magiorkinis, E. et al., 'Scurvy: Past, present and future', *European Journal of Internal Medicine*, *22*(2), pp. 147–52, 2011.
3. White, M., 'James Lind: The man who helped to cure scurvy with lemons', *BBC News*, 2016, https://www.bbc.co.uk/news/uk-england-37320399 [accessed: 10 Jun. 2020].
4. Lind, J., *A Treatise of the Scurvy in Three Parts*, A. Kincaid & A. Donaldson, 1753.
5. Magiorkinis et al., cited note 2.
6. Léger, D., 'Scurvy: Reemergence of nutritional deficiencies', *Canadian Family Physician*, *54*(10), pp. 1403–6, 2008.
7. Stevens, G. A. et al., 'Trends and mortality effects of vitamin A deficiency in children in 138 low-income and middle-income countries between 1991 and 2013. A pooled analysis of population-based surveys', *The Lancet Global Health*, *3*(9), pp. e528–36, 2015.
8. Osterhues, A. et al., 'Shall we put the world on folate?', *The Lancet*, *374*(9694), pp. 959–61, 2009.
9. Durga, J. et al., 'Effect of 3-year folic acid supplementation on cognitive function in older adults in the FACIT trial: A randomised, double blind, controlled trial', *The Lancet*, *369*(9557), pp. 208–16, 2007.
10. Gómez-Pinilla, F., 'Brain foods: The effects of nutrients on brain function', *Nature Reviews Neuroscience*, *9*(7), pp. 568–78, 2008.
11. Wang, X. et al., 'Fruit and vegetable consumption and mortality from all causes, cardiovascular disease, and cancer: Systematic review and close-response meta-analysis of prospective cohort studies', *BMJ*, *349*, p. g4490, 2014.
12. Miller, V. et al., 'Fruit, vegetable, and legume intake, and cardiovascular disease and deaths in 18 countries (PURE): A prospective cohort study', *The Lancet*, *390*(10107), pp. 2037–49, 2017.
13. Boffetta, P. et al., 'Fruit and vegetable intake and overall cancer risk in the European Prospective Investigation into Cancer and Nutrition (EPIC)', *Journal of the National Cancer Institute*, *102*(8), pp. 529–37, 2010.

14. Evert, A. B. et al., 'Nutrition therapy for adults with diabetes or prediabetes: A consensus report', *Diabetes Care*, 42(5), pp. 731–54, 2019.

15. Afshin, A. et al., 'Health effects of dietary risks in 195 countries, 1990–2017: A systematic analysis for the Global Burden of Disease Study 2017', *The Lancet*, 393(10184), pp. 1958–72, 2019.

16. Baquero, F. and Nombela, C., 'The microbiome as a human organ', *Clinical Microbiology and Infection*, 18(Suppl 4), pp. 2–4, 2012.

17. Wells, J. C. et al., 'The double burden of malnutrition: Aetiological pathways and consequences for health', *The Lancet*, 395(10217), pp. 75–88, 2020.

18. Cotillard, A. et al., 'Dietary intervention impact on gut microbial gene richness', *Nature*, 500(7464), pp. 585–8, 2013.

19. Allegretti, J. R. et al., 'The evolution of the use of faecal microbiota transplantation and emerging therapeutic indications', *The Lancet*, 394(10196), pp. 420–31, 2019.

20. Wu, G. D. et al., 'Linking long-term dietary patterns with gut microbial enterotypes', *Science*, 334(6052), pp. 105–8, 2011.

21. Zmora, N. et al., 'You are what you eat: Diet, health and the gut microbiota', *Nature Reviews Gastroenterology & Hepatology*, 16(1), pp. 35–56, 2019.

22. Koh, A. et al., 'From dietary fiber to host physiology: Short-chain fatty acids as key bacterial metabolites', *Cell*, 165(6), pp. 1332–45, 2016.

23. Afshin et al., cited note 15.

24. Miller et al., cited note 12.

25. Lee-Kwan, S. H. et al., 'Disparities in state-specific adult fruit and vegetable consumption – United States, 2015', *Morbidity and Mortality Weekly Report*, 66(45), pp. 1241–7, 2017.

26. Kellogg's, 'Can everyone access affordable, nutritious food?', pp. 1–11, 2018.

27. https://www.worldwater.org/conflict/map [accessed 14 Oct. 2020].

28. Amnesty International, 'Dead land: Islamic State's deliberate destruction of Iraq's farmland', 2018.

29. https://www.unwater.org/water-facts/scarcity/ [accessed 28 Apr. 2020].

30. FAO, 'Towards a water and food secure future: Critical perspectives for policy-makers', World Water Council, pp. 1–76, 2015.

31. Ibid.

32. Ibid.

33. Brown, E. G., 'California agricultural statistics review 2017–2018', *California Agricultural Statistics Review*, pp. 1–121, 2018.

34. Stokstad, E., 'Deep deficit', *Science*, 368(6488), pp. 230–3, 2020.

35. Ibid.

36. FAO, 'Water for sustainable food and agriculture', 2017.

37. Williams, A. P. et al., 'Large contribution from anthropogenic warming to an emerging North American megadrought', *Science*, *368*(6488), pp. 314–8, 2020.

38. Stahle, D. W., 'Anthropogenic megadrought', *Science*, *368*(6488), pp. 238–9, 2020.

39. FAO and World Water Council, 'Towards a water and food secure future. Critical perspectives for policy-makers', 2015.

40. Baulcombe, D., 'Reaping the benefits: Science and the sustainable intensification of global agriculture', The Royal Society, 2009.

41. Hellmich, R. L. and Hellmich, K. A., 'Use and impact of Bt maize', *Nature Education Knowledge*, *3*(10), p. 4, 2012.

42. Ibid.

43. Yang, X. et al., 'The *Kalanchoë* genome provides insights into convergent evolution and building blocks of crassulacean acid metabolism', *Nature Communications*, *8*(1), p. 1899, 2017.

44. https://www.bbc.co.uk/news/business-48592391 [accessed 22 Jul. 2020].

45. https://www.fastcompany.com/90485666/the-united-arab-emirates-is-100-million-in-indoor-farming-as-it-tries-to-become-more-resilient [accessed 22 Jul. 2020].

Chapter 6: Animal Protein

1. Ritchie, H. and Roser, M., 'Environmental impacts of food production', Our World in Data, 2020, https://ourworldindata.org/environmental-impacts-of-food [accessed 10 Jun. 2020].

2. Bar-On, Y. M. et al., 'The biomass distribution on earth', *PNAS*, *115*(25), pp. 6506–11, 2018.

3. Ritchie, H., 'Half of the world's habitable land is used for agriculture', Our World in Data, 2019, https://ourworldindata.org/global-land-for-agriculture [accessed 10 Jun. 2020].

4. Ritchie, H. and Roser, M., 'Meat and dairy production', Our World in Data, 2017, https://ourworldindata.org/meat-production [accessed 10 Jun. 2020].

5. Milton, K., 'Role of meat eating in evolution', *Evolutionary Anthropology*, pp. 11–21, 1999.

6. Larson, G. et al., 'Current perspectives and the future of domestication studies', *PNAS*, *111*(17), pp. 6139–46, 2014.

7. Ritchie and Roser, cited note 1.

8. Roser, M. et al., 'World population growth', Our World in Data, 2013, https://ourworldindata.org/world-population-growth [accessed 10 Jun. 2020].

9. Crisp, J., 'Parents who raise children as vegans should be prosecuted, say Belgian doctors', *The Telegraph*, 16 May 2019.

10. Royal Academy of Medicine of Belgium, 'Clarification on the vegetalian [sic] diet for children, pregnant and breastfeeding women', 2019.

11. Ritchie and Roser, cited note 4.

12. Howes, O., 'The truth about supermarket chicken', *Which?*, pp. 19–23, 2019.

13. Bradsher, K. and Tang, A., 'China responds slowly, and a pig disease becomes a lethal epidemic', *The New York Times*, 17 Dec. 2019, https://www.nytimes.com/2019/12/17/business/china-pigs-african-swine-fever.html [accessed 4 Sep. 2020].

14. Diamond, J. M., *Guns, Germs and Steel: A Short History of Everybody for the Last 13,000 Years*, W. W. Norton & Company, 2005 [revised edition].

15. O'Neill, J., 'Antimicrobials in agriculture and the environment: Reducing unnecessary use and waste', Review on Antimicrobial Resistance, 2015.

16. Ibid.

17. Ibid.

18. Perkins, C., 'Is that WHO cancer report to blame for bacon sales slump?', *The Grocer*, 16 Dec. 2016, https://www.thegrocer.co.uk/meat/bacon-salesslump-is-that-who-cancer-report-to-blame/546296.article [accessed 3 Sep. 2020].

19. https://www.who.int/mediacentre/news/statements/2015/processed-meat-cancer/en/ [accessed 23 Jul. 2020].

20. https://scienceblog.cancerresearchuk.org/2015/10/26/processed-meat-and-cancer-what-you-need-to-know/ [accessed 4 Sep. 2020].

21. Ibid.

22. Global Panel on Agriculture and Food Systems for Nutrition, 'Food systems and diets', 2016.

23. Sinha, R. et al., 'Meat intake and mortality: A prospective study of over half a million people', *Archives of Internal Medicine*, 169(6), pp. 562–71, 2009.

24. Abete, I. et al., 'Association between total, processed, red and white meat consumption and all-cause, CVD and IHD mortality: A meta-analysis of cohort studies', *British Journal of Nutrition*, 112(5), pp. 762–75, 2014.

25. Reinicke, C., 'Beyond Meat extends its post-IPO surge to 734%, breaking the $200-a-share threshold for the first time (BYND)', *Business Insider*, 23 Jul. 2019, https://markets.businessinsider.com/news/stocks/beyond-meatstock-price-breaks-200-per-share-2019-7-1028376980 [accessed 4 Sep. 2020].

26. González, A. and Koltrowitz, S., 'The $280,000 lab-grown burger could be a more palatable $10 in two years', *Reuters*, 2019, https://uk.reuters.com/article/us-food-tech-labmeat/the-280000-lab-grown-burger-could-be-a-more-palatable-10-in-two-years-idUKKCN1U41W8 [accessed 10 Jun. 2020].

27. Poore, J. and Nemecek, T., 'Reducing food's environmental impacts through producers and consumers', *Science*, *360*(6392), pp. 987–92, 2018.

28. Data source: Ibid; Diagram: https://ourworldindata.org/food-ghg-emissions [accessed 27 Oct. 2020]. Reproduced under Open Access license CC BY by Hannah Ritchie.

29. Volpicelli, G., 'The strange war against cow farts', *Wired*, 1 Dec. 2018, https://www.wired.co.uk/article/the-strange-war-against-cow-farts [accessed 4 Sep. 2020].

30. https://edition.cnn.com/videos/tv/2019/02/16/exp-gps-0217-gates-on-cow-farts.cnn [accessed 4 Sep. 2020].

31. Sutton, M. A. and Ayyappan, S., 'Our nutrient world: The challenge to produce more food and energy with less pollution', UK Centre for Ecology & Hydrology, 2013.

32. Ritchie and Roser, cited note 1.

33. Ibid.

34. Eating Better, 'We need to talk about chicken', *96*, pp. 60–1, 2020.

35. Canadian Cattlemen's Association. 'Feedlot operation', www.cattle.ca/cca-resources/animal-care/feedlot-operation [accessed 10 Jun. 2020].

36. Mottet, A. et al., 'Livestock: On our plates or eating at our table? A new analysis of the feed/food debate', *Global Food Security*, *14*, pp. 1–8, 2017.

37. Fry, J. P. et al., 2018 *Environ. Res. Lett.* 13 024017.

38. Mottet et al., cited note 36.

39. Durrell, G., *The Drunken Forest*, Penguin, 1956.

40. https://www.worldwildlife.org/stories/the-story-of-soy [accessed 17 Feb. 2020].

41. The Observatory of Economic Complexity, 'Brazil', https://oec.world/en/profile/country/bra [accessed 17 Feb. 2020].

42. Bradsher, K. and Tang, A., 'China responds slowly, and a pig disease becomes a lethal epidemic', *The New York Times*, 17 Dec. 2019, https://www.nytimes.com/2019/12/17/business/china-pigs-african-swine-fever.html [accessed 4 Sep. 2020].

43. 'A meaty planet', *The Economist*, pp. 57–9, 4 May 2019.

44. Eshel, G. et al., 'Land, irrigation water, greenhouse gas, and reactive nitrogen burdens of meat, eggs, and dairy production in the United States', *PNAS*, *111*(33), pp. 11996–2001, 2014.

45. Mottet et al., cited note 36.

46. Gibbs, H. K. et al., 'Brazil's Soy Moratorium', *Science*, *347*(6220), 2015.

47. Ibid.

48. Soterroni, A. C. et al., 'Expanding the Soy Moratorium to Brazil's Cerrado', *Science Advances*, *5*(7), p.eaav7336, 2019.

49. Romero, S., 'Taps start to run dry in Brazil's largest city', *The New York Times*, 16 Feb. 2015.

50. Watts, J., 'The Amazon Effect: How deforestation is starving São Paulo of water', *The Guardian*, 28 Nov. 2017.

51. Davidson, E. et al., 'The Amazon basin in transition', *Nature*, *481*, pp. 321–8, 2012.

52. Gatehouse, G., 'Deforested parts of Amazon "emitting more CO2 than they absorb"', *BBC Newsnight*, 11 Feb. 2020, www.bbc.co.uk/news/science-environment-51464694 [accessed 11 Feb. 2020].

53. Ibid.

54. Borunda, A., 'See how much of the Amazon is burning, how it compares to other years', *National Geographic*, Aug. 2019.

55. FAO, 'Status of the world's soil resources', 2015.

56. Interview with Dr Emma Keller, WWF, 5 Mar. 2020.

57. Poore, J. and Nemecek, T., 'Reducing food's environmental impacts through producers and consumers', *Science*, *360*(6392), pp. 987–92, 2018.

58. Sutton and Ayyappan, cited note 31.

59. Mottet et al., cited note 36.

60. European Nitrogen Assessment, 'Nitrogen on the table', 2016.

Chapter 7: Other Sources of Protein

1. Kigo, G. and Lace-Evans, O., 'Climate change: Why are tomato prices in Africa increasing?', *ECWA*, 26 Feb. 2020.

2. Ibid.

3. Jones, B., 'Kenya bears the brunt as floods devastate east Africa', *The Guardian*, 13 May 2020, https://www.theguardian.com/news/2020/may/13/kenya-bears-the-brunt-as-floods-devastate-central-africa [accessed 4 Sep. 2020].

4. Phillips, N. and Nogrady, B., 'The climate link to Australia's fires', *Nature*, *577*, 2020.

5. Sanderson, B. and Fisher, R., 'A fiery wake-up call for climate science', *Nature Climate Change*, *10*, pp. 175–7, 2020.

6. Cai, W. et al., 'Increased frequency of extreme Indian Ocean Dipole events due to greenhouse warming', *Nature*, *510*, pp. 254–8, 2014.

7. Kappelle, M. et al., 'WMO statement on the state of the global climate in 2019', 2020.

8. FAO, IFAD, UNICEF, WFP and WHO, 'The state of food security and nutrition in the world 2019. Safeguarding against economic slowdowns and downturns', FAO, 2019.

9. Myers, S. S. et al., 'Increasing CO2 threatens human nutrition', *Nature*, *510*(7503), pp. 139–42, 2014.

10. Ritchie, H. and Roser, M., 'Seafood production', Our World in Data, 2019, https://ourworldindata.org/seafood-production [accessed 20 Jun. 2020].

11. Surette, M., 'The science behind dietary omega-3 fatty acids', *CMAJ*, 178(1), pp. 1486–90, 2008.

12. Willett, W., 'Food in the Anthropocene: The EAT–Lancet Commission on healthy diets from sustainable food systems', *The Lancet*, 393(10170), pp. 447–92, 2019.

13. Afshin, A. et al., 'Health effects of dietary risks in 195 countries, 1990–2017: A systematic analysis for the Global Burden of Disease Study 2017', *The Lancet*, 393(10184), pp. 1958–72, 2019.

14. Wallace, D. F., *Consider the Lobster*, Little, Brown and Company, 2005.

15. Hawthorne, D., *The Inexhaustible Sea*, Macdonald, 1954.

16. IPBES, 'Summary for policymakers of the global assessment report on biodiversity and ecosystem services of the Intergovernmental Science-Policy Platform on Biodiversity and Ecosystem Services', 2019.

17. Ritchie and Roser, cited note 10.

18. Pérez Roda, M. A. [ed.] et al., 'A third assessment of global marine fisheries discards', FAO Fisheries and Aquaculture Technical Paper No. 633, 2019.

19. Ritchie and Roser, cited note 10.

20. Stentiford, G. D. et al., 'New paradigms to help solve the global aquaculture disease crisis', *PLoS Pathogens*, 13(2), pp. 1–6, 2017.

21. 'Grub's up: Beetles and flies are becoming part of the agricultural food chain', *The Economist*, 6 Jul. 2019.

22. Coburn, C., 'A bug in the system', *The Spectator*, 3 Aug. 2019.

23. Ritchie, H. and Roser, M., 'Environmental impacts of food production', Our World in Data, 2020, https://ourworldindata.org/environmental-impacts-of-food [accessed 10 Jun. 2020].

24. World Meteorological Association, 'WMO Provisional statement on the status of the global climate in 2019', 2019.

25. Gamito, R. et al., 'Trends in landings and vulnerability to climate change in different fleet components in the Portuguese coast', *Fisheries Research*, 181, pp. 93–101, 2016.

26. https://oec.world/en/profile/country/grl [accessed 22 Jul. 2020].

27. Raven, J. et al., 'Ocean acidification due to increasing carbon dioxide', *The Royal Society*, 2005, https://royalsociety.org/~/media/royal_society_content/policy/publications/2005/9634.pdf [accessed 27 Oct. 2020]

28. Bednaršek, N. et al., 'Extensive dissolution of live pteropods in the Southern Ocean', *Nature Geoscience*, 5(12), pp.881–5, 2012.

29. https://www.nhm.ac.uk/discover/quick-questions/why-are-coral-reefs-important.html [accessed 22 Jul. 2020].

30. World Meteorological Association, 'WMO Provisional statement on the status of the global climate in 2019', 2019.

31. Bednaršek et al., cited note 28.

32. Raven et al., cited note 27.
33. Laffoley, D. and Baxter, J., 'Ocean deoxygenation: Everyone's problem', International Union for Conservation of Nature, 2019.
34. Storhaug, C. L. et al., 'Country, regional, and global estimates for lactose malabsorption in adults: A systematic review and meta-analysis', *The Lancet Gastroenterology and Hepatology, 2*(10), pp. 738–46, 2017.
35. Ritchie, H. and Roser, M., 'Environmental impacts of food production', Our World in Data, 2020, https://ourworldindata.org/environmental-impacts-of-food [accessed 10 Jun. 2020].
36. Data source: Poore, J. and Nemecek, T., 'Reducing food's environmental impacts through producers and consumers', *Science, 360*(6392), pp. 987–92, 2018; Diagram: https://ourworldindata.org/less-meat-or-sustainable-meat [accessed 27 Oct. 2020]. Reproduced under Open Access license CC BY by Joseph Poore and Hannah Ritchie.
37. European Nitrogen Assessment, 'Nitrogen on the table', 2016.

Chapter 8: The World on Your Plate

1. 'Mayor confirms ban on junk food advertising on transport network', 2018, https://www.london.gov.uk/press-releases/mayoral/ban-on-junk-food-advertising-on-transport-network-0 [accessed 27 Oct 2020].
2. Thomas, F. et al., 'A prime time for action: New evidence on the link between television and on-demand marketing and obesity', Cancer Research UK, 2018.
3. Fagerberg, P. et al., 'Ultra-processed food advertisements dominate the food advertising landscape in two Stockholm areas with low vs high socioeconomic status. Is it time for regulatory action?' *BMC Public Health, 19*(1), pp. 1–10, 2019.
4. Mills, S. et al., 'Frequency of eating home cooked meals and potential benefits for diet and health: Cross-sectional analysis of a population-based cohort study', *International Journal of Behavioural Nutrition and Physical Activity, 14*(1), p. 109, 2017.
5. Boseley, S., 'The chicken shop mile and how Britain got fat', *The Guardian*, 28 Jan. 2016.
6. Hashem, K. M. et al., 'Cross-sectional survey of the amount of sugar and energy in cakes and biscuits on sale in the UK for the evaluation of the sugar-reduction programme', *BMJ Open, 8*(7), p. e019075, 2018.
7. The Eat–Lancet Commission, 'Healthy diets from planet; Food planet health', *The Lancet*, p. 32, 2019.
8. Public Health England, 'A quick guide to the government's healthy eating recommendations', p. 7, 2018.

9. https://www.vegansociety.com/resources/downloads/vegan-eatwell-guide [accessed 4 Sep. 2020].
10. Clark, M. A. et al., 'Multiple health and environmental impacts of foods', *PNAS*, *116*(46), pp. 23357–62, 2019.
11. Buranyi, S., 'The future of meat in a plant-based world', *Financial Times*, 13 Jun. 2019.
12. https://www.msc.org/home [accessed 14 Oct. 2020].
13. Henderson, E., 'Anti-meat agenda damaging farmers' mental health, says NFU', *Farmers Weekly*, 12 Feb. 2020.

Chapter 9: Enough

1. Le Guin, U., *No Time to Spare*, Houghton Mifflin Harcourt, 2017.
2. Buranyi, S., 'The future of meat in a plant-based world', *Financial Times*, 13 Jun. 2019.
3. Baulcombe, D., 'Reaping the benefits: Science and the sustainable intensification of global agriculture', The Royal Society, 2009.
4. https://www.un.org/sustainabledevelopment/sustainable-development-goals/ [accessed 4 Sep. 2020].
5. Project Drawdown, 'Reduced food waste', www.drawdown.org/solutions/reduced-food-waste [accessed 10 Jun. 2020].
6. Ibid.
7. Springmann, M. et al., 'Options for keeping the food system within environmental limits', *Nature*, *562*(7728), pp. 519–25, 2018.

INDEX

Page numbers in **bold** indicate references where definitions are provided.

ABOUT THE AUTHOR

Dr Cassandra Coburn is a scientist, writer and editor. She obtained her PhD in Genetics from the Institute of Healthy Ageing at University College London, UK. She joined *The Lancet* in 2013, where she was Deputy Editor at *The Lancet Oncology*, and Acting Executive Editor of *The Lancet Haematology*. She left the group for two years to focus on writing but returned in 2020 to become the founding Editor-in-Chief of *The Lancet Healthy Longevity*.

Cassandra has given talks on health in China, Japan, the USA and Europe, and has led multiple specialist commissions to address inequities in healthcare provision. A career highlight was launching a research programme for cancer care at the United Nations, alongside former US Vice President Joe Biden.

She writes for both academic and general publications, including *The Spectator*, *The Observer* and *The Reader's Digest*. Cassandra is passionate about using science to inform and drive change in the world and believes that scientific knowledge can and should be interesting and accessible to all.